EXCURSIONS IN
EASTERN
SPAIN

30 Great Trips from the
Costa Blanca and Valencia

by Nick Inman and Clara Villanueva

Illustrations by Nick Inman

SANTANA BOOKS

/

Published in March 1996 by Ediciones Santana S.L.

Graphic design and typography by Bruce Williams, Mijas Costa 258 6653.

Printed by Gráficas San Pancracio, S.L.,
Pol. San Luis, C/.Oratova 17, Málaga.
Depósito Legal: MA-330/1996

ISBN: 84-921229-3-5

Writer, editor and photographer Nick Inman has been writing about Spain for newspapers, magazines and guidebooks since 1986. He is a specialist on eastern Spain, an area he feels deserves to be better known to travellers.

Valencia-born writer Clara Villanueva was seven months pregnant when she crossed the snowbound passes of Albarracín and Cuenca to research this book.

They are married and live in London with their daughter, and travel frequently to Spain.

For Amy who travelled (almost) everywhere with us.

Thanks to Peter, Ana and Tamara Baker for providing us with a forward base; to Miguel of Detalle in La Cañada for the map typesetting; to our co-pilots Toni, Vincente, Pepe, Angel and Puri Villanueva; to our culinary expert Purificación Ribes; and to Josefina Fernández and Encarna Molina for their unconditional support.

■ CONTENTS ■

Half-day Trips:

Day Trips:

Day Trips *continued . . .*

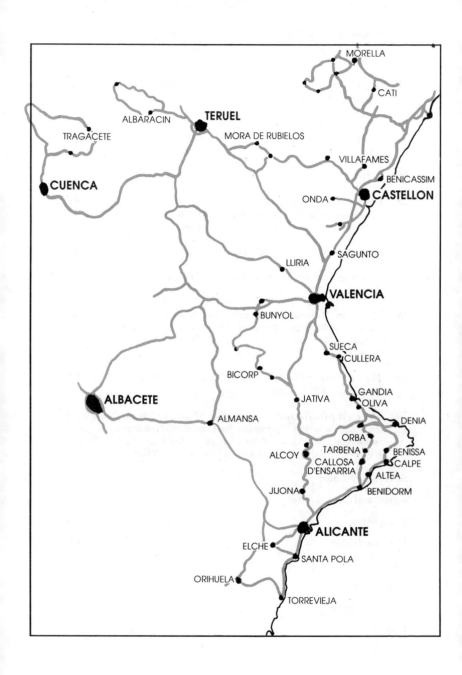

■ USING THIS GUIDE ■

Behind the tourist resorts of the Costa Blanca, Valencia and the Costa del Azhar lies one of Spain's least celebrated and least travelled regions. The countryside, towns, cities, villages and other sights may not be the most famous of Spain but that doesn't mean they are less attractive, interesting or spectacular. Until they are better known, they are yours to discover.

The excursions in this book explore Eastern Spain from the borders of Catalonia to that annexed sea, the Mar Menor; from the coasts of Valencia and Alicante inland as far as Don Quixote's La Mancha. Most of the routes criss-cross the three provinces that make up the region of the Comunidad Valenciana: Valencia, Castellón and Alicante, but ten take you much further afield: to Murcia, Albecete, Cuenca, Teruel; as far east as the borders of Toledo; and across the sea to Ibiza.

As well as visiting the best-known places of the region, the 30 routes also take you to little-known towns and villages, monuments, nature reserves and natural features of the landscape. Wherever possible, the roads linking these places are chosen because they pass through picturesque countryside.

The routes are mainly for car travellers but most take quieter backroads which are also ideal for those cycle tourists who are not put off by steep gradients (unavoidable in such a mountainous country as Spain). Some of the upland areas of the interior are good for rambling.

Apart from background information about the places visited you will find practical information on possible overnight stops and where to eat. At the end of the book we have included advice on driving in Spain, as well as useful basic vocabulary and a list of fiestas worth experiencing.

To simplify planning your excursions, the book has been organized into sections. First come half-day and day trips which start from, and return to, key points along the coast: Valencia, Denia, Benidorm, Alicante and Torrevieja.

Two of the longer trips (to La Mancha and Ibiza) are round trips. The others can be travelled in reverse to return to your starting point or you can link them together. The appropriate links are mentioned in the text and also in the suggested seven-day tour at the end of the book.

Finally, there are five side-trips originating from the destinations of the weekend trips. There are also circular routes which can be made into a day. Some of the best routes begin in Valencia. If you are starting from the northern Costa Blanca you can still manage them with an early start if you take the motorway. Allow an hour and a half extra each way from Denia and two hours from Benidorm. When you reach Valencia follow the blue signs for Barcelona on to the by-pass. This will bring you back on to the A-7 motorway north or the N-340 (for Routes 16, 17, 24 and 25). For Route 23, turn off the by-pass for Ademuz.

When following the excursions you will come across some names printed in bold, e.g. **Valencia.** Full information on these places (sights, hotels, restaurants and services) is given in the Town and City Guide at the end of this book.

Place Names

Many villages and towns in the Comunidad Valenciana now prefer to be known by their names in the local Valencian language. Where this varies significantly from the common Spanish (Castilian) name it is given in brackets.

Eating Out

Because there are constant changes in prices and exchange rates we do not give prices of meals and accommodation.

Instead, we give a rough indication of price.

After the name of a restaurant you will find its address, telephone number, opening times, etc. in brackets. At the end of this is a letter. B stands for budget, indicating that a three course meal, without wine, costs under 1,500pesetas; M is for moderate, in the 1,500 to 3,500 range; E means expensive, more than 3,500; VE means that if you have to ask about the price you probably can't afford it.

The cheapest places to eat are often where the locals go. Bars in Spain are plentiful, inexpensive and functional, and most (but not "pubs") serve *bocadillos* (sandwiches) and *tapas* -- ask for a ración if you want a plateful -- at all hours. Some also serve lunch and dinner, probably without formality or a written menu. You can also eat in a *venta* or *mesón*, but you may not be able to pay by credit card. Wherever possible we give the opening times of restaurants; in general Spaniards take meals late: lunch is any time between 1 and 4pm; dinner from 8 onwards.

Where to Stay

Every town of any size has at least one *fonda, hostal* or *pensión*, where you will find basic accommodation, probably with a communal bathroom. A blue plaque outside indicates the category of the establishment: F for fonda, P for pension, Hs for hostal and H for hotel. Among the country's best hotels are the *paradores*, which are state run and often located in attractive refurbished old buildings such as castles and convents.

The categories and stars used to identify Spanish hotels refer to whether or not they have certain facilities required by the tourist authorities. They give only a rough indication of price and no idea of quality of reception, service, decor, atmosphere, comfort or value for money. Hotel prices vary greatly according to the category, the time of year and the room you choose, but as a rough guide only, you can expect to pay the following for a double-room:

pension or one-star hostal: 2,000 - 4,000 pesetas;
one star hotel or two star hostal: 3,000 - 8,000 pesetas;
two star hotel or three star hostal: 4,000 - 10,000 pesetas;
three star hotel: 5,000 - 18,000 pesetas;
four star hotel: 9,000 - 22,000 pesetas;
five star hotel: 16,000 - 24,000 pesetas;

Parador: 10,000 - 14,000 pesetas.

Most hotel prices exclude VAT (IVA) currently 16% or 7%.
For more accurate information on hotel prices, consult the *Guia Oficial de Hoteles* (see further reading).

Maps

Although detailed road directions are given it is advisable to carry a map with you in case you lose your way or want to take a short cut. Almost every road is on Michelin's 1 : 400,000 (1cm to 4 km) map of central and Eastern Spain (section 445). Only three of our routes stray off it. You'll need section 444 for part of Route 21. Ibiza and Formentera (Routes 22 and 30) are on a section of 443 but you would be better off buying a local map on the islands.

A good map of the eastern seaboard is the 1 : 300,000 *Comunidad Valenciana Mapa Turistico* produced by Plaza and Janes in association with the regional tourist board, ITVA. Firestone produces a 1 : 200,000 map of the Costa Blanca but, although it is more detailed than the others, it is also less accurate.

Also, bear in mind that there are a few roads too new or too small to feature on any of these maps.

For walking, you will need 1 : 50,000 maps produced by the Spanish armed forces *(mapas militares)*, which are the nearest equivalent to ordinance survey maps. These are available from Regolf, C/ de la Mar, 22, Valencia.

Let Us Know

We welcome your help in keeping this guidebook as up-to-date as possible. If you come across any changes, if you discover a restaurant worth recommending or a hotel with special appeal, please let us know. We will take your comments and suggestions into account when preparing the next edition. Write to us c/o Ediciones Santana S.L., Apartado 422, 29640 Fuengirola (Málaga), Spain ❑

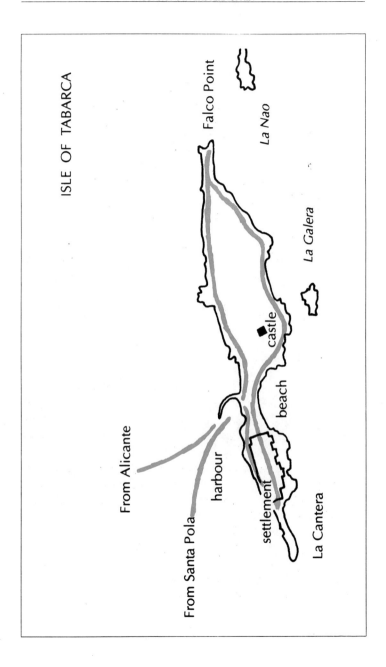

ISLE OF TABARCA

Excursion 1- The Phantom Ship:

Alicante - Santa Pola - Tabarca - Santa Pola - Alicante
(44km by car and 1/2 hour ferry trip each way)

Four and a half nautical miles are all you need to get away from the madding crowds of the Costa Blanca. With no cars and only one telephone, the Isle of Tabarca preserves a sense of peace and traditional living. Although in summer it's clear waters are popular with day-trippers, from autumn to spring - and on summer nights - it's the perfect place for a pensive stroll to the sounds and smell of the sea.

You can get there from Alicante Port directly. During the summer (July to mid-September) boats leave every 2 hours, the first at 9.45am, the last returning at 8pm. From April-July the first is at 11.30am, the last at 5pm. In winter (November-March) there's only one boat each way on Thursdays and Sundays, which leaves at 11.30am and returns at 4pm. (Tel. 96- 521 63 96 or 96-522 25 90 for more information).

The journey takes one hour, but the trip is shorter if you go down the coast on the N-332 to Santa Pola (Pop. 14,250). Lying low in the water and once described poetically as a strange phantom ship", Tabarca (*l'Illa* to the locals) is easily visible from the harbour and the journey there takes just 30 minutes. Summer sailings (July-September) are every half hour from 9am to 7pm. From April to June sailings are less frequent and start at 10am. In winter there's only one boat a day, which leaves at 11.30am and returns at 2pm. The two hours this gives you on the island is just enough time to see everything there is to see. (Tel 96-541 23 38 or 96-541 11 13 to find out more about sailings from Santa Pola).

Leaving Santa Pola the boat turns sharply to port and follows the coast at a distance. For the whole journey, the island's church, dominating a settlement of low houses enclosed by sturdy sea-walls, can be clearly seen. You may also spot the castle and lighthouse behind.

17

Tabarca is divided into two distinct parts: the settlement and what is grandly called *el campo* ("the countryside"), a stony, treeless area of flattish ground rising to 17 metres above sea level near the lighthouse. A narrow neck of land joins the two parts: on one side is the harbour, on the other the beach. Turn left when you leave the harbour and follow the north coast. This is formed by very low cliffs and rocks running into the sea. Unfortunately, the shore is badly polluted in places by litter thrown over the side of ships.

Falcó Point, which marks the end of the island, just beyond the tiny, white sailors' cemetery, is about half an hour's stroll from the harbour. From here you have a good view of a large flat-topped off-shore rock called La Nao. Beyond this an area of sea-bed has been declared a marine nature reserve. Once these waters were home to the monk seal and dolphins, but sadly now the largest animal you are likely to encounter is a sea turtle. You can see a selection of the Costa Blanca's underwater wildlife in Santa Pola's excellent municipal aquarium (see Excursion 9).

Return along the south coast, which has much higher cliffs with some pretty views looking back to La Nao and south to another islet, La Galera, where a surviving colony of rabbits can still be found (all the ones on Tabarca were shot by the Dukes of Maqueda). There are also large colonies of birds - especially gulls and cormorants - which you may glimpse skimming across the waves.

As you approach the settlement you pass the "castle", the Torre de San José (now occupied by the *Guardia Civil*). Masses of prickly pear, the largest plant on the island, grow around it. The plant's red fruit is delicious when ripe (early spring) but is heavily defended by fine spines which are maddeningly difficult to pick out of your fingers.

Crossing the neck of land between the beach and the harbour you'll pass a solar power station which contributes part of the island's electricty needs. It was originally hoped that Tabarca would be Europe's first entirely solar-powered island, but the station is big enough to produce only a few hours of power a day.

The 18th-century settlement is entered from this side by a monumental gateway, the Puerta de San Rafael. You emerge onto the unsurfaced main street and enter a square partly shaded by thirsty palm trees. This minute fortified village - built to a strictly rational plan - was established on the orders of Charles III after he had declared Tabarca to be Spanish territory. Before then it was occupied by the Sultan of Algiers. Charles wanted to make sure that an island so close to shore would never be used as a base for pirate attacks on the mainland. Strictly, by the way, this is Nueva Tabarca as there is another Tabarca off the North African coast. Many of today's inhabitants are descended from captives held on the original Tunisian Tabarca.

The settlement was once home to an industrious, close-knit community which made a meagre living from tuna fishing and such farming as the scant acreage could afford. During this century most of Tabarca's indigenous inhabitants went off to live in Santa Pola, letting their island houses as holiday homes.

The only restaurant you are likley to find open out of season is Don Jeronimo II, on the main street. Open all year for lunch and dinner but with no set opening times. No cards. B). In summer, there's much more choice of places to eat and drink around the beach.

The settlement finishes with another square and then you pass through the Puerta de San Gabriel leading to the flat promontory of La Cantera. If you look up at the gateway from the seaward side you'll see that it is carved with a sword and

the words "Hispania Rex Edific": "The King of Spain built this".

From the gateway, climb the wide, tapering sea-walls and walk along to the church (open only on Sundays and at Easter - the priest, who lives on the mainland, keeps the keys) which has basements connecting to the sea. Continuing along the wall, you pass over the top of a third gateway, the Puerta de San Miguel, and drop quickly back down to the harbour, where, if you've timed it right, your boat will be waiting to whisk you back to the mainland and perhaps to a late lunch ❑

Excursion 2 - Woods and Water:

Alicante - Sierra de Maigmó - Tibi - Jijona - Alicante

(85km)

A short way inland from Alicante there are two secluded beauty spots lost among the hills: a thickly wooded sierra and Europe's oldest dam.

From the centre of Alicante follow the signs on to the A-213 for San Vicente del Raspeig. Here you have a choice of route - either carry straight on for Maigmó (15.5km), or take a detour via the A-220 to Agost (11.5km. pop. 3,800), a town famed for its pottery of white porous clay which is made into drinking jars or *botijos*. A Pottery Museum is situated just off the road by-passing the town (open 11am-2pm and 5-8pm in summer; 12am-2pm in winter. Closed Mon.). Then follow the A-221 to Maigmó (11km), turning left on to the A-213 again.

Restaurante Maigmó (Ctra. de Alicante a Castalla, km 21. Tel: 96-561 72 83. Visa. B-M) specialises in game and barbecues.

The magnificently wooded Sierra de Maigmó (rising to 1,296 metres) dominates the view to the left of the road. The pines and evergreen oaks go right up to and over the heights. Only the steepest crags are bare. The trees give the Sierra a gentle, harmless appearance but they conceal mighty precipices and deep ravines.

Parallel with the road runs the route of the Alicante-Alcoy railway line - a line on which no train ever ran. Building began in the 1930s over bridges and through cuttings and tunnels, but was never completed. There are hopes of turning it into a footpath or cycle track.

Carry straight on past the right turning to Tibi and take the left turning sign-posted for Parque Natural del Maigmó (Maigmó Nature Reserve). At first the road climbs past almond terrace and weekend villas but it soon plunges into those slopes of enchanting pine woods.

Turn left at the next junction (straight on takes you on a bumpy and tortuous ride high into the Sierra). After climbing in steep curves for 4km through the trees, the road levels out to give views over the Foya de Castalla (the valley of the River

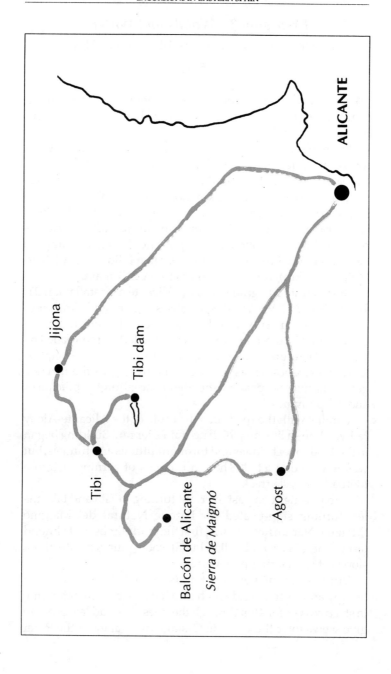

Monnegre), which is filled with vaporous almond blossom in late February and early March. Eventually, you will reach the Balcón de Alicante, a picnic and barbecue area looking over the other side of Maigmó onto the Vinalopé valley. Footpaths lead off into the woods.

Returning back to the main road at the foot of the slope, turn right back towards Alicante but turn left at the next junction for Tibi (5km) and right again after 1km (still for Tibi (pop. 1,000). You can eat at La Alameda (La Alameda, 3. Tel: 96-561 71 19. No cards. B).

From Tibi take the road for Jijona. A short way out of town turn right at the signpost for "Pantano" and "Castillo". The 10th century castle is disappointingly ruined but surrounded by an informal nature reserve.

After four kilometres of narrow, bendy, but well-surfaced road there is a dark, glassy reservoir picturesquely fringed by the rocks of Mos del Bou and Las Peñas. The last few yards to the parking place by the waterside are along a dirt track.

The dam, reputedly the oldest in Europe, is a thick curving wall 43 metres high and 34 metres wide at the base. Built by the city of Alicante between 1580 and 1594 to provide irrigation water, it has long since blended into the landscape. One of the architects responsible for it is Juan de Herrera, the Renaissance all-rounder famed for his work on the Escorial and at Aranjuez.

Returning the way you came, turn right again on to a small road which crawls round the side of Peñarroja (1226m) before dropping down to Jijona (pop. 7,400), which is famed for the manufacture of *turrón*, Spain's typical Christmas sweet made from almonds. This sweet traditionally comes in two varieties: *Alicante*, hard and nougat-like, and *Jijona*, soft, sticky and sweet. There's a whole museum dedicated to the stuff in one of the factories (Turrones El Lobo and 1880, C/Alcoy, 62. Open daily 9.30-1pm and 4 to 8pm). The town also boasts a centuries-old evergreen oak tree. Turn right on to the N-340 to return to Alicante ❏

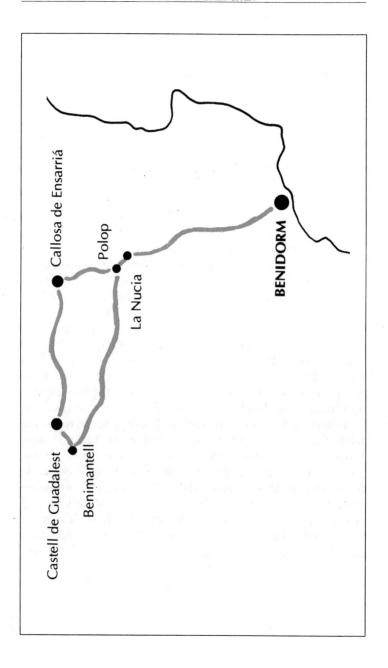

Excursion 3 - The Eyrie of the Costa Blanca:

Benidorm - Polop - Callosa d'Ensarriá - Castell de Guadalest
- Benimantell - Benidorm
(54km)

The pretty mountain village of Guadalest is one of the Costa Blanca's star attractions but, despite drawing coachloads of tourists, remains relatively unspoilt and just as spectacular as always.

Part of the draw is Guadalest's proximity to the coast - in no time at all you can exchange the skyscrapers and beach umbrellas of Benidorm for the long views and pure air of the mountains. There are also several good places to eat included on this route.

Leave Benidorm from the big crossroads near the bullring on the C-3318 which crosses the railway line and heads inland between estates of white villas towards the massive bulk of Mount Ponoch. This road has recently been improved and takes you quickly into the hills. As you go around its base, have another look at Ponoch and you may be able to see why it is known locally as "The Sleeping Lion". La Nuciá (pop. 5,300) stages a popular flea-market on Sunday mornings. Bar Chato in the main square opposite the church serves tasty tapas and bar meals.

Around the next corner is the picturesquely-located Polop de la Marina (pop. 1,900). Although the village is blighted by new developments the old quarter has some pretty streets to wander around. There is also a zig-zagging path up to the cemetery in the ruins of the old Moorish castle. From here you can get good views of the surrounding lush hills. Polop also has a singular fountain with 221 spouts and a "medieval basement" (C/Posito, 8. Open 10am-9.30pm).

Ca L'Angeles (Gabriel Miró, 16, Tel 96-587 02 26. M-E) on the main road is the best place to eat here. There is no written menu as the dishes are made from the freshest ingredients and vary from day to day and season to season.

The road takes a circuitous route through citrus orchards down to a long bridge over the inconspicuous River Guadalest.

Callosa d'Ensarriá (pop. 15,300) on the other side, is famous for its production of medlars. From a distance the town looks horribly modern but it hides a heart of brightly painted houses, one of which is an art gallery (Galería Arrabal Tel: 96-588 07 68). Turn left at the roundabout in the town centre for Guadalest. All the way up the valley there are attractive views of the Sierra Aitana which is topped by rocky crags and often speckled with snow in winter.

Shortly after leaving Callosa, look out for road-side stalls selling local honey. You will be invited to try several different varieties before choosing which one to buy.

The road dips down to a bridge to cross the Guadalest river again and then climbs steadily up through the trees (ravaged recently by fire). Ahead you will soon see the old castle and belfry of Castell de Guadalest (pop. 170), perched precariously on a rock outcrop from which they command the whole valley.

It is only possible to visit the village on foot - and by a single entrance. Park in the car-park surrounded by souvenir shops and follow everyone else along the narrow street on the opposite side of the main road.

What appears to be half a white-washed house stuck on to

the cliff-face turns out to be the entrance to a short, sloping tunnel cut through the rock over 1,000 years ago. The village's inaccesibility has saved it from invasion by cars and property developers. Leaving the modern world behind for a while, you emerge from the tunnel into a square surrounded by well-kept houses, most of which are now craft and souvenir shops, bars and small museums.

To begin with, go straight to the parapet flanking the right side of the square and have a look over. Below is a vivid turqoise reservoir, overlooked by the lonely stump of a watchtower which was stranded for evermore on its own pinnacle of rock by the 1644 earthquake, which shook Guadalest's fortifications apart.

Of the various shops, one of the more interesting is the glass shop at the end of the square. Here, you will find a range of cheap, green glass which has a rough and ready handmade quality and far more character than the mass-produced commodity. Other shops sell leather, pottery and textiles.

Beside the glass shop, a flight of steps leads up past the stations of the cross to the castle. Most of the summit of the rock is occupied by the town cemetery which is the highest in Spain - although there are plans to move it to a less-frequented location. You can by-pass it if you want to get directly to the castle keep. There are views through 360 degrees.

Looking back down towards the coast, with the hooked nose of Mount Bernia standing proud of its own range to the left, it takes some believing that Benidorm and all the commotion of the coast are just half an hour's drive away.

Further up the valley lie four or five unspoiled little villages (Excursion 11 goes that way) overlooked by the military communications base crowning Mount Aitana. Hill terraces and trees - laid out by the Moors and still irrigated by the same merrily gurgling ditches - go right up to the craggy heights, with only an isolated house here and there.

You will have realised by now that Guadalest's distinctive turret, the church's annexed bell-tower, is stuck on another outcrop of rock and is inaccessible to visitors. But you can still take a good snap of it from where you are and trace the long cord with which they toll the bell on special occasions.

Guadalest has another bizarre claim to fame. It has not one but two museums of microscopic works of art. The Mundo de Max (open daily from 10am. Tel: 96-588 08 08) is in the main carpark and features such wonders as dissected and dressed fleas and Leonardo da Vinci's *Last Supper* painted on a grain of rice. Manuel Ussà's Microminiature Museum (open daily 10am-9pm) is in the old village. Here, displays include a sculpture of a camel passing through the eye of a needle and Goya's *Maja Desnuda* painted on the wing of a fly. Needless to say, you can only view these objects through powerful lenses. Both of the collections are small and quickly visited.

To return to the coast, continue through Guadalest on the same road as before and take the steep left turning on to the unclassified (but well surfaced) backroad to Polop.

If you want to eat in the mountains, take the small lane just after this turning to the Trestellador (Closed Tues. No cards. B), which does a succulent roast lamb. It also
has a terrace offering a magnificent view, on clear days, all the way back to Altea and the coast 16km away.

The nearby village of Benimantell has several restaurants popular with foreigners and locals alike. Our favourite is L'Obrer (on the main road at the end of the village. (B-M), which serves a hearty menu of mountain food.

The back road to Polop is shorter, less busy and more scenic than the outward route, and also avoids passing through Callosa. There are good views to the right of the Sierra Aitana and Ponoch. When you get to Polop, turn right and you are on the C-3318 back to Benidorm ❑

Excursion 4 - Rock of Ages:

Benidorm - Albir - Altea - Calpe - Peñón de Ifach - Benidorm

(52km)

A Gibraltar look-alike, the Peñón de Ifach is a massive rock which rises vertically out of the sea to tower 300 metres above the Costa Blanca. If you have a good pair of legs a walk to the top affords stupendous views. If you'd rather stay in the car the Peñón is still highly photogenic, and there are other sights to see on this route.

Leave the centre of Benidorm on Avenida del Mediterráneo, which runs along Levante beach. At the end, by the statue of the naked woman with her arms held aloft, turn left and after 2km turn right onto the AP-1535 to Altea and Playa del Albir.

Go straight over the small crossroads next to what looks like an aircraft hangar (in fact it's a restaurant). Further on you'll pass a fake castle with a cluster of red-roofed turrets. This is a popular place for mock "medieval" banquets (Castell Compte D'Alfás. Tel: 96-588 85 92). Turn right at the next T-junction and you are heading for the beach.

The visit to Albir lighthouse, from which there are views of a long sweep of coastline, involves a 5km round trip on foot. To get there fork right just before you reach the sea front into Camí del Far (sign-posted "Faro de Albir"). Follow this road all the way up the hill until it ends. A small surfaced lane goes off to the left. You can drive a further 100m along this to a turning - parking space but from then on you have to walk. The 2.5km to the lighthouse take you through a tunnel and past a Phoenecian ochre mine (below the track on the left). For the adventurous walker there is a cliff-top route from the lighthouse to Benidorm, passing by the 438-metre summit of the Sierra Helada (marked by a TV mast).

From Albir follow the road along the head of the beach which takes you past *Altea* (pop. 12,300) harbour and brings you out at a crossroads with traffic lights. Go straight over and up the hill to visit the narrow, stepped streets of Altea's old town. Alternatively, turn right on to the N-332 to head for

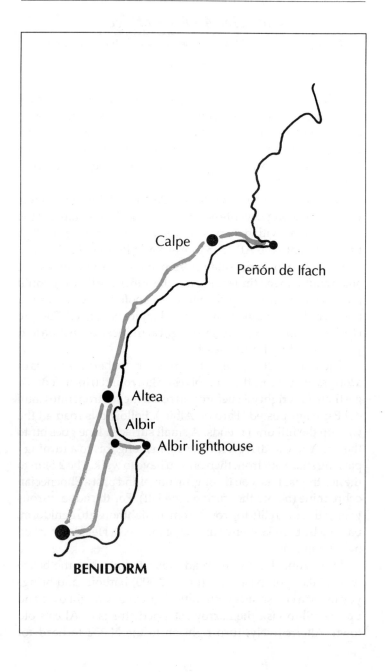

Calpe directly.

After a turn-off for the motorway the road climbs in sharp curves, passing the entrance to a cactus and tropical plant garden which hangs over the cliff-top (Cactuslandia. Tel: 96 584 22 18. Open daylight hours). When the road levels out there are fine views over the sea and the two rocky islets off Altea.

The road now passes through three short tunnels piercing a great wall of rock, the Morro de Toix - the final buttress of the Sierra Bernia. In between the tunnels comes a bridge over an extremely deep and narrow gorge, the Barranco de Mascarat. It is possible to catch only a quick glimpse of it because there is nowhere to stop (a better view can be had from below - as well as of the great sea cliffs of Toix - by taking the road down to the Pueblo Mascarat estate on the Altea side of the tunnels.)

About 3 km after the gorge turn right into *Calpe* (pop. 11,000) and stay on the dual carriageway down the hill, skirting the town centre. Follow the signs for "Port" and "Peñón. Reaching sea level, the road passes by old salt pans on the left. Turn right at the traffic lights for "Puerto Pesquero" (Fishing Port) and the Peñón de Ifach. The tourist information office is just before this turning, also on your right. Fork left by the Hostal Bar Ancla and carry straight on up the hill past the Torre Alejandro apartment block.

Park where you can near the sign for the Parque Natural del Peñón de Ifach (Peñón de Ifach Nature Reserve) and continue up the unsurfaced road on foot to the visitors' reception centre (open Mon-Sat 10am-2pm. Limited parking space for disabled and elderly people only). The centre has a permanent exhibition and video film on the nature reserve, a specialised reference library and a children's room. You can also arrange a guide to meet you here and take you on a tour of the reserve (Tel: 96-386 60 03. Small groups only).

The Peñón was privately owned until it was bought by the regional government in 1987. Its unique eco-system is now protected by law. This colossal block of limestone, seemingly disconnected from the surrounding geography, is home to 300 kinds of wild plants, including several rare species. One, the Calpe carnation, which flowers in spring, grows only here.

Migrating birds use the Pen as a landmark. If you are lucky you might sight an Audouin's gull, identified by its dark green legs and red bill with a black band.

The walk to the top (332m) sets off to the left of the visitors' centre. It presents no special difficulty, although it helps to have a head for heights. It should take a minimum of an hour to get to the exposed summit. Allow two to three hours for the ascent and descent. From the bottom, the rock looks unclimbable without ropes and pitons, as it was until a short, unilluminated tunnel - invisible until you reach it - was built in 1918 to let walkers through to the much gentler slopes on the seaward side of the rock. The footpath is well-worn and takes you across slopes of juniper and fan palm high above the crashing waves. The view from the summit takes in the northern half of the Costa Blanca. Calpe looks like Toy Town below. On a clear day you can even see the hazy hills of Ibiza.

Getting back down is much quicker. If you've built up an appetite there are several restaurants bordering Calpe's little harbour below. Return to the N-332 the way you came and turn left on to it. This will take you straight back to Benidorm.

You can stop at another viewpoint on the way back. You have to follow your nose through the private estate of large, white villas covering the north-facing slopes of the Morro de Toix. Keep going upwards and seawards until you see the road climb steeply ahead to an exposed corner. Park just beyond the last house and walk up to this corner, around which are fabulous views of the coast ❑

Excursion 5 - Cape to Cape:

Denia - Mount Montgó - Cabo San Antonio - Jávea -
Cabo de la Nao - Jesús Pobre - Denia
(67km)

Cliffs, coves, caves, two capes with lighthouses and a mountain national park: Denia and Jávea's pretty coastline is varied but easily seen in a morning. There are plenty of good places to stop - and to eat - on the way which could make this excursion a leisurely day-trip instead.

Leave *Denia* (pop. 24,800) by the A-132, the road behind the tourist information office, which passes the yacht club and at first follows the beach. Soon it winds through undulating hillocks, between ageing, walled-in villas.

After about a kilometre the A-132 heads into the hills towards Jávea (7km) - you'll be going that way shortly - but for now, keep straight on for Las Rotas (Les Rotes), Denia's prettiest beach, which has shelves of rocks offshore making for magnificent skin diving. The beach is overlooked by the Torre del Gerro, which used to be a look-out for pirate attacks. The road ends at Las Rotas. From here the rocky shore line rises into the whitish cliffs of Cape San Antonio.

Return to that junction and head for Jávea on the A-132 which now winds into the Mount Montgó Nature Reserve. The peak itself (753m) rises on the right - a strenuous walk if you are in the mood. Montgó presents a different aspect to north and south. An enormous wall of white cliffs forms the backdrop to Denia. On the Jávea side the cliffs are rose-coloured and especially vivid at sunset. The vegetation on the more gentle, seaward slopes is thick and varied. Montgó's floral wealth attracted the Great Caliph Abd-ar-Rahman III to come and pick medicinal plants here.

After going over a saddle, the road begins to drop down towards Jávea. Turn left for Faro de San Antonio (3.5km). To your right, a line of 17th-century windmills runs along the crest of the hill above Jávea; they were used to grind grain until the beginning of this century, when citrus crops became more

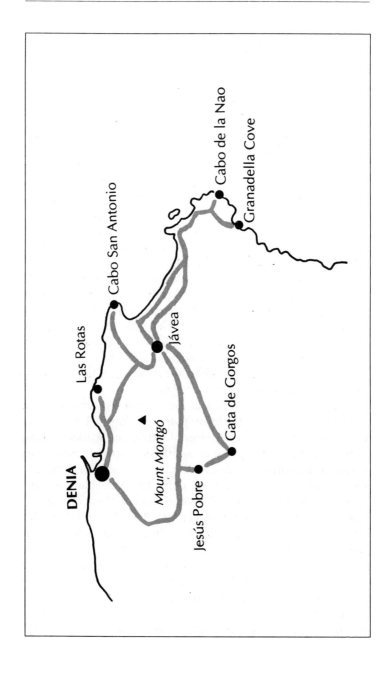

profitable than cereals.

Just before you reach the lighthouse there is a car-park on the right. From here there is a splendid view over the port of Jávea with its modern church, Santa María de Loreto, which was inspired by the ribs of a ship's hull. Return to the main road and carry on down around the bends, past a blue-domed chapel, into the town.

Denia and Jávea may be neighbours but they could not be more different. Whereas Denia is essentially urban, commercial and maritime, incorporating its main tourist services and commercially important harbour in one expanding metropolis, *Jávea* (Xabia. pop. 16,500), is quaint, retiring and prim, with its town centre set discreetly inland from a modest port. Its older buildings are all made of an attractive, locally-ocurring sandstone, *tosca*.

Go straight over the first junction you come to and turn left for "Puerto" (immediately after passing the arched doorway of the market). A long, straight road brings you to the port. Bear to your right along the seafront lined with fancy villas, heading
south. Behind, you have good views of the cliffs of Cape San Antonio. If you stop and look at the beach you'll see where blocks of *tosca* have been carved out.

After passing the Parador and crossing a water channel crammed with boats, you'll come to an area of low-lying touristy restaurants. Round an S-bend and the beach becomes more rocky. Just before the telephone box fork right onto a street which is not sign-posted (it's the last turning before the end of the beachhead road) and you will come out in front of a chemist that is fronted by arches supported on *tosca* columns. Turn left up the hill for Cabo de la Nao. The road climbs towards the coast and upwards into an area of pine woods scattered with villas.

After a few kilometres you'll see a stone cross on a bend on the left. Pull over and from the balcony overhanging the cliffs have a look at the tree-clad Isle of Portichol and the rugged coastline.

At this corner the road turns inland again. After many more

curves, it eventually straightens out and passes a T-junction on the right, sign-posted to the pretty cove of Granadella (4km).

The road comes to an abrupt halt not much further on at Cape de la Nao, from which there are more cliff-top views. There is a bar-restaurant (B-M) next door to the lighthouse.

Turn round and follow the same road back down through the pine trees. When you get to the chemist shop with stone arches you can either turn right and go back along the beach to the town centre the way you came, or carry straight on for a shorter, though less interesting, route.

If you choose the latter, a long straight road takes you parallel with the coast. Turn left by the basket shop (after the mock windmill) for "Xabia". If you're hungry, one of Jávea's best *tapas* bars (also a small, friendly, family restaurant), Bar Paco, is on the right beside the car showrooms (see Town and City Guide).

When you get to the centre of Jávea, follow the one way system for Alicante and Valencia, passing the turning to Cabo de San Antonio, the road you came down earlier. You've seen the coast and you could return to Denia this way if you wish.

The rest of the route completes the circuit around the base of Mount Montgó. If you haven't done your souvenir shopping you can make a detour from Jávea to Gata de Gorgos, a town filled with basket-work shops. Afterwards, follow the signs to Jesús Pobre, pass the village and turn left at the T-junction to rejoin the route.

To follow the main route, however, turn right in Javea into Avenida del Colomer for Jesús Pobre and Denia at the triangular traffic island with an olive tree planted in the middle. Keep straight on along this road which hugs the foot of the slope, passing one of Jávea's classier restaurants, El Gaucho (Ctda. Jesús Pobre, Partida Valls, 62. Tel: 96-579 04 31. Closed Monday and November. Master, Visa. E-VE).

Go over the level crossing and at the next junction bear right for Denia (3.5km) through orange groves scattered with the odd palacial farmstead and whitewashed wellhead. This fertile land is of a premium and not to be wasted - most of the roads are reduced to narrow lanes to take up a minimum of space.

Quite suddenly, you will come to an unusual tower rising into the sky: a minaret, with its copper-coloured dome glinting in the sun. You would be forgiven for thinking that this is a last enclave of the Moors or the private palace of a sheik. La Muntanyeta may be authentic-looking but it is no more than a folly.

The first sign of Denia as you approach it is a view of the castle, standing proud of the coastal plain. Two or three kilometres further on you enter the outskirts of the town ❏

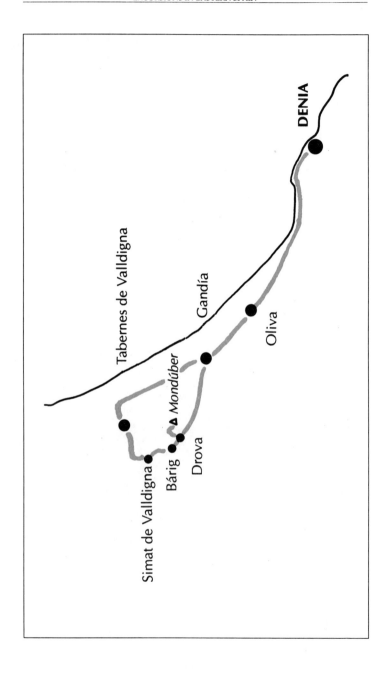

Excursion 6 - The Mountain over the Sea:
Denia - Oliva - Gandía - La Drova - Mondúber - Bárig -
Simat de Valldigna - Tabernes de Valldigna -Denia
(103km

The historic city of Gandía and a mountain top with a spectacular view are the destinations of this trip.

From Denia, take the N-332 north. You can either join it at Ondara (by taking the C-3311 from Denia) or follow the road along the coast. For the latter option, turn left at the waterfront in the town centre, passing the old fishermen's quarter with its quaint rows of brightly-painted houses. Carry straight on along this road behind Las Marinas beach. After a few kilometres the hotels, restaurants, discotheques and apartment blocks thin out. Take the next left turning sign-posted to Valencia (about 10km from Denia). Turn right on to the N-332.

As it crosses into the province of Valencia, the road skirts Pego marshes. The orange trees give way to reed-beds and you may see the occasional snow-white egret winging over them. Eight kilometres after Oliva (pop. 21,000), which has a ruined 14th-century castle, you come to Gandía (pop. 51,800).

Follow the signs for "centro ciudad" and "ayuntamiento," which will take you into the cobbled streets of the old part of town and past the magnificent, arcaded, neo-classical façade of the town hall; a large, white building presiding over the Plaça Constitució.

A little beyond this stands the Palacio Ducal (on Calle Sant Duc). With its richly decorated halls, ornate floors and ceilings, this palace is the thing to see in Gandía. However, you can only visit it on a guided tour (see Town and City Guide).

A little beyond the palace you will strike the Passeig de les Germanes, a wide boulevard cutting across the town. Turn right on to it and follow it all the way up (away from the river). You will find yourself on Carretera de Barx: the main road to Bárig (Barx).

The beginning of this road is lined with holiday villas and restaurants, but soon it curves through a wild neck of land, the

Barranc Sant Nicolau, to enter a U-shaped upland valley.

As you approach La Drova, a cluster of homes becoming popular with Britons, you will see a tall TV booster antenna on the top of the mountain to your right. This marks the summit of Mondúber (Montdúver).

Standing at 841 metres, Mondúber is not particularly high compared with other mountains in the area, but its proximity to the coast makes it an incomparable viewpoint for surveying the Gulf of Valencia. Most of the way up can be travelled by car, but you'll need to walk the last part (about a mile).

Take the last turning on the right in La Drova: Carrer de L'Esparterola. It's sign-posted for "Residencia de 3ª Edad Mondúber" and passes an estate agent's office. Go straight up this steep and badly-surfaced road and soon you will come across a smooth new road without white lines or crash barriers (take care, there's a steep drop to the side) going up the mountainside.

This road finishes at a parking place high up (although there are plans to extend it to the summit). Continue on foot along the broad track which describes wide loops on its way to the peak. There is a short cut (marked by an arrow on a rock) but it is more of a scramble through the undergrowth than a footpath. Close by is the Parpalló cave where a remarkable collection of prehistoric etchings on 5,000 limestone slabs was discovered, which were made over a period of 12,000 years. The cave is not open to the public but some of the slabs are on display in Valencia's Museum of Prehistory.

At the top, next to the TV antenna, is a small white cabin used as a look-out for forest fires during the summer.

On an average day you can see almost 100km of coast from the outskirts of Valencia to Denia; from the Albufera and its rice fields to Mount Montgó. When the air is at its clearest you can even see Ibiza. Inland and to the south, in every direction, there are mountains and more mountains.

The dry slopes of Mondúber are covered with wild flowers and shrubs. Surprisingly, even the mountain-top itself is swarming with wildlife - butterflies, crickets, lizards and vipers - but be careful not to lift any stones or you may surprise a scorpion.

Coming down to the valley again, continue along the road to   Bárig (Barx. pop. 945). If you didn't get to the top of Mondúber, you can get a more limited view of the coast without walking by taking a detour after the town. Look out for a turning to the left on to a surfaced road, which can't be missed as there is a pine tree planted in the middle of the junction. This road curves upwards around the side of the mountain, passing a spring, and levels out after 3.5km to traverse an area of holiday homes. Keep going and you will come to another spring: Font Nova. The road continues to the left of this for another 4.5km through attractive countryside - suitable for picnicking, camping or walking - to a smaller TV antenna. Near the end you have views of the sea and coast southwards to Mount Montgó.

Back on the main road, you now descend in hairpin curves to the flat valley of Valldigna, which is densely planted with orange trees - a sharp contrast to the mountains left behind. Surveying such a fertile sweep of land it is easy to believe that the province of Valencia produces 70 per cent of Spain's citrus fruit. James II of Aragón is said to have seen this view and declared that this was a *"valle digno de un rey"* - a valley fit for a king.

Simat de Valldigna (pop. 3,300) sits on the edge of the coastal plain. The former Cistercian monastery, now in public ownership, is being restored and can be visited only with special permission. Follow the signs through the town for Tabernes de Valldigna. Turn right at the T-junction with the C-3322 and go straight through Tabernes. Turn right onto the N-332 to Gandía and then Denia.

There is still one more curious sight to see on the way home. Just after joining the N-332, take the first surfaced road to the right between the orange trees (near to the km 236 marker). Turn left after passing under the motorway. There you will find the charming Villa Pechina, now in a sad state of repair, which someone has lovingly encrusted with shells, decorated with strange sculptures and crowned with a model steamship.

Retrace your steps to the main road and head south again.

If you want to avoid the traffic snarl-ups in Gandía and Oliva, take the first motorway entrance you come to (number 60). Denia is the next exit but one ❏

Excursion 7 - A Watery Labyrinth:

Valencia - El Saler - La Albufera - El Palmar- Monte de los
Santos - Sueca - Cullera - Valencia
(82km).

The ultimate objective of this excursion is to eat a good paella. To build up an appetite for it you're going to travel first through the paddies where the rice is grown for Valencia's internationally-famous dish. The fields are at their best in June and July, when the vivid green crop is well advanced. It's a particularly enjoyable area to amble about on foot or by bicycle at sunset. This route also takes you through a nature reserve rich in wildfowl and up to two viewpoints from which to survey the flat, watery labyrinth.

Leave Valencia on the short motorway (V-15) that heads for the resort of El Saler (from the end of Angel Custodio bridge). As you cross the new course of the River Turia (diverted after disastrous flooding of the city centre in 1957) you'll see the first rice fields. Don't turn off for El Saler but keep on the motorway as it merges into the B-road along the coast. Passing the town (on your left) look right and you'll see a colourful huddle of rowing boats in a small harbour. This whole area is criss-crossed with tiny navigable canals.

The road skirts La Albufera, a singular freshwater lake that is - despite pollution from surrounding factories and the seasonal havoc wreaked by hunters - still one of Europe's most important coastal wetlands and a vital stop-over for migrating birds. It was given limited protection when it was declared a nature reserve *(parque natural)* in 1986. There's a parking place and viewpoint on the right of the road next to a fisherman's hut. The long poles sticking out of the water are used to fish for eels, mullet and bass.

The lake is extremely shallow - only 1-2.5 metres deep - and is gradually shrinking (in the Middle Ages the lake was ten times its present size). Not only does it silt up naturally but farmers around its fringes are also reclaiming land. Even so, La Albufera owes its continuing existence to the cultivation of

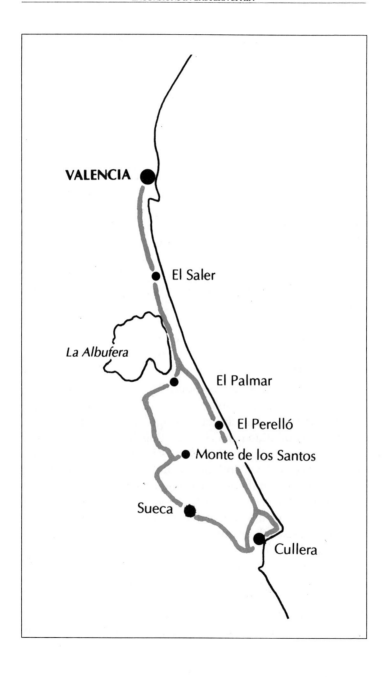

VALENCIA

El Saler

La Albufera

El Palmar

El Perelló

Monte de los Santos

Sueca

Cullera

rice. Without the paddy fields the water would be diverted to other crops elswhere and the lake and the birds would disappear.

La Albufera is connected to the sea by three channels (or *golas*) and you now cross one of them. It's fitted with sluice gates to control the water level in the lake.

Between the road and sea stretches the Dehesa, a biologically-rich habitat of wooded sand dunes, which was partially built up in the '60s and '70s with unsightly apartment blocks.

Take the right turning to El Palmar. Near this junction there is a nature reserve information centre, Raco de l'Olla (open daily, 9am-2pm), with a glass-domed observation tower. Wall panels tell you about the ecology of La Albufera and the species to be seen. About 250 kinds of birds have been recorded here, 90 of which breed. There are large numbers of egrets, herons, terns and ducks. Some years, between 50,000 and 60,000 ducks gather here (including up to three quarters of Europe's population of red-crested pochard).

If you want to get closer to the birds, the fishermen of El Palmar organise boat trips of La Albufera (Tel: 96-386 37 38 or look out for signs on the road).

Continuing towards El Palmar there are several secluded places to pull over on the right and creep into the reeds, binoculars at the ready. Many of the birds congregate on and around the lake's six islands or *matas*.

The road crosses three more water channels and there are good views of the reed-beds from the bridges. As you approach El Palmar you'll see several *barracas* - traditional Valencian houses with steeply-pitched thatched roofs - among the neat market gardens. In days gone by the inhabitants of these houses around La Albufera inspired the Valencian novelist Vicente Blasco Ibañez.

You may be forgiven for thinking that El Palmar's main occupation is serving paella. There are plenty of restaurants to choose from around the main square including La Isla (Pl. Sequiota, 10. Tel: 96-162 00 40. Visa. M) and Cañas y Barro (Caudete, 7. Tel: 96-161 10 97. Closed Tuesday. Visa. B-M) As well as paella you'll find another speciality of La Albufera on the menu: *all i pebre* (eels in a spicy sauce). If you can wait, good paellas can also be found further south in Cullera.

Go all the way through the village and down Calle Redolins. When you can go no further, turn right onto a small road which crosses a bridge and sets off in a dead straight line across the paddy fields (not marked on the map). As you cross the bridge look out for the brightly-painted narrow boats used to navigate the channels around La Albufera.

After the next bridge the road jerks 90 degrees round to the left and for a while runs beside an irrigation ditch. From April, (when the fields are first flooded) until July (when the rice leaves blot out the water) this little lane is a causeway across a glassy maze. One third of Spain's rice (short-grain for Valencian cuisine) is grown here.

Although the drained and muddy fields are less inviting during the winter months, plenty of birdlife can be found all year round. Most common are the flocks of snow-white little egret pecking among the mud or standing motionless. Solitary herons fly above you on slow wings or stand one-leggedly in

corners like statues. Black-winged stilt, easily-identifiable because of their improbably long pink legs, peck at the squelchy earth.

Although there are many inviting tracks that zig-zag erratically around the edges of the fields, don't be tempted to stray off the surfaced road. It's easy to get lost around here.There are few landmarks (just a handful of farmhouses and the odd disused rice factory) with which to orient yourself - although you can usually spot the line of high-rise apartments along the beach.

Eventually, you come to a junction where the main surfaced road turns right across the water channel for Sollana. If you've had enough of rice fields you can follow this to the N-332 and turn left for Cullera to continue the route more rapidly.

Straight on is an unsurfaced road bound for Sueca, which follows the water channel. It's slightly bumpy but easily passable by car. If you look in front you will now see two more useful landmarks. To your left is a prominent hill, Mount Zorras, at the base of which stands Cullera. Nearer to hand, a conspicuous concrete water tower marks a dimple of a hill among the rice fields. This is the Monte de los Santos (Muntanyeta dels Sants), your next objective.

Ignore all turnings as before. When you come to the next T-junction, turn left then a quick right: in effect travelling straight on towards the Monte de los Santos. This brings you to a wide, new, smooth-surfaced thoroughfare, which looks like a main road but is only a glorified agricultural access road cutting across the rice fields from north to south. Turn right onto this road. When you come to a crossroads turn left towards the Monte de los Santos. Take your bearings because you will be coming back to this crossroads shortly.

On reaching the base of the hill, turn right towards the rice silos and you'll find a left turning taking you to a car park. Steps lead up to a chapel and a panoramic view of the paddy fields. The pretty 17th century Ermita de la Pedra (open only on Sundays) is dedicated to Saints Abdon and Sennen. They are the patrons of the rice fields and, according to popular lore, are the "Stone Saints" who specialise in protecting crops from

47

hailstones. On July 30th the people of nearby Sueca flock here for a fiesta to mark the saints' feast day. In early September they return to prepare a giant paella as part of their Rice Festival.

Return to the wide access road and go straight over the crossroads (and over the railway line) to join the N-332. Turn left on to the N-332 and keep on it through Sueca (pop. 23,000), capital of the rice belt. After three or four kilometres turn off for Cullera (pop. 20,200), which, above all else, has a good rice restaurant in a picturesque spot. (If you want to cut the route short take the left turning in front of a futuristic night spot, built of black girders, and turn left at the T-junction to join the coast road to Valencia.)

As you enter Cullera follow the signs for "*centro ciudad*." These take you under an iron bridge and on to the banks of the River Jucar, which is lined with moored boats. Soon you have to choose between veering right over another bridge across the river or forking left for "Platges" (beaches) along Diagonal País Valencià. Choose the former if you're ready for a paella or the latter if you want to go up to the castle.

To find the restaurant, cross the river and turn left immediately. Take the left turning for "Marenyet", which begins by following the river but then leads you through fields and round an old tower (the 16th century Marenyet). From here, follow the signs for the restaurant and for Estany de Cullera. Casa Salvador (Tel: 96-172 01 36. Open daily 1-11pm. M), is sited on a pretty inlet, in two joined *barracas*. If you dislike rice, Les Mouettes (Tel 96-172 00 10. On the way up to the castle. Closed Sunday evening and Monday. E) specialises in French cuisine.

From Cullera you can either follow the signs for "Valencia per la Costa" (Valencia via the coast) - a quicker route. Or you can take a more torturous road around the beaches of Cullera: follow the signs beneath the castle for *Far* - lighthouse. This road winds around the headland to meet the coast road. Turn right on to it.

There are more rice fields along this road but orange groves and apartment blocks are steadily gaining ground. For most of the way until La Albufera you have a long line of developing high- rise holiday resorts to your right and intensive agriculture to your left. As you pass through El Perelló, look left for a view of a photogenic fishing hut stranded in the water.

A few kilometres further on you pass Valencia's Parador which is surrounded by a golf course. Keep going and you will find yourself on the road you came down earlier, along the shore of La Albufera. Take the motorway again, just before El Saler, to return to the centre of Valencia ❑

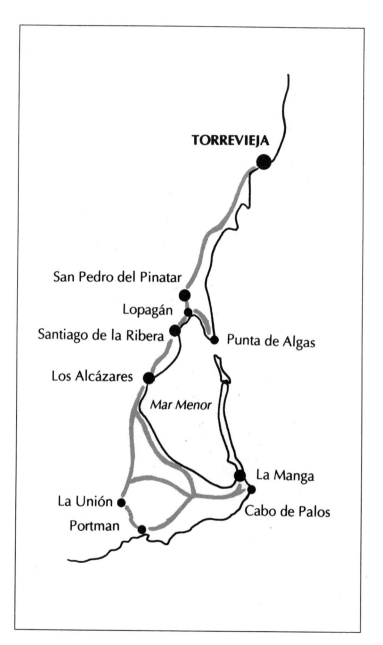

Excursion 8 - The Smaller Sea:

Torrevieja - San Pedro del Pinatar - Punta de Algas -
Santiago de la Ribera - Los Alcázares - Cabo de Palos -
La Manga - Torrevieja
(130km)

The Mar Menor is a large salt-water lagoon annexed from the main body of the Mediterranean by a long, sandy strip (now a thriving tourist resort), La Manga. The landscape is dead flat, but far from uninteresting. If you can spend more than a day you can extend the route to explore further into the little-known province of Murcia.

Leave *Torrevieja* (pop. 25,000) by the N-332 in the direction of Cartagena. This road heads down the coast past intermittent apartment blocks before emerging on an agricultural plain which straddles the border between the provinces of Alicante and Murcia.

In San Pedro de Pinatar (pop. 4,000) take one of the several turnings on the left for "Mar Menor". The one-way system through the backstreets is badly sign-posted but you should come out on a main road, flanked by brick buildings, which leads to Lopagán.

When you get to the waterfront at Lopagán (pop.730) turn left up the first narrow street on to an avenue lined with palm trees. This takes you to the atmospheric, windswept causeway of Punta de Algas. From here there are views of the resorts of the Mar Menor and the tip of La Manga - which seems tantalisingly close but is still a long drive away. Punta de Algas also has a ruined windmill and extensive saltflats, the only part of the Mar Menor protected as a nature reserve.

Do not be surprised if you see people around here caking themselves in slimy mud; these mud baths are famous for their curative powers (especially for arthritis and rheumatism). The water of the Mar Menor has a high concentration of mineral salts and iodine.

Return down the avenue and find your way back to the harbour through the one-way system and carry on along the shore. The road becomes a *paseo* (promenade) beside the beach, shaded by more palm trees, and enters Santiago de la Ribera (pop. 2,200) where there are pretty painted wooden jetties (the brown concrete yacht club creates a sharp contrast to them).

From Santiago de la Ribera you can visit two of the Mar Menor's six islands. They are largely rocky and treeless but have good beaches. The largest, Isla Mayor, which has a tower and a 108-metre viewpoint, is also called "The Baron's Isle" because, according to legend, a Tsarist aristocrat fleeing from the Russian Revolution fell in love with it. There are boats twice a day in summer. For details contact the tourist information office (C/ Padre Juan. Tel: 968-57 17 04).

Keep on the road by the beach and follow it as it turns inland past the airforce training base (on the left). Turn left at the T-junction along the other side of the base, passing Murcia's airport. The road turns sharply to the right at Los Narejos to meet the N-332. Turn left for Cartegena.

In Los Alcázares (pop. 720) the beach is very close behind the town but you'll have to park and walk a few yards as there is no road along it. It has a particularly attractive landing stage.

Balneario La Encarnación (C/Condesa, 1. Tel 968-57 50 07. Open summer only), arranged around a courtyard dripping

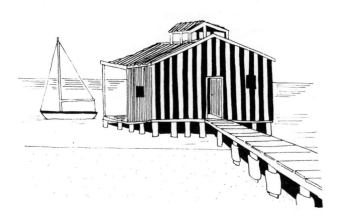

with flowers and foliage, was the first hotel built on the shores of the Mar Menor. Ostensibly it's a spa although it in fact provides heated sea-water. It's so popular with its regular clients that it is virtually impossible to book a room less than a year in advance.

On the main road through the town you will find one of the best-value restaurants on the shores of the Mar Menor: Ramón (Tel 968-574 173. B) is renowned for its seafood.

Carry on along the N-332 out of Los Alcázares. Just after the petrol station there is a track to the right leading to the 16th century Torre del Rame, one of many neglected defensive towers to be seen in this area.

Take the left turn (opposite the campsite) for Los Urrutias. This lane brings you close to the shore and affords views across the water to the surreal, jagged skyline of La Manga whose skyscrapers seem to march across the middle of the sea.

Go straight through Los Urrutias and in Los Nietos follow the signs for Cartagena and La Manga. This brings you to a pair of roundabouts, one at either side of a new dual carriageway, which will speed you along the next few kilometres. Follow the signs for La Manga.

Just before you enter La Manga, turn right on to a one-way road for Cabo de Palos, where a lighthouse stands on a low, rocky headland. There's a car-park and playground at its base. From here you have a view of La Manga stretching into the sea and, offshore on the Mediterranean side, a conical island.

Return the way you came and take the only road into La Manga. Not so long ago this was a desolate strip important for its wildlife. Now, however, it's a one-way, high-rise holiday strip dormant in winter, bustling in summer. Tourists, say the brochures, can choose between two seas to bathe in.

You can follow the road for 18km towards the tip of the sand bar which almost meets the Punta de Algas. But there is only one way back. When you have satisfied your curiosity, take the dual carriageway towards Cartagena.

If you are ready to head back, follow this road until you reach the junction with the N-332 at El Algar and turn north for Torrevieja. But if you are in the mood to explore a very different region - a harsh but compelling landscape of industrial archaeology - turn off the dual carriageway at the same exit that you joined it on earlier (sign-posted "Golf" and "Escombreras" coming from La Manga).

A shaky road leads you up to the luxurious La Manga Club, a leisure complex with a hotel and restaurants (Tel: 968- 56 45 11. All cards. M-E) and a golf course. The road becomes smoother between the greens and fairways but then returns to its bone-rattling state.

After passing through some low hills (which, surprisingly, conceal the last woods of one of the rarest trees in Europe, the Barbary arbor-vitae) you begin to drop down towards the sea. Suddenly, you are in quite a different landscape after the flat and gentle countryside around the Mar Menor. Above, on the right, looms the bulk of Mount Cenizas, a headland towering 337 metres above the sea.

Down below, the infamous Portman sits at the head of beach blackened by years of unchecked pollution. At one time, the mines in this valley produced most of Spain's lead and zinc, and the refining process pumped out 90 per cent of the country's marine contamination. The houses surrounding the abandoned works are now becoming holiday homes and, although the landscape has been permanently changed by industry, the former natural beauty of the area is reasserting itself.

Just before you get to Portman, double back left on to the narrow road which goes to Faro de Punta Negra. You can't get all the way to the lighthouse because it is surrounded by a military base, but you can get down to a pretty beach-cum-harbour, from which you have a fine view of the mountainous Murcian coast towards Cape Tinoso in the distance.

Continue through Portman for La Unión (pop. 11,800). The road twists through hills badly scarred by mining with old shafts and ruined pit-head buildings littered everywhere. The Carthaginians (after whom Cartagena is named) were the first to mine here. Later, some 40,000 men slaved away for the Romans in the extraction of lead and silver. The trees which once cloaked these slopes were cut down to make pit-props and to feed fires for smelting.

When you reach the main road at La Esperanza ("Hope" is a reassuring name for a town on the edge of such a desolate landscape) turn right and follow the signs for Alicante round the mining town of La Unión (which stages an annual miners' song festival in August), connecting with the main route again at El Algar.

A short way out of El Algar you'll see one of the Mar Menor's best-restored windmills to the left, standing guard over an orange grove. To look at the windmill, take the unmarked turning after the white house. The windmill is private and screened from the lane by a wire fence but you can get very close to it.

Further on, the main road takes you past another of the Mar Menor's towers, the Torre del Negro - on to which a house has been attached. Soon you pass the turning to Los Urrutias which you took earlier, and enter Los Alcázares. Carry straight on back to Torrevieja by the N-332 ❑

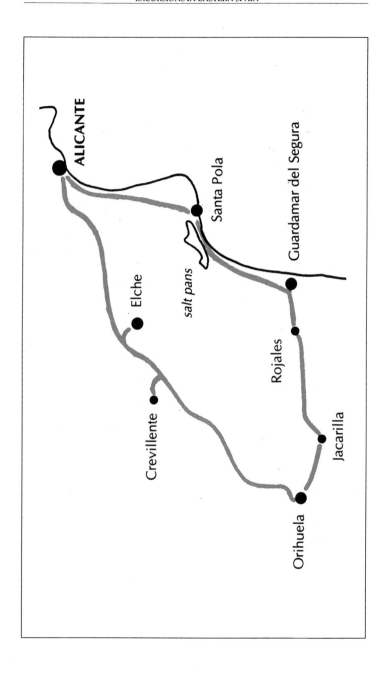

Excursion 9 - Palms and Palaces:

Alicante - Santa Pola - Guardamar del Segura - Rojales -
Jacarilla - Orihuela - Elche - Alicante
(125km)

The fishing port of Santa Pola and its salt flats could justify a half-day's visit by itself. Orihuela and Elche are worth at least the same, if not a day. If you don't have time, this route takes you on a lightning tour of these and other interesting places south of Alicante.

Leave the city on the N-332 for Cartagena which first crosses the flat, marshy coastal plain on which Alicante airport (El Altet) stands. After passing through the village of El Altet the road climbs over the headland of Cape Santa Pola. A left turning takes you on a brief detour to the lighthouse, 143 metres above sea level, from which there are views of the coast and the Isle of Tabarca. The main road then drops down towards a vast area of salt pans. A bacteria, *halofila*, turns the evaporating water a shade of pink as the concentration of salt builds up. This colour switch is sometimes enhanced by weather conditions. The salt pans are particularly striking at sunset.

Turn left into Santa Pola (pop. 14,250). In Roman times this was the port of Elche, but now it's a thriving town in its own right, with one of the most important fishing fleets on Spain's Mediterranean coast. You can buy fresh fish from the day's catch at quayside auctions. This is the closest point of departure for Tabarca (see Excursion 1).

Santa Pola castle in the town centre was built in the 16th century to defend the sea-faring community against attacks from Berber pirates. It now houses the fascinating Municipal Aquarium (closed Monday morning). Upstairs there's an Archaeological Museum and a Fishing Museum.

The best thing about this aquarium is that there is not a tropical fish in sight. The 80-odd different species represented in its seven large tanks are all locals: they have been taken from the Bay of Santa Pola or the waters off Tabarca.

The aquarium not only provides a fascinating display, but

it has a lot to do with conservation: sometimes sick animals - turtles especially - are brought in for nursing back to health. The population of the tanks changes frequently as these creatures are released back in the wild. What you see depends on when you visit: sharks, turtles, cuttlefish and octopus (which, we were told, are wont to slither out of their tanks and go walkabout) are all visitors from time to time.

The thing to eat in Santa Pola - if you can face it after the aquarium - is seafood. The best restaurants are pricey. They include Varadero (Santiago Bernabéu s/n. Tel: 96-541 17 66. All cards. E-VE), Miramar (Avda. Pérez Ojeda 8. Tel: 96-541 10 00. All cards. E) and Batiste (Avda. Pérez Ojeda. Tel: 96-541 14 85. All cards. M).

A more economical restaurant is Cervecería Loroy (C/ Muelle 27. Tel. 96-541 20 91. Open May-September, 1-4pm and 7-12pm. B), a pleasant and modern bar with large windows on a corner opposite the port..

From Santa Pola go back to the N-332 and continue south along the causeway that crosses the salt flats. The grounds of the little chapel near the salt works are carpeted with a purple-pink creeper in springtime.

The salt works straddle the road. On the left you will see enormous, brilliant white conical piles of crystals. The Romans began the industry to produce salazón - salted fish. A fourth-century salting factory has been excavated near Santa Pola. The salt pans that you can see now were constructed at the beginning of this century and produce up to 100,000 tonnes of salt a year. Much of it is exported to northern Europe.

Apart from their commercial importance, the lagoons also support a great variety of birds: a welcome example of economics and ecology working together. Large flocks of flamingoes (up to 3,000) make a vital stop-over here en route between their two European breeding grounds: the Camargue in France and Fuente de Piedra in Málaga. This is also one of the last European breeding sites of the rare marbled teal.

Halfway across the salt pans is the stranded stump of the 15-th century Tamarit tower which once stood on the coast - the sea has receded since it was built. Park in the lay-by if you want to have a leisurely look at the salt flats and their birdlife.

Leaving the salt flats the road climbs up to an area of cultivated land and crosses La Marina. On the left the coast is now densely covered with pine woods.

Turn left into Guardamar del Segura (pop. 5,700) and on entering the town turn left by the supermarket into Calle Dunas (sign-posted "playa" and "dunas"). A maze of roads leads around an extensive area of dunes covered with pine woods. Part of this area has been turned into a park with lakes and a nature trail.

Guardamar del Segura used to be situated on the coast, but following an earthquake which destroyed almost all its 550 houses - as well as its church and castle - the survivors built inland. Having survived one natural disaster, the town was then faced with another: blizzards of sand. The pine trees were not planted as a civic amenity but to stabilize the creeping dunes.

The best-known restaurant is Rincón de Pedro (Urbanización Las Dunas. Tel: 96-572 80 95. Closed Wednesday in winter. Amex, Visa. M), which specialises in seafood and rice.

Return to the main road and cross over it on to the C-3323 which winds through flat, well-irrigated land towards Rojales (6km). When you reach the small square in the centre of Rojales (pop. 5,000) turn left across the bridge spanning the River Segura. But do look at the bridge itself as you cross; it was built in the 18th century and is lined with noble stone benches.

The road on the south of the River Segura is unclassified but good. Follow the signs for Benijófar, then Algorfa, then Benejúzar. Turn left at the roundabout in Benejúzar for Jacarilla (4km). The road turns away from the river and crosses and overgrown railway line. Ahead, two mountains rise above the plain. Callosa de Segura sits at the foot of the nearer one, and Orihuela of the one furthest away. When you get to Jacarilla, turn left opposite Bar Curro into Calle Duque de Cubas which becomes Avenida de la Cruz. Behind the church a surprise awaits. A gateway guarded by a pair of lions lets you into an avenue lined with palm trees and low, clipped hedges. These cool, elegant gardens (open from 8am to 6pm) with their statues and grotto, once belonged to the Marquis of Fontalba.

At the end of the main avenue, over to the left, is the marquis' cream-coloured palace decorated with unusual yellow and blue ceramic balustrades. Beside the house, down the steps, are old cages with miniature, decorated houses for large animals to live in - although we could find no one to tell us what beasts were kept there.

Return to the main road and carry on for *Orihuela* (pop. 49,500), joining the A-332. The last stretch of road runs in a dead straight line towards the Seminario de San Miguel (a school for clergymen) which overlooks Orihuela.

Turn right, crossing the River Segura again, following the signs for Alicante. The city centre is on the left. The cathedral and Easter Week Museum are worth stopping to visit even if you don't have time to stroll around the rest of this once grand city.

You can see some of the sights as you drive through. Look out left for the old casino (a gentleman's club). Further on you pass the former university, now a school, which is glimpsed through a stone arch gateway, the Puerta de la Olma (again on the left).

The road leaves Orihuela through extensive palm groves (somewhat smaller than those of Elche - still to come - but nevertheless impressive). Six kilometres from Orihuela take the A-7 motorway (toll-free) which speeds you to Elche. Crevillente (pop. 22,000), on the way, is important for its carpet industry. If it is still daylight, take exit 74 for *Elche* (pop. 188,000), a large city famed for its thousands of palm trees. From Elche you can either continue on the motorway and take Exit 71 into Alicante, or take the old main road, the N-340, which brings you into the south of the city ❏

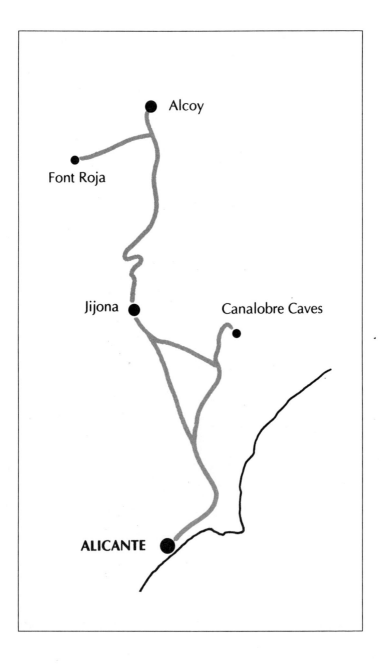

Excursion 10 - The Red Fountain:

Alicante - Font Roja - Alcoy - Alicante
(125km)

Alcoy, the province of Alicante's second city, is picturesquely located among beautiful mountains. Of the many areas of natural beauty nearby, the most outstanding is Font Roja, the destination of this trip.

Leave Alicante on the N-340 which sets off across scruffy badlands of mud carved by the elements into ravines. If you want to see one of the region's best caves, take the turning for Cuevas de Canalobre (and Busot) just after Muchamiel. The caves, at a height of 700 metres, are 7km from Busot. There is a good view from the entrance.

The caves (open daily: April-September, 10.30am-8.30pm; October-March, 11am-6pm. Closed Christmas and New Year's Day) are on various levels and there are many steps. They were formed seven and a half million years ago and discovered by the Arabs in 740 AD. Inside, the temperature is a constant 16 degrees, making them a cool refuge in summer; indeed, before refrigerators were invented they were used for cold storage. Subtle lighting displays the stalagmites and stalactites, one of which is said to resemble a candelabrum (*canelobre* in Valencian). Concerts and dances are held in the main cave, a chamber over 300 feet high.

Head for Alcoy and you'll come out again on the N-340. The mountains converge on the town of Jijona (pop. 7,400), famed for its manufacture of *turrón* (see Excursion 2).

After Jijona the landscape - now the upper valley of the River Torremanzanas - becomes more green and interesting, with many almond trees. The road climbs in long zig-zags to a pass, the Port de la Carrasqueta (1024 metres above sea level), giving views back over Jijona and, in the distance, the coast. On the way you'll pass Venta de Teresa (Puerto de la Carrasqueta. Tel: 96-561 26 63. As well as traditional cuisine you can taste home-made *turrón*. B).

On the other side of the pass you descend through attractive wooded scenery leading into the Barranc de la Batalla, part of the Font Roja nature reserve. The road goes through a tunnel and over a bridge. As soon as you reach Alcoy turn left up the hill for Font Roja.

Having been protected by the city of Alcoy since 1332, Font Roja must rank among the world's longest-running ecological success stories. The nature reserve, at 1,000 metres of altitude, is a unique eco-system of mixed woodland. Fifteen different kinds of trees - including oak, ash, maple and even yew (reaching the south of its range in Europe) - and 40 species of shrub occur here.

Its mainly deciduous foliage comes as a welcome contrast in autumn to the evergreen forests that cover most slopes in Eastern Spain. These woods are inhabited by many birds, among them woodpeckers, firecrests, nightingales and two species of eagle. Curiously, the humble robin has few other places to nest in the province of Alicante. A rare and solitary pair of wild cats also have their den amongst the trees.

Little has changed since the 18th century botanist Antonio José Cavanilles commended the "beautiful views, thick woods all along the slopes and abundant springs of pure water: the best in the kingdom, so cool in summer that it is impossible to hold your hand under it for two minutes."

Font Roja, "the Red Spring," is named after one particular water source (now a fountain) which is surrounded by red clay. As well as a nature reserve, Font Roja has been a place of pilgrimage since 1653 when a priest saw a vision of the Virgin Mary in the bulb of a lily. A little chapel was built on the spot at the end of last century.

The most conspicuous building, nowadays, is the 1920s hotel which protrudes from the slope and is capped by a gigantic white statue of the Virgin of the Lilies, Alcoy's patroness. Although it fell into a state of disrepair, the building is to be renovated as a centre for conferences on wildlife and ecology.

There's a car-park, viewpoint and picnic site near the chapel and hotel. There's also a campsite (apply to Alcoy town hall for permission to use it. Tel: 96- 554 52 11). From here you can follow a 13km trail which takes you through the woods and high up the slope before delivering you back at your starting point.

Near the start of the walk (on the left) is the Cueva Helada, or Freezing Cave. You only need to step into the entrance on a hot day to appreciate why it was so named.

Further up you come to a clearing in which the ground is stained black as testimony to the ancient forest craft of charcoal burning.

There are six ice pits in Font Roja, one of which lies near the path, higher up the slope. Built in the 18th century, these holes were used for storing perishable items in the summer months and for preserving ice for sale in the cities.

Near the highest point of the trail another path branches off to the summit of Mount Menetjador (1,352 metres) from which the view is incomparable.

When you have had your fill of nature, come back down the hill to the crossroads and turn left into the centre of Alcoy (pop. 62,300). Although it is an industrial city and doesn't have a tourist information office, Alcoy is picturesquely sited in a deep valley at the confluence of three rivers and it's streets exude the charm of a well-to-do textile city. In April it holds one of the most visually-memorable fiestas in Spain (see Town and City Guide).

The quickest way back to Alicante is the way you came along the N-340. A longer, scenic alternative is to turn left on to the C-3313 in the Barranc de Batalla and then take the A-170 (s ee Excursion 11) from Benasau to Villajoyosa. From there the motorway or N-332 will whisk you back to the capital ❏

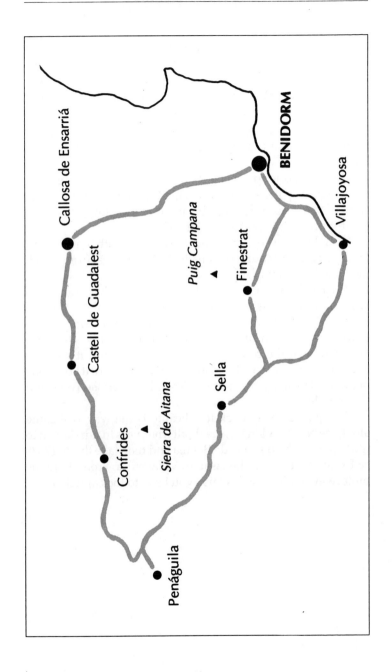

Excursion 11 - A Secret Garden:

Benidorm - Callosa d'Ensarriá - Castell de Guadalest -
Confrides - Penáguila - Alcolecha - Sierra Aitana - Sella -
Finestrat - Benidorm
(105km).

This is a mountain circuit around Alicante province's highest peak, Aitana (1,558m), with the possibility of visiting a secret garden (phone to arrange a visit in advance - see below) and a high-altitude safari park.

Take the C-3318 from Benidorm through Callosa de Ensarriá and continue up to Guadalest and Benimantell as in Excursion 3. Carry on along the same road up the valley.

Over the centuries the slopes of the upper Guadalest valley have been carved into thousands of small hill terraces, each supported on time-worn stone walls and watered by a furtive irrigation ditch. The best time to see it is in February at the height of the almond blossom.

The well-surfaced road follows the contours of the slope. When you approach the end of the valley the terraces thin out and the land becomes more wild. A right turning takes you to Abdet (1.2km) from where there is a view back down the whole valley to the sea.

Confrides (pop. 345), with its ruined castle (on a ridge on the left of the road), stands at the head of the valley. There are two economical restaurants on the main road: Jamí (San Antonio No phone. Open daily. No cards. B) and El Pirineo (San Antonio. No phone. Closed Tuesday. No cards. B), which also has rooms.

The valley suddenly ends in a rocky gorge. The road follows this, still climbing towards an enormously high wall of rock. At the end of the gorge the landscape is truly bleak and mountainous. On the next tight corner is an incongruously-sited bar-restaurant serving Canary Islands dishes: El Rincón del Olvido (No phone. Open weekdays and Sunday 10am-5pm. Friday and Saturday 10am-5pm and 8-12pm. Closed Monday).

Crossing over the 966-metre pass, Puerto de Ares, you come down a series of hairpins through what was once (and hopefully will be again) beautiful wooded scenery, badly burnt by a forest fire. Soon the almonds and olives reappear. Take the next left turning for "Alcoleja" and "La Vila Joiosa". When you come to a T-junction, turn right on to the A-164 for Penáguila (3km).

Penáguila (pop. 400) now seems like just another small town lost in the hills but it was once an important country seat and it retains a hint of its lost grandeur in the aristocratic coats of arms over some of its doorways. Parts of the old defensive walls, including one gateway, have been incorporated into the houses. It's overlooked by a high, rocky pinnacle from which it gets its name - "Eagle Rock" - although sadly there are no eagles around here any more.

The main reason to come to Penáguila is to see a small but engaging, garden which sits like an oasis amongst the parched hills. The Jardín de Santos was laid out by a wealthy aristocratic family in the 18th century (their descendents still live in the tallest house in the village) but has recently passed into the hands of the town hall.

The mayor, Enrique Picó Gisbert, has been in love with the garden since he was a small boy. Then, the commonfolk were allowed into the garden on only one day a year. He is determined to restore it to its former splendour and open it to everyone. Until the restoration is complete, however, you can visit the

garden only by phoning Sr Picó in advance (Tel: 96 551 30 03).

If you can't contact him, or you would like just a glimpse of the garden, you can still peer through the gate. There are two routes to get there. Either way, leave the village the way you came. If you are on foot or bicycle, take the track just before a white bridge which snakes down through the woods and passes between two stone gate-posts. This is the formal drive, flanked all the way by cypresses.

If you are in a car, carry on over the bridge and look out for an unsurfaced track to the left with a 20km/h sign which leads down the hill from a bend (about 1km from the village). The garden surrounds a rectangular green pond with a water-spout that casts rainbows in the sunshine. By the entrance gate is a brilliant-blue summer house. Behind it is an ornamental maze of concentric rectangles of yew and cypress hedges leading to a Cedar of Lebanon.

Elsewhere you'll find an old conservatory; a mossy woodland walk between chestnut, yew, magnolia and spindle trees; a Baroque grotto decorated with stalactites taken from a local cave; and a large, circular wrought iron birdcage.

After visiting the garden, go back along the road you came on. Turn right on to the A-170 for Alcolecha (Alcoleja. pop. 350), which gathers around a lovely round stone tower with a conical roof - part of the palace of the Marquis of Malferit. The road now starts to climb towards the mountains of the Sierra Aitana, through woods and underneath cliffs flushed salmon-pink.

After the entrance to the military base (the top of the mountain is given over to antennae and two radar domes), on the left you come to a crossroads 1,207m up at the Puerto de Tudons. The right turn takes you to a safari park (Safari Aitana. Open daily). Its tigers and elephants could not seem more out of place at an altitude of 1000 metres.

Keep straight on for Sella (12km). The road immediately drops down in curves with splendid views of the southern slopes of the Sierra Aitana on the left - much gentler than the northern slopes which you saw earlier coming up the Guadalest valley.

As you approach Sella (pop. 620) you'll see a large, lonely mountain ahead which looks as if a slice has been cut out of the summit. This is Puig Campana, the 1,410m peak behind Benidorm. The "missing" slice is called La Cuchillada de Roldán - Roldán's Gash. According to legend, the giant Roldán was in love with an Arab princess. One day a curse was placed on the princess: she was to die that very evening as soon as darkness fell. When Roldán saw the sun going down behind Puig Campana he struck a slice out of the mountain top to give him and his love a last few minutes of daylight. In his grief he hurled the slab of rock that he had carved out into the sea where it became the Isle of Benidorm.

Continue on the main road through Sella, which has a castle with a shrine built in it. Restaurant L'Hort (on the main road. No phone. Closed Monday. B) is popular with the Costa Blanca's foreign residents.

You now come down into a landscape carved into ravines of soft, red earth. Six kilometres after Sella you can choose your route back to Benidorm. Straight on, after Orcheta reservoir, is Villajoyosa. Turn left on to the N-332 to return to your starting point.

The left turning takes you across badlands to the pretty village of Finestrat which sits at the base of the now pyramidal Puig Campana. Turn right into the village centre. (A road to the left takes you half way up the mountain. It can only be climbed by an excruciatingy long bed of scree.)

Finestrat (pop. 1,100) has narrow streets of well-kept houses and an exceptionally quaint square which has been recently marred on one side by the insensitive construction of a new town hall. Hostal La Costera (San José, 1. Tel: 96-587 80 76. B) is a cheap and unpretentious place to eat.

Don't take the old backroad to Benidorm, but go down the hill past the sports centre to the next crossroads and turn left to pick up a fast new road to the La Cala end of Benidorm ❏

Excursions 12 - Blossoms and Bodegas:

Benidorm - Callosa de Ensarriá - Fuentes del Algar -
Tárbena - Coll de Rates - Parcent - Alcalalí - Jalón - Sierra
Bernia - Benissa - Benidorm
(115km)

High mountain views; a lush valley of vines and almonds; a swim if you wish; and a choice of inexpensive eating. What more could you want from a day out?

Take the C-3318 from Benidorm to Callosa de Ensarriá and turn off the mini-roundabout in the town centre for three points on the route: Fuentes del Algar (2.9km), Tárbena (12km) and Coll de Rates (20km). The road is still the C-3318.

As you leave Callosa, the Sierra Bernia appears ahead. The poet Gabriel Miró described the range as "an upturned galleon, its keel broken." Much later on the route you'll be up there looking back down at where you are now.

Immediately after the brick factory take the right turning to Fuentes del Algar (1km). This pretty waterfall has been developed into a weekend resort with several restaurants specialising in paella. Casa Marcos (Open all year. Tel: 96-588 08 68. B-M) has a swimming pool for a pre-lunch dip. You can also bathe in the chilly water at the bottom of the waterfall.

Resume the C-3318 which follows a lush valley of medlars, citrus trees and almonds, between towering mountains.

After Bolulla the road climbs in hairpins through attractive scenery. On the left a long, thin waterfall is etched against a wall of rock and overlooked by an impossibly-located cliff-top house. There are great views back down the valley.

Gradually, Tárbena (pop. 760) comes into view: a town perched right on top of the mountains. There has been a settlement in these hills since pre-historic times. When the Moors were expelled from Spain, Tárbena became a refuge for Moriscos (Moors who nominally converted to Christianity and stayed behind in Spain after the Reconquest) until they were summarily expelled in 1609. The area was then re-populated with settlers from the Balearic Islands. The local dialect retains

71

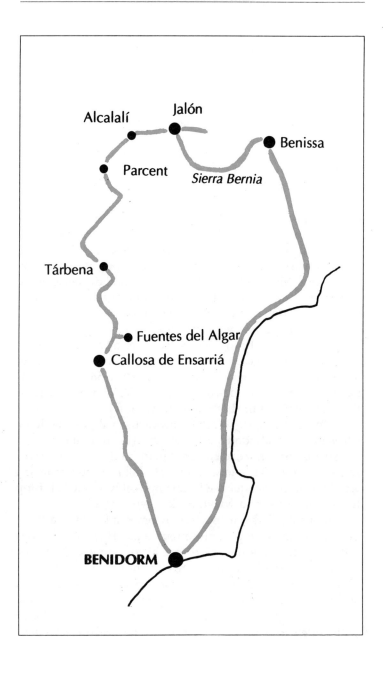

an influence of island speech. Another of the Mallorcans' legacies is a particular kind of Tárbena sausage.

Can Pinet (Avda. Constitución 11. in the town centre. Tel: 96-588 41 31. B.) is a lively restaurant run by Pinet, a Communist who doesn't take himself too seriously. A more conventional choice is Sa Canterella (Partida Foya Gavach. Tel: 96-588 40 62. B-M.). on the main road, which has a swimming pool and a terrace giving views of the mountains.

After Tárbena the road crosses into another valley crammed with terraced fields. It loses some of its height but soon climbs again curling around wild slopes of dwarf fan palms and rocks towards the wind-swept Coll de Rates (540m) where, improbably, there is a restaurant, the Merendero de Coll de Rates. The road goes down now and gives splendid views over the Jalón valley, known for its almond blossom (late February to early March, depending on the weather), its wine and its restaurants.

Arriving at Parcent (pop. 650) turn right onto A-142 for Alcalalí (2km) where you're sure to find a restaurant to suit your palate and your purse. Among the more popular in the valley are: Valbon (Partida la Solana Gardens. Tel: 96-573 17 71 and 648 2271. Closed Monday. B- M), Los Almedros (Paseo Joaquin Ferrando. Tel: 96-648 22 69. Closed Monday. B-M) and Benarrosa (Partida la Solana Gardens. Tel: 573 01 06 and 648 20 06. Closed Saturday. B-M).

More bars and restaurants can be found in the next village, Jalón (pop. 1,800). There's also a renowned *bodega* where you can taste and buy the local wines. Molino de Vino (opposite the *bodega*, Tel: 96-648 04 09. Evenings only 7-11pm. E) is a restaurant in a restored 200-year-old water mill set in its own garden. Specialities include lamb, salmon and steak.

Turn right in Jalón between two buildings into a narrow street, Calle de la Iglesia, sign-posted for Bernia (if you're short of time, you can skip this drive through the mountains and go straight down the valley to Benissa).

This small road, a bit rough in places, climbs gently through a sparsely-populated area of almond terraces. Five kilometres from Jalón it passes through the hamlet of Maserof, now a vineyard and wine club run by Englishman Peter Pateman and his wife Maria (Tel: 96-578 18 87).

A few kilomtres further on the road climbs more steeply, past abandoned terraces. At one point you have a view back towards Callosa de Ensarriá. After this, the slopes become less inclined. There are even a few tall pine trees growing up here, and almonds again. On your right, all the while, are the summits of the Sierra Bernia. There's plenty more to see if you want to set off on foot: an old castle on the Altea side, just below the summit, and a natural tunnel, or *forat*, passing through the top of the sierra from one side to the other.

Turn left at the next junction for Pinos on the AV-1425. You come down now from the wild mountains on a steep road through the tiny village of Pinos. There are stunning views over Calpe and the Peñón de Ifach.

Cross the motorway and turn right for Benissa (pop. 7,200) and right again on to the N-332 for Alicante. Benidorm is about 32km. If you want to take the motorway, the nearest entrance is in the opposite direction, north of Benissa ❏

Excursion 13 - Castle of Castles:
Denia - Cueva de las Calaveras - Benidoleig -
Orba - Castell de Castells - Vall de Alcalá - Vall de Ebo -
Pego - Denia
(100km)

This route takes you quickly from the developed coasts into the bleak, high mountains, on a circuit of one of the more remote areas behind the Costa Blanca.

Take the C-3311 from Denia, cross the main road at Ondara and look for signs to Benidoleig. Just before entering the village you come to the Cueva de las Calaveras (the Cave of the Skulls. Open 9am-dusk. Tel: 96-640 42 35).

When the cave was first discovered, there were 12 skeletons in a circle and three more - an adult and two youths - at the far end of the cave. According to legend, these were the remains of the Moorish king of Castell de Castells who hid in the cave while fleeing from the Christians. The 12 skeletons are supposed to be those of the king's wives who killed themselves, and the other bones those of the king and his servants.

Near the entrance you can see numerous half-excavated bones which are 50,000 years old. Pre-historic man left paintings on the walls of the cave but, sadly, they have since faded. The only other signs that he inhabited the cave are the sooty stains on the ceiling.

A concrete path leads you down a 400-metre corridor which opens into chambers up to 20 metres high. The rock has dripped and flowed into massive red bosses and semi-recognisable shapes. At the end of the path you come to a fenced-off underground lake.

In Benidoleig (pop.780) you can eat at Maxis (Aldea de las Cuevas. Tel: 96-588 38 94. Closed Monday. B) which has its own swimming pool.

Continuing through Orba (pop. 1,600), overlooked by the stump of a castle, you strike the AP-1437. Turn left towards Benidorm.

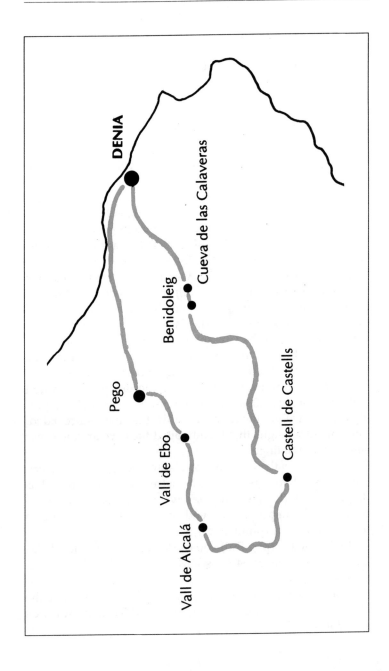

The road zig-zags past a horse-breeding ranch (on the left). After El Portet restaurant, turn right on to a quiet road for Castell de Castells (16km). The road first heads for a twin-peaked conical mountain then passes through the pretty village of Murla (pop. 360). Look out for the church which was built on the walls of an old fortress and has two old towers attached to it.

Murla marks the eastern end of the Caballo Verde ridge, scene of the battle in 1609 in which the last Moriscos in Eastern Spain were defeated (the survivors being deported to Africa via Denia). The ridge is named after a spectral Moorish knight supposedly seen mounted on a green steed.

From here the road follows a lightly-wooded valley in between rocky mountains to Benichembla. Keep right on the A-120 for Castell de Castells (11.5km).

As you climb into the mountains away from the coast, following the stony bed of the River Jalón, the land becomes less cultivated and the scenery prettier. The almond and olive trees are interspersed with pinewoods and ancient, gnarled carobs.

You seem to be heading for even wilder mountains; but approaching Castell de Castells the landscape suddenly becomes crammed with well-kept terraces of almond trees, which creep towards the rocky summits.

Castell de Castells (literally "Castle of Castles", pop 700) commands the head of the valley and is surrounded by mighty peaks. It has some pretty houses and cool, narrow streets. It also has a small, British-run hotel. Jan and Eric Wright only have eight beds in their Pensión Castell (Calle San Vicente, 18. Tel: 96-551 82 54). It's a popular place for hikers and nature-lovers. Buzzards and eagles soar over the mountains and genets and wild boars roam the slopes. Mozarabic trails and mule tracks, ingeniously scaling even the steepest gradients, provide paths for walkers.

Castell de Castells may seem prosperous but it shares the fate of many villages around this area: its young people are deserting the land for life and work on the coast. Some years ago a British documentary film-maker chose the village to make a film about rural depopulation in Spain.

There are not many restaurants ahead and this may be a good opportunity to stop. El Raconet (Avda de Denia, 8. Tel: 96-551 80 93. B) serves a good range of food at reasonable prices.

If you want to explore off the route, a new road, the AV-1203 connects Castell de Castells with Tárbena (see Excursion 12), passing near the natural rock arch of Arc de Atanços (a 20-minute walk from the car).

Follow the A-120 from Castell de Castells. It goes on climbing through neat olive and almond terraces until it reaches the barren, rocky slopes of gorse and pine under the summits of the Sierra de Aixorta and the Sierra de Serrella (which separate this valley from that of Guadalest). The ruined Castillo de Serrella (1,050 metres) - the "castle of castles" - sits between the two ranges. You can reach it by walking about three and a half kilometres along forestry tracks.

The road skirts past Facheca (pop. around 150), a village which made a name for itself not so long ago when its few remaining inhabitants elected an all-female town council.

You now descend through high, bleak country. Take the right turning, the A-122, for Tollos, a village that has suffered the drift to the cities and coasts more than others and has a

neglected air about it - half its houses are abandoned.

Keep on the road which takes you round the village for Beniaya (4km). You are once again high in the mountains with impressive views. The road climbs over a pass of pretty slopes and falls down into a new valley in which the next stop is Beniaya (Beniaia).

Traverse the village and when at last you come to a T-junction turn right onto the AV-1042 for Alcalá de la Jovada (2.5km). This village and Beniaya together are also known as Vall de Alcalá. Turn left before you enter Alcalá for Vall de Ebo (11km) and Pego (15km).

The road now crosses an area of dry upland scattered with white rocks, the odd pine tree and a few gorse bushes. The high mountain on the left with the red and white antennae is Almisera (757 metres).

After a while you come out high above Vall de Ebo (pop. 430) and drop down quickly to the village. For eating and drinking, there is only a simple bar in the main square. Turn left along side the river (in spring, filled with croaking frogs), and left again over the bridge for Pego.

The road climbs again giving fantastic views back over Vall de Ebo. Look below right and you will see that the lower valley is carved into a series of superb gorges.

Now you head for a pass and suddenly have views of the coast a long way below. Pego marshes, squeezed on all sides by agriculture, show up as a brown belt between the orange groves and the sea.

It takes many twists and turns to get down to Pego. There's another gorge to look at on the right. Finally, the road descends past a ruined castle and through pine woods to the fertile orange groves of the coastal plain.

If you've made it all the way without refreshment, Pego (pop. 9,400) provides at least a modest choice of eating and drinking. Bar Rafael (Avda Fontilles 11. Tel: 96-557 12 36. B) lays on a succulent *cordero al horno* (roast lamb) ❏

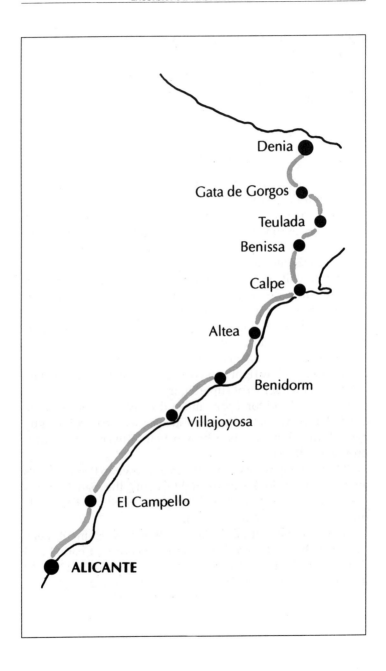

Excursion 14 - Stopping Train:

Alicante - Benidorm - Altea - Calpe - Gata de
Gorgos - Denia (and back again) by train
(93km each way)

If you haven't got a car or want a day out without driving, why
not rumble along the Costa Blanca by train on the narrow-
gauge line from Alicante to Denia? Apart from the excellent
views of the coast and the countryside, you can stop off at a
number of beaches and interesting towns on the way.

For a guided tour take the Limón Exprés, a tourist train
using re-conditioned, old-fashioned rolling stock which runs
from Benidorm to Gata de Gorgos and back again (see page 83).

The route for this excursion is the whole line, taking the
ordinary stopping train, the Costa Blanca Exprés, which shuttles
back and forth along the 93km of track, giving you a chance to
explore independently.

You can start from either end of the line or from any station
in between. If you want beaches, you'll find most of them on the
southern section, the first few kilometres out of Alicante
(although the stations at Paradis and Altea are not far from the
beach either). If you want scenery and views of the coast, take
the train from Benidorm northwards.

The first train out of Alicante is at 6.15am and the first one
from Denia at 6.40am. Trains then run every hour until around
8pm. (These times may vary; check before you travel). The full
trajectory takes around two-and-a-quarter hours. In summer
there is also a nocturnal service between Altea and Alicante -
the Trensnochador - for late-night revellers returning from
pubs and discotheques.

It helps to be armed with a timetable-map (available from
any station), as many of the halts are request stops - you have
to press a button to advise the driver - and some are not clearly
named on the platform. Full information is available from
Estación de la Marina, Alicante (Tel: 96-526 29 43 or 526 26 78).

The metre-wide line was built by a French company between
1914 and 1915 to transport fruit, vegetables, raisins, wines and

fish to the port of Alicante and to return with imported guano, grains and flour. For most of its length it is single track. The main stations have a second track for trains to pass. It is now operated by FGV - not Renfe, which runs Spain's inter-city railways. The two companies' stations are at opposite ends of Alicante. The only forward connection from Denia is by bus; the closest Renfe station at this end is Gandía although there are plans to extend the narrow-gauge line to meet it.

From Alicante the line first runs along the rocky shoreline close to the city and passes through two tunnels, in between which comes a large hotel.

Near Albufereta look out for a couple of houses which have been built around restored watchtowers. The line describes a loop through an area of wasteland and swings round on to the very edge of a very long, wide, sandy beach. The next few stops - Palmeral, Carrabiners, Sant Joan (in which the station is more or less a bar in summer) are right on the beach - you only have to cross the road to start digging in the sand.

The train pulls up and away from the shore in Les Llances but the beach is still within walking distance from Salesians station. The resort of El Campello (pop. 9,300) is the first major halt.

Following the coast at a short distance, the line passes between estates of modern villas, one of which is a lavish oriental fantasy. Further on, after Calapiteres, a bright white mansion with the façade of a classical temple stands proudly above the breaking waves.

The track now crosses a long, iron girder bridge, the first of seven viaducts. The derelict tram car (left), mounted on a block of concrete, once ran along the streets of Alicante until it was moved here as an advertising hoarding.

The beaches to the south of Paradís (literally "Paradise") are quiet and secluded. One of the Costa Blanca's most comfortable hotels, El Montiboli (Urb El Montibolí, 32. Tel: 96- 589 01 86), stands above a cove.

Villajoyosa (La Vila Joiosa, pop. 21,700) is the next stop. Fifty years ago it was a far more important centre than Benidorm, which has now all but eclipsed it. Villajoyosa, however, has the

Costa Blanca's only casino. The old town of Villajoyosa is a tight, tiered cluster of houses that intermeshes with the medieval ramparts. It's as if everything had been melted together with a church, a corner tower and a handsome pink arch mixed in. Unfortunately, these buildings have been neglected over the years, although there are now plans to restore them.

Villajoyosa possesses the oldest chocolate factories in Spain. You can taste the authentic product (in liquid or solid form) in Chocolatería Valor on the main road through the town (Avenida Pais Valencia, 14. Tel: 96-589 40 99).

In August, the town stages a maritime variation of the ubiquitous mock battles between Moors and Christians (see Fiestas at the back of this book).

As soon as the train pulls out of the station and crosses a bridge over the trickling River Sella, look left across the road bridge and you will see a line of hanging houses painted in bright colours. They were individualised, the locals will tell you, so that the fishermen who lived in them could keep an eye on their homes from far out at sea.

The line swings inland again, under the shadow of Puig Campana (1,410m - see Excursion 11 for the legend attached to the peak), and back towards Benidorm. You get good views of the Mediterranean's largest resort from the railway, including La Cala (the first group of skyscrapers you pass), the Isle and the Sierra Helada (the mountains beside the sea immediately to the north).

Benidorm station is quite a way out of town and far from the beaches but there is a regular bus service connecting with both. This is the starting point of the Limón Exprés which runs to Gata de Gorgos and back along the most scenic stretch of the line four times a week (Tuesday to Friday) leaving at 9.35am. (Tel: 96-585 18 95 for information.).

The Limón Exprés, started by Briton David Simpson in 1971, has since been taken over by FGV. Its green-liveried coaches date from the 1930s. They have restored wooden interior fittings and wrought iron balconies at each end (as in western films). A guide accompanies you on the journey, pointing out sights on the way.

As you leave Benidorm you'll catch a glimpse of the new Parque de L'Aigüera (beside the bullring). This monumental work was built as part of the resort's plan to create a more up-market image. Classical music concerts and operas are staged in its open-air amphitheatre. A little further on you may be able to make out the resort's two biggest discotheques, one of them shaped like a flying saucer.

Alfaz del Pi (L'Alfás del Pí, pop. 7,000) has a large, new station with a terrace bar. Both the town centre and the beach, however, are a fair distance away. Alfaz has more foreign residents than native citizens, it is "twinned" with Oslo and 18 different nationalities of children attend its school. It also runs an ambitious film festival each summer which attracts famous Spanish screen stars.

Drawing into *Altea* (pop. 12,300) you have views of the old town with the blue and white dome of its church glinting in the sunshine. Its narrow, pretty streets are a fair stroll from the station, which is in the modern part of town close to the harbour and the sea front promenade.

The train goes through two tunnels to pass underneath Altea and then crosses the River Algar. On the other bank of the river the line starts a steep climb through luxuriant vegetation hiding numerous villas. As you gain height, there are spectacular views of the coast from Altea to Albir, with the Sierra Helada in the background.

The line edges along a corniche, which in 1990 was blocked for six months by a landslide. Passing through a tunnel the train emerges above the clear, green sea with a marina full of yachts almost directly below.

Another tunnel feeds the line abruptly on to a metal bridge: at 105 metres it's the highest on the line. If you look quickly before the train disappears into the next tunnel you can see the deep and narrow Mascarat gorge.

For the next few kilometres there are fine views of the Peñón de Ifach, that mighty rock which rises from the sea in great vertical cliffs (see Excursion 4). The station at *Calpe* (pop. 11,000), sheltering under the flat-topped summit of El Olta, is a long way from the town and even further from the beaches and the Peñón. However, there is a bus service to meet each train and bring you back to the station later.

After Calpe the train turns away from the coast and rattles around a large curve through pretty countryside and over another high viaduct. This stretch of the line is fringed with wildflowers: in every ravine there are reeds and oleanders; thirsty century plants keel over on embankments; and thistles, chicory and valerian poke out of the grass.

The train reaches its maximum height of 300 metres as it crosses the terraces of vines around Benissa (pop. 7,200). Teulada (pop. 4,300) has two 16th century towers and a church with a hexagonal tower. From here the line weaves along a pretty steep-sided valley of desolate slopes scarred by two quarries.

Leaving that brief wilderness behind the line crosses the River Jalón and comes to Gata de Gorgos (pop. 5,200), the final destination of the Limón Exprés. Look over to your right and there are views of Mount Montgó, that impressive hump of rock which separates Denia from Jávea.

Gata station is a one-minute walk from the town centre and five minutes from numerous souvenir shops which specialise in wicker, raffia and basket work, but also sell many other craft goods.

If you arrive here by Limón Exprés you will be taken on a tour of a family-run guitar factory close to the station. All the instruments are made by hand and there are miniature guitars for children to take home as souvenirs. The Limón Exprés departs again at around 12.25pm (but check with the guide as the time varies). The return journey seems to be quicker as passengers are more interested in the sparkling wine being served than taking snaps of the view.

From Gata de Gorgos the line curves around Jesús Pobre (hidden behind a hill with three ruined windmills on its crest) and slices through the middle of a golf course. After skirting around the end of Mount Montgó it rattles through the final orange groves towards *Denia* (pop. 24,800). Look left for the mock-minaret at La Muntanyeta. As you approach Denia the castle comes in sight.

Denia station is close to the harbour and the town centre,

where there are plenty of bars and restaurants to relax in before the journey home. The tourist information office is also just around the corner.

During the return journey you can enjoy the same sights - or close your eyes and snooze as a soft breeze blows through the train windows ❏

Excursion 15 - Cherry Trees:

Denia - Pego - Vall de Gallinera - Planes -
Beniarrés - Castellón de Rugat - Gandía - Denia
(130km)

Inland from Denia there is a magnificent green valley filled with cherry trees and lush vegetation.

Turn left at the waterfront in Denia along Las Marinas beach (see the start of Excursion 6). Follow the signs for Valencia briefly joining the N-332 but get ready to turn off left soon afterwards for Pego on the AP-1066.

This road climbs a bridge over the motorway giving a view of an extensive marshland spread out before you. Although an important habitat for wildlife, this land is under pressure from local farmers who want to reclaim it for orange groves.

Keep straight on. If you stop anywhere in the next two or three kilometres you will hear innumerable small birds hidden among the reedbeds clucking, chirping, squawking and warbling to each other. You may see egrets and herons flying overhead.

After the marshes the orange groves resume. When you come to a crossroads, turn right on to the C-3311 for Pego (pop. 9,400). Its blue-domed church stands on the edge of the coastal plains, with a wall of mountains behind it. Go around the town following the signs for Muro de Alcoy and Cocentaina (keep on the C-3311).

As you leave Pego the hills begin. The fertile coastal plain densely carpeted with citrus groves is about to end. After Absubia the road enters a small gorge and meanders beside a river bed filled with pink-flowering oleander. There are crags and rocks all around.

Take the right turning to Forna (3.5km) for a short detour. Forna is a pretty, peaceful village of white houses lost among the hills and is popular with foreign residents. It is plunged in foliage and overlooked by the walls of a castle (one of the few in this area to survive a great earthquake in the 17th century). Restaurante Nautilus (Tel: 96-557 13 66. 1.30-3.30pm and 8pm

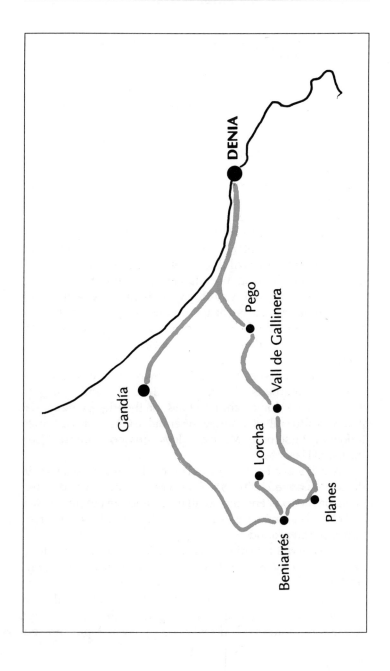

until late. No cards. Paella and Valencian cuisine. B) is in the square: a simple, no-frills restaurant with some shady tables outside.

After the gorge, the C-3311 gradually ascends the valley - keeping just above the level of the river. It then starts to climb steeply passing a string of mountain villages whose houses huddle together for security: Benirrama, Beniali (where there is a bar to stop for tapas), La Carroja and El Patro.

In between the villages and up and down the hillside are terraces of innumerable cherry trees which blossom in early spring and are laden with fruit by May.

Eventually, the road reaches a height and runs more on a level. Across the valley are the wild, steep slopes of the Sierra del Almirante.

Dropping down at last you pass a turning to Margarida and enter a soft landscape of terraced fields bordered by old stone walls overgrown in places with lush grass and brambles. You could, for an instant, be somewhere in the north of Europe.

Just before arriving in Planes you cross Barranc de l'Encantada. A little road goes off to the right to a picnic area. Soon after this there's a right turning to Beniarrés (10km), which you will be coming back to after having had a look at Planes.

Planes de la Baronía (pop. 940) clusters organically around a rock surmounted by a ruined medieval castle. It is a small and somewhat neglected village, but it does have an outstanding feature: a 15th-century aqueduct. To get there take the first right turning as you enter the village (C/Virgen de los Dolores also called Carrer de la Mare de Deu dels Dolors) and turn left down the hill from the small square. There is space to park and turn at the bottom.

Although there is a sign warning not to drink the water that flows across the aqueduct into the communal laundry, the locals claim that this water is healthier than the stuff that comes out of the taps.

This route lacks eating places. There is a rough village bar in Planes, another ahead in Beniarrés and straightforward restaurants in Castellón de Rugat. But if you want more than a

simple meal, your best bet is to make for L'escaleta in Cocentaina (17km; see Alcoy in the Town and City Guide). The road to get there - straight along the C-3311 past Benimarfull to Muro de Alcoy - is a pretty drive.

From Planes go back along the C-3311 and take that turning to Beniarrés. The road goes around the back of the village and then climbs to give views across Beniarrés reservoir to the village of the same name, marked by the white steeple of the church. The prominent peak behind is Mount Beniarrés (1,104 metres) which presents a markedly different profile from each direction.

The road dips down close to the water's edge and crosses the dam, then follows the other side of the lake before heading for the village (pop. 1,600). You can get a basic meal here in the Bar Crespo (C/ San Antonio, 5. Tel: 96-551 50 36. B). Lorcha (pop. 900), a 16 km detour along the leafy Serpis valley, has an impressive ruined Templar castle but the village itself, at the end of the road, is disappointing.

From Beniarrés take the A-101 to Castellón de Rugat (12km) which ascends the slopes of dry almond terraces in tight bends. Behind, there are views over the village you have just left and the lake. In the distance to the south you can still see Planes. To your right you can see the Sierra Mariola and Cocentaina castle all alone above the valley.

The Puerto de Beniarrés (a pass of 594 metres) marks the boundary between Valencia and Alicante provinces. The slopes on the other side of the Sierra de Benicadell are prettily wooded. At the T-junction in Castellón de Rugat (pop. 2,150) turn right for Gandía (22km).

A straight, fast road now heads for the coast following a line of mountains, the Sierra de La Safor, to the south. Citrus trees reappear as you leave the interior uplands behind.

On the left after Rótova (pop. 1,140) you will see the fawn-coloured former monastery of San Jerónimo de Cotalba (now private property and not open to the public). A bumpy dirt track takes you to a leafy picnic spot outside the monastery's high walls from which a shady avenue of plane trees leads up to a locked gate. Founded by Alfonso of Aragón, the monastery hides Gothic and Renaissance cloisters. Follow the avenue of pine trees in front of the monastery to resume the main road.

Seven kilometres further on you reach Gandía, a troublesome, and badly sign-posted traffic bottleneck. Turn right on to the N-332 south and turn off it onto the C-3311 in Ondara for Denia (8 km) ❑

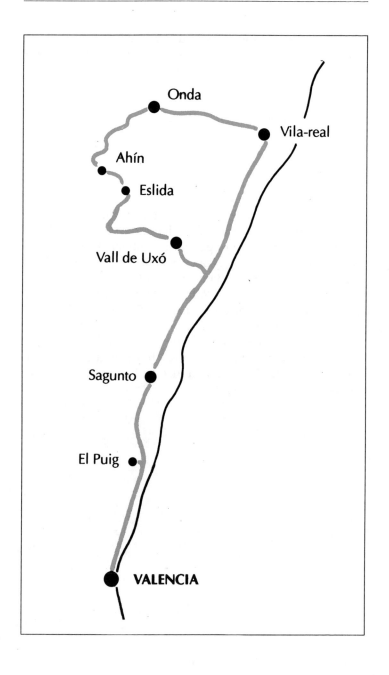

Excursion 16 - A Subterranean Boat Trip:

Valencia - El Puig - Sagunto - Vall de Uxó -
Sierra de Espadán - Onda - Benicassim - Valencia
(180km)

This trip takes you north-west into the pretty and unfrequented Sierra de Espadán, stopping on the way at a citadel famous in ancient history, taking a subterranean boat ride and visiting a curious natural history museum run by monks.

Leave Valencia on the A-7 motorway (toll-free for the first 24km) to Barcelona. Take Exit 4 for a short detour (4km).

King Jaime I besieged the Moorish castle at El Puig on the eve of his conquest of Valencia in October 1238. The Mercedarian monastery he founded on the site houses a collection of 240 paintings. Its Museum of Graphic Art and Printing (open weekends 10am-1pm and 4-6pm) commemorates the printing of the first book in Spain in Valencia in 1474, of which it has a facsimile. The museum includes antique printing presses, printers' blocks, posters from the '20s and '30s, fascinating old maps of the eastern seaboard, a replica of Jaime I's sword and a copy of the smallest book in the world.

Take Exit 5 (just before the toll motorway begins) for Sagunto, on the N-340. Sagunto (pop. 55,500), originally an Iberian settlement, pre-dates Valencia and played a crucial role in Spain's ancient history. Although the two great powers of Rome and Carthage had agreed to divide Spain between them, the Carthaginian general Hannibal (he of the elephants) stormed and sacked Saguntum, an important Roman outpost on the Via Augusta. All the inhabitants of the town were said to have died in the assault, the last throwing themselves on to fires rather than fall into the hands of Hannibal's brutal troops. The attack provoked the wrath of Rome and thus sparked off the Second Punic War which ended (despite Hannibal's valiant invasion of Italy) with 600 years of Roman civilisation for Spain.

Roman Sagunto is on the hill above the town centre. The 1st-2nd century amphitheatre, in a natural depression in the hillside, has seating for 4000 people and such good acoustics that every August it is used as the venue for a classical theatre festival. It has, however, been controversially restored using modern building materials. A road to the left leads to the castle which spreads out accross the crest of the hill. (Both monuments are open 10am-2pm and 4-6pm, Tuesday to Saturday; Sunday 10am-2pm; Monday closed.

One of the best restaurants in Sagunto is L'Armeler (C/ Castillo, 44. Tel: 96-266 43 82. Closed Sunday. All cards M-E), which provides both French and Valencian cuisine. A cheaper alternative on the same street is Mesón Casa Felipe (C/ Castillo, 21. Tel: 96-266 4765. Closed Wednesday. No cards. B), which serves paella and a varied menu of home-cooking which changes frequently according to the season.

After Sagunto the N-340 travels across a vast plain of orange trees which stretch from the beach to the hills inland. Almenara castle, on top of a high hill with two watch towers distanced from the main fortification, cuts a dramatic silhouette.

A little further on, turn left on to the small road to Vall de Uxó (La Vall d'Uixó. 8km) which has some of the best caves in eastern Spain. You don't have to go into the centre of the town (pop. 27,800) to visit them. Keep on the by-pass, the C-225, which heads for the hills. The left turning to "Coves de San Josep" is sign-posted. The caves are about 200 metres off the main road.

The caverns are open 10.50am-1pm and 3.20-5.30pm in winter, but open later during the rest of the year.(Closed Monday and after heavy rains. Tel: 964-69 05 76 for information). They have been explored to over two kilometres and probably extend much further, although at the moment you can only travel a quarter of the distance. Still, the subterranean boat excursion is a singular experience, especially if you are lucky enough to get a quiet time. The boatman steers you expertly down the serpentine course of the cave, over the sandy bottom, pointing out sights of interest and warning you to duck your head to avoid vicious projections. The water reaches its deepest point (12 metres) in the Lago Azul. Now and then the cave opens out into large chambers, such as the Hall of the Bat -- there used to be bats and eels here until the floodlights were installed - and the Gallery of the Syphons.

There are bars, restaurants and souvenir shops outside the caves. Restaurant Las Grutas (Open 1-4pm weekdays, 1-4pm and 8.30-11pm Friday and Saturday. Closed Monday. Amex, Visa. M) is in another cave and serves fish, seafood and rice.

From the caves, turn left at the end of the access road up the hill, and left again at the stop sign, back on to the C-225 which you left earlier (sign-posted Teruel).

After passing through Fondeguilla (which has a brilliant white chapel and an ancient aqueduct) the road takes you up into the magnificent Sierra de Espadán: a land of ancient hill terraces (decorated with pink almond blossom in February); pine, carob and cork oak trees; rock outcrops and dense undergrowth.

Turn right onto the CS-231 to Eslida (13.6km). First comes Chovar (pop. 430), which clusters at the base of a conical hill. As you go through the village you will notice an unusal monument on the left. The fat trunk of a pine tree, 1.25m in diameter, is all that remains of acres of forest which were destroyed by a fire in 1981. Fortunately, there are still extensive woods of cork oaks left to lose yourself in. The bark is surgically skinned once every nine years by expert tree surgeons.

As you twist upwards through these magical woods, new summits and ridges seem to appear above all the time. After the Puerto de Eslida (620 metres) the road drops down into the next valley and brings you to Eslida (pop. 900), a village of narrow streets and steps; and mineral springs. Bar Paquita (B), at the end of the village on the right, is a spacious place serving simple meals.

Turn left at the bottom of the village on to the CS-230 for Ahín (5km). After more wooded hills you enter an unlit tunnel, which curves tightly round to bring the road back over itself.

The well-kept village of Ahín (pop. 140) is surrounded by field-terraces laid out by the Moors. The only place for refreshment is one small bar in the square. Continue to the T-junction and turn right to L'Alcudia de Veo, which has a two-star pensión, Pico Espadán (Tel: 964-62 91 68. B).

The next village on the route is the under-populated Veo.

Many of its fine old stone houses are now abandoned or ruined but it's worth stopping to wander around its sloping streets. A very old line of the stations of the cross climbs through nearby woods.

For a while the road follows a small, green reservoir. Turn right for Onda at the T-junction before Tales. Suddenly, after the wild sierra, you find youself back in a tame valley of orange groves and carob trees.

Keep straight on through Artesa. After 2km, just before reaching Onda, you will come across a large building of yellow brick, the Museo del Carmen. (Open June-October 9.30am-2pm and 3.30- 8pm; October-March 9.30am-2pm and 3.30-7pm; March-June 9.30am-2pm and 3.30-7.30pm. Closed Monday, except fiestas, and December 20- Jan 20).

It would be strange enough to find a natural history museum here but stranger still is that it is part of a Carmelite monastery. Step inside and a pair of leopards snarl at you ferociously. An eagle descends on its prey, its talons outstretched. A large shark lunges at you out of the gloom. On the three floors of the museum you'll find representatives of just about every animal family you can imagine. There are over 1,500 species of mammals, birds, fish, reptiles and crustacea on show here. Not to mention all manner of preserved creepy-crawlies, bones galore, biological specimens, skeletons, mutant births, grisly human organs, mineral specimens, insects and other curios.

The collection was started in 1952 for the private scientific study of the Carmelite fathers. A decade later it had grown so big that it was decided to rehouse it here at El Carmen and open it up to the public. The museum's subdued lighting lends dramatic effect to each glass case with its inhabitants set in life-like poses against naturalistic backdrops. The museum has a bar- restaurant attached.

Onda (pop. 18,000) is known for its ceramics and stucco, and you'll see some fine examples of both if you wander through its streets. It also has medieval porticoes of Gothic arches in the Plaza del Almudí or Plaza de Isaac Peral. Above the town is the evocatively - but exaggerately - named Castle of the Three Hundred Towers.

Take the C-223 from Onda to Villarreal. Ceramics and tile factories follow you all the way to the coast. This could be the place to buy your next kitchen floor. When you get to Villarreal (Vila-Real, pop. 38,000), you can either take the N-340 or the A-7 motorway back to Valencia (there's an entrance 4km south). Before doing so, you may feel like a dip on Burriana beach (7km off route), a quiet stretch of shore except in high season. ❏

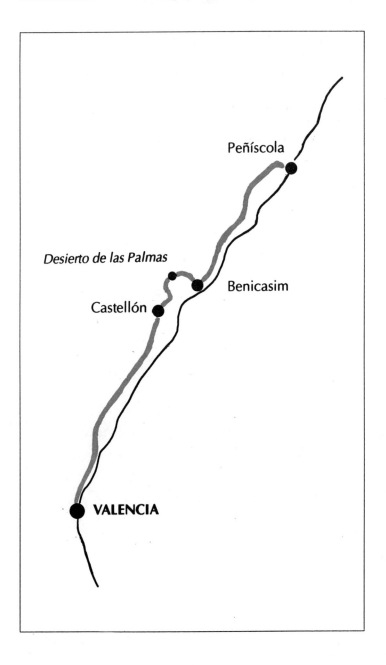

Excursion 17 - City in the Sea:

Valencia - Castellón - Desierto de las Palmas - Benicassim -
Peñíscola - Valencia
(315km)

This route may seem exceptionally long; but most of it can be travelled without stopping and the destination is worth the distance. Peñíscola, the "city in the sea", is a fortified outpost with a distinguished history. On the way there is a short and unsuspected mountain detour giving superb views of the coast.

From Valencia you can either take the main coast road - the N-340 - which can be snarled with lorries, or the A-7 (toll) motorway which will speed you past the congested city of Castellón. If you choose the motorway, leave it at Exit 46 beyond Castellón and join the N-340.

After a petrol station on the right you'll come to a left turning to Desierto de las Palmas. From here it's straight on past a little chapel on a hill and quickly up into the mountains.

This nature reserve was, until recently, a favourite beauty spot. Hopefully it will be again. Most of the trees were destroyed by a forest fire in 1985, and another fire devastated the area in late 1992. A drive around the Desierto de las Palmas will not, for the time being, be the same magnificent experience it once was, but it still affords great views of the coast.

The highest point is Mount San Miguel (also called Mount Bartolo) reaching 729 metres. Beneath the summit, at 459 m, is the Monasterio del Desierto de las Palmas which was built in 1796. The museum and church are open to visitors (open 10am-1pm and 4-6.30pm - you have to ring the bell. Closed during services: Saturday 6pm. Sunday and feast days: 9.30am, 12am and 6pm. Also closed Wednesday in winter).

From here, you start to descend. Turn right for Bar Restaurant Desierto de las Palmas (Tel: 964-30 09 47. Open 1- 2.30pm. Open for dinner only in summer. Closed Tuesday in winter. Visa. M-E), which belongs to the monastery and has a glass-enclosed dining room giving more panoramic views. On a clear day you can see the Columbrete Isles, 70km out to sea.

Below the restaurant, in the valley, you'll see the pink ruins of the former 17th century monastery which was inadvertently built on a fault line and fell down twice before the monks moved to more secure ground up the hill.

Losing height as rapidly as it gained it, the road snakes inexorably down towards sea-level. All the way there are impressive views of the coastal plain looking south to Benicassim.

Turn left at the bottom of the hill and pass under the main road to reach Benicassim (pop. 5,300), a resort dating back from long before the days of mass tourism and which is still popular for its benign micro-climate.

You can stop here to sample liqueur courtesy of the Carmelite Monks of the Desierto de las Palmas. They moved production down to the coast in 1913 and, in the 1980s, rented out the business to another company. The monks may no longer work in the factory but you are still welcome to visit the Bodegas Carmelitanas (visits every 10 minutes from 9am-1pm and 3-6.30pm) in the outskirts of Benicassim for a whistle-stop tour concluded by a wine-tasting session. Production is still on a small scale and traditional. The brew-house smells agreeably of coffee liqueur. Benicassim has a bar specialising in all types of ham (Benijamon, C/Bayer). Restaurante La Manduka (C/ Santo Tomas, 69. Te : 964-30 17 18. M) serves pizzas and a tasty cheeseboard.

However, save the best part of the day for Peñíscola, a town which is as picturesque as it is historic. Although now a tourist resort, the old Peñíscola retains all its charm. To get there, carry straight on up the N-340 north from Benicassim (after about 10km there's a motorway entry, if you prefer to speed up your journey)and turn off for Peñíscola.

The old quarter of white houses, surrounded by walls and fortifications, clusters around a promontory jutting into the sea. In the middle of it stands the castle which was once home to the controversial 15th century papal pretender Pope Benedict XIII - better known in Spain as *Papa Luna*.

Pedro de Luna, cardinal of Aragón, was elected Pope during

the Great Schism that split the Christian Church at the end of the 14th century. When he was branded an anti-Pope in 1409 he withdrew from Avignon to his stronghold in Peñíscola to await a call to return that was never to come. He died here in 1422, a nonagenarian, as obstinate as ever, even naming his own successor. One of his more memorable and long-lasting acts was to confirm the foundation of St. Andrew's University in Scotland.

The castle, built by the Knights Templar, has been skillfully restored. From the battlements you look down on a labyrinth of rooftops clustering around the rock almost cut off from the mainland.

And you have a privileged view of the Costa del Azahar (the "Orange Blossom" Coast). The wide beach to the north was used to film *El Cid*, starring Charlton Heston (the castle being in the background). To the south, the small beach near the harbour is followed by a steep, rocky coastline at the foot of the Sierra de Hirta (Irta), which is punctuated by unspoilt coves.

The narrow streets surrounding the castle are all steeply sloping or stepped and are dotted with ramparts, gun batteries, watchtowers and coats of arms. You may hear a disturbing booming sound coming from the Bufador: a rocky blow-hole in a corner behind the harbour.

Back down at sea level you can watch the return of the fishing boats and the auction of the day's catch. Peñíscola and neighbouring Vinarós are famous for the variety of their seafoods: there are many local dishes to try including spicy fish, king prawns and date mussels. The best restaurants are in the Paseo Marítimo.

Having got this far you may like to venture further. Inland is the incomparable Maestrazgo region (see Excursions 24 and 28). Just over 25km up the coast to the north you enter the Catalan province of Tarragona, which has two nature reserves: Puertos de Beseit and the Ebro Delta.

If you've travelled enough for now, return to Valencia along the coast the way you came, either by the N-340 or by the A-7 motorway ❑

Excursion 18 - Játiva's Revenge:

Valencia - Játiva - Valencia
(125km)

If one town could encapsulate the history of Eastern Spain it is *Játiva*, a city of old palaces and churches, which has one of the most extensive castles in Spain.

Take the N-340 dual carriageway (known locally as the Pista de Silla) which leaves Valencia for Alicante and turn off for Albacete (still on the N-340). After the industrial outskirts the road cuts through extensive orange groves, passing the Moorish Espioca tower on a hill to the right.

In Masalavés (pop. 1,500) and Alberique (pop. 8,700) you will notice many shops advertising *panquemado* - a local variety of sweet cake something like brioche.

Shortly after Alberique you cross the mighty Río Júcar which by this stage has been reduced to an insignificant trickle. Most of its waters have been diverted into a wide irrigation canal to feed the orange groves.

The road climbs to a low pass of 180 metres and drops down to the turn off for Játiva (5.5km, still on the N-340). Játiva (Xátiva, pop. 24,400) squats at the bottom of a tall ridge, Mont Vernissa, which is covered with the walls of an ancient castle. This is your first destination.

When you reach the city centre follow the purple signs for "Centro Histórico" which take you on a tortuous, but well-indicated, route along modern streets.

Passing through two small squares follow the signs to the castle which bring you suddenly out of the city and on to a pretty little lane which quickly climbs a green hillside in hairpin bends. Leaving two very old whitwashed churches behind (for the moment) you enter attractive pine woods. Looking back you have views over the rooftops of Játiva.

Follow this road all the way up until you come to the car-park of the castle. (Open Winter: 10am-2pm and 3.30-6pm. Summer: 10am-2pm and 5-8pm. Closed Monday and the day after each public holiday).

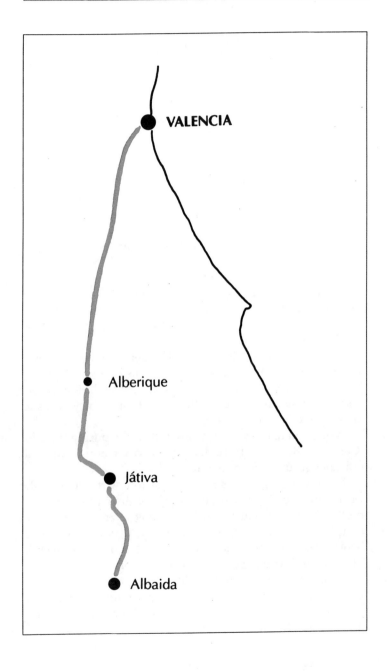

Your journey isn't over. The castle spreads out above and it is a kilometre on foot to the uppermost ramparts. The extensive ruins, interspersed with 30 towers, are in varying states of preservation and restoration, and also a little overgrown. The whole area is filled with wildflowers, butterflies and birds in spring.

From the entrance gateway, turn left to visit the oldest part of the castle (Castillo Menor). The Iberians first fortified the site. From then on all the major civilisations to subdue Spain displaced each other in succession to occupy this privileged vantage point. Carthaginians, Romans, Visigoths, Moors, Christian reconquerors - all held this famous citadel until, in 1707, King Felipe V burnt it (and the town) in revenge for Játiva picking the losing side of the War of the Spanish Succession. Játiva has been getting its revenge on Felipe ever since (see below).

Return to the main entrance and follow the stepped walk that climbs up the hill past what was once a private mansion to the later parts of the castle (Castillo Mayor). A chapel contains the remains of the Conde de Urgel, heir of the crown of Aragón, who was imprisoned and died here in 1438.

You can explore his cell a little further up. Above it a lone *ajimez* window is all that's left of the Sala del Duque where several nobles were executed and which was destroyed by an earthquake in the 18th century. From the very top of the castle you can see down both sides of the slender ridge.

Leaving the castle, go back down the road and stop to visit the two little churches: San José (with more views of the city) and, down a short track, San Felix (San Feliu. Open Winter 10pm-1pm and 3-6pm. Summer 10am-1pm and 4-7pm) which dates from the 13th century but stands on the site of a much earlier pagan temple.

Continue until you reach the built-up area and park in the second or third square you come to. From here, it is a short stroll to the museum housed in what was once a granary (Open Tuesday-Friday 11am-2pm and 4-6pm. Saturday and Sunday 11am-2pm. Closed Monday.) There is an important archaeology collection (including arches taken from some Moorish baths) and paintings. The renowned painter José Ribera, El Españoleto, was born in Játiva.

Speaking of paintings, do you want to know how the people of Játiva got their revenge on Felipe V? Easy: they hung his full-length portrait upside down in this otherwise serious art gallery and it will remain that way until the King of Spain comes in person to put it the right way up.

If you are in the mood to wander along Játiva's narrow streets filled with palaces, stone arches, gardens and running water follow the Carrer de la Corretgeria to the Collegiate Church (open 6.30-8pm). The old hospital opposite has an ornate Plateresque façade. The tourist office (in a 17th century chemist's) is near here.

Go round the Collegiate Church by Calle Abad Plá and down Calle San Vicente, Calle de Bruns and Calle de Segurana and you come to a fountain with 25 spouts irrigating a pretty garden.

Return along Portal de Cocentaina, Calle de San Pedro, Plaza Alejandro VI, Carrer de L'Angel, Plaça de la Trinitat (which has a medieval fountain) and Calle de Moncada.

Játiva can fill the best part of the day. If you still want to see more sights, take the N-340 round the end of Mount Vernissa into an area of trees dotted with villas and down across a gentle agricultural plain.

Albaida (25km further south) has a remarkable fortress-palace and a quaint museum. The Palace of the Marquises of Albaida, with its three stout tapering towers, forms an imposing wall across the main square.

Go through the main archway and beside the church you'll find a small, fenced off alleyway, the middle house of which has been inspired by Moorish fantasies. This was the house of artist José Segrelles, who was born in Albaida and, having achieved international fame, returned here to shut himself away with only his imagination for company.

After having illustrated the Arabian Nights and various works of Spanish literature he devoted himself to depicting religious visions and sci-fi scenes. The house-museum (Plaza

Pintor Segrelles, 13. Tel: 96-239 00 40. Open 10am-1pm and 4pm- 7pm), run by the painter's nephew, is no less revealing about the man than the collection of paintings. The cosy library, open to the public twice a week, contains almost 11,000 books. Fonda Comercio in the main square (Tel: 96-239 10 90. B) is an inexpensive and unceremonious place to eat.

Albaida's chief industry is candle-making. Albaida's candles find their way into churches and processions all over the Spanish Levant.

To return from Albaida you can take the C-320 to the coast and pick up the A-7 motorway. But the shortest route to Valencia is back along the N-340 to Játiva, the way you came. This could be the moment to stop in Masalavés to buy a *panquemado* for tea ❑

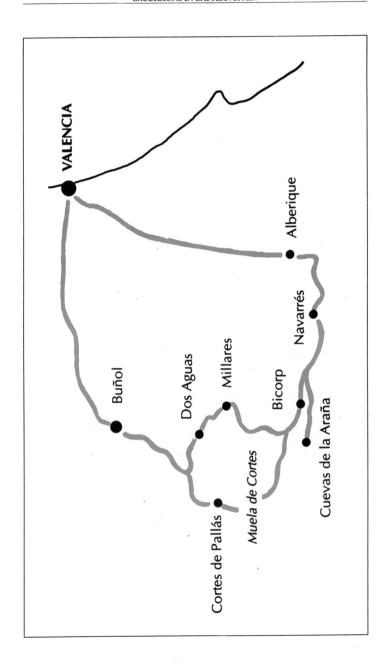

Excursion 19 - Mediterranean Moors:

Valencia - Sumacárcel - Navarrés - Quesa - Cuevas de la
Araña - Bicorp - Cortes de Pallás - Buñol - Valencia
(210km)

The object of this trip is to cross the vast, wild plateau of the Muela de Cortes. It is a route for part-time adventurers as it includes 16km of dirt track - easily passable in car but bumpy nevertheless and taking you ever further away from civilisation (there is a less scenic alternative route).

Leave Valencia on the N-340 for Alicante and Albacete and keep on this road as it peels off for Albacete.

After Alberique turn right onto the VP-3072 to Cárcer and then Sumacárcel (Sumacárcer, pop. 1,400). Just before reaching the latter the road runs beside the green-flowing River Júcar. There is an unusual cemetery before the village, on the left, built around a group of miniature towers and spires.

Turn left at the junction in Sumacárcel and head up the hill for Navarrés (10km). For the next few miles this road curves up a beautifully-wooded valley littered with crags.

Turn right into Navarrés (pop. 2,700) at the stop sign and carry straight on for Quesa. (If you want a swim, turn left and look out for the sign on the right to Playamonte, a small lake which is used as a natural swimming pool, 3km from the town.)

As you approach Quesa (pop. 900) the high plateau of the Muela de Cortes rises before you. Carry straight on for Bicorp through a landscape of red earth and the last few orange trees. Bicorp comes in sight. Just before you get there you will see a left turning marked to the Cuevas de la Araña. This road leads to a series of caves in which there are a number of pre-historic paintings. The most famous shows the first domestic scene recorded by a pre-historic artist: the honey collector. A man or woman, high up on a rope and holding a basket, plunders a hive while bees buzz around him or her. You'll have to visualise this scene yourself because the painting has been all but obliterated by careless sightseers throwing water at it to make the colours more visible. Other paintings show hunters with bows and arrows confronting deer, goats and a bull.

The caves are covered with grilles, which are kept locked to protect them from further damage. The keys are kept in Bicorp town hall; at weekends they are left in the Bar Navalón (Avda la Carretera, 19. Tel: 96-216 90 33). To borrow them you will have to leave your passport, identity card or a photocopy. You may be able to recruit a guide in the village as pre-historic paintings tend to be difficult to discern if you don't know where to look. The best time of day to visit the caves is in the morning before the sun is high.

Even if you if you don't intend to have a proper look at the caves, the little road up to them is worth following for its scenery alone. It takes you deep into a most attractive valley between beautiful, thickly wooded hills. On the way you pass a fountain on the right. A track climbs from there towards the Barranco del Buitre - "Vulture Valley" - where there are more cave paintings.

The road surface ends after 3km. The caves are a further 10km along a rough track. The first part is passable by car but sooner or later it's best to park and continue on foot. The track is mostly sign-posted for the cave but, in any case, it follows the stream, fording it several times.

If you decide to go without the keys or a guide you will have to peer hard and use your imagination. There are no paintings in the first cave you come to and only a few in the second. The third is in two halves; the one on the right has the best paintings - look for a long vertical line marking the rope with the honey collector at the top.

Return down the track, turn left into Bicorp (pop. 800) and keep straight on around the town for Millares. The road becomes more narrow and bumpy, and climbs on to the plateau in tight bends. When it seems to have reached its highest point, you will see a broad, dirt track setting off to the left beside a small stone wall and a sign saying "Reserva Nacional de Caza Muela de Cortes" (Muela de Cortes Game Reserve).

If you don't fancy 16km crawling along a dirt track you can carry straight on to Millares through rather drab scrub and farmland, dropping down into a gargantuan gorge. From there follow signs to Millares, Dos Aguas and then Buñol. On the way you will meet the main route back to Valencia (see below).

This dirt track, not marked on maps, cuts right across the middle of the plateau from one side to the other, making it the ideal way to see the impressive and varied scenery of the Muela de Cortes. You are almost guaranteed to be by yourself for the next 40 minutes or so. There are no real obstacles; the gradients have been constructed to take cars although there are one or two corners which are badly eroded.

The Muela de Cortes is perhaps the nearest thing in Spain to moorland. The landscape, bordered by lofty peaks, has the same air of desolation as upland Yorkshire or the Scottish Highlands. The lack of surface water would make this dry and stoney land forboding but for the abundance of Mediterranean shrubs and wildflowers, partridges and songbirds, innumerable butterflies and mammals. The bigger animals you could see are genets, badgers, wild boar and mouflons (introduced in 1976). This is also one of the few refuges of the Spanish ibex, a wild mountain goat with lyre-shaped horns.

The desolation has its oases. The plateau is cut here and there by dry gulleys filled with oleanders and deep valleys with pine trees: shady spots to stop and rest.

After a long way you pass an almond plantation. If you look right you'll see what could be an earth-coloured flying-saucer or a pristine megalithic earthwork on the skyline. This is the raised bed of a reservoir above Cortes de Pallás which feeds a hydroelectric station in the valley below.

Shortly, you come to the crude gateway of a forestry plantation with a fire watch-tower in the middle. Fork right here.

After a further 1.5km, including some of the worst stretches of track, you come out on to a surfaced road. Turn left for Cortes de Pallás (16km). Right takes you up to the locked gate of that reservoir and no further.

Take care not to squash any snakes as you drive down to Cortes de Pallás. They are wont to slither on to this road and bask in the sunshine.

After 9km you arrive at the lip of the plateau. The landscape caves away into a gigantic canyon carved by the River Júcar and now partially-filled by a turquoise reservoir. On your right is the isolated ruin of the Castillo de Chiret on top of a bluff. The road drops down towards Cortes de Pallás with great views of this enormous valley all the way.

Cortes de Pallás (pop. 900) has a sprinkling of bars and restaurants. Casa Fortunato, on the main road (Avda Dr Sánchez Urzaiz, 12. Tel: 96-251 70 26. No cards. B), is both - and it has rooms.

The road continues to descend beneath salmon-coloured cliffs and curves through a tunnel which emerges directly onto a modern concrete bridge over the reservoir, the Embalse de Millares.

Coming off the bridge the road climbs up the other side of the gorge and then makes its way through the adjacent tree-filled valley, passing above El Oro. The enormous cliffs fringing the flat-topped meseta - and that superimposed reservoir - are still visible far off but have now shrunk into perspective.

The road reaches the level and comes to a crossroad. Turn right onto the VV-3046 towards Buñol. After about 4km you come to another junction. This is where the alternative route meets the main one.

Take the VV-3085 for Buñol. As you approach Macastre there are views of Forata reservoir and a picturesque crossing over the River Magro. Macastre (pop. 900) has an old stone church tower and a hill crowned by a ruined castle.

It is only 6km to Buñol (pop. 9,700) which is most famous for its annual fiesta, the Tomatina, in which hundreds of people pelt each other with ripe tomatoes. From here take the N-111 dual carriageway back to Valencia ❏

Excursions 20 - Spain's Grand Canyon:

Alicante - Almansa - Alcalá del Júcar - Cuenca
(315km)

The picturesquely-sited city of *Cuenca* would be a destination in itself, even if it were not the capital of a green and unspoilt province. And what better way to get there than via Spain's own Grand Canyon, a spectacular gorge eroded by the River Júcar in Albacete - a sight not to be missed.

From Alicante take the N-330 (toll-free) motorway towards Madrid. Leaving behind the outlying industrial estates you pass through an area of arid, stony badlands. After a few more kilometres the landscape becomes more gentle with the semi-desert giving way to an an agricultural plain planted with olive groves, almond orchards and vineyards.

One stop worth making along here is Novelda (pop. 21,300), the heart of Spain's marble industry. As you enter the town you'll see Cylopean blocks of the precious rock waiting to be sliced into highly polished wafers. The main reason to visit Novelda is to see its Art Nouveau house (Calle Mayor, 24, behind the town hall. Open Monday-Friday 11am-2pm and 5-9pm). Built in 1903, it has now been immaculately restored, complete with period furniture.

The motorway continues up the industrial Vinalopó valley following the Sierra del Maigmó (to the right). From this side the mountains give little indication of the lush woodlands that cover their north-facing slopes.

At one time, this valley was a frontier between Moorish and Christian lands. A line of castles, more impressive from a distance than close up, still stands guard along the route. Most are kept locked and to visit them you have to ask for the keys from the town hall. Sax (pop. 8,000) castle, overhanging a jagged rock, is particularly dramatic. The Castillo de la Atalaya in Villena (pop. 30,400), which stands on the remains of a Moorish fortress, has double walls. To get there you have to follow a tortuous, badly sign-posted route through narrow back streets.

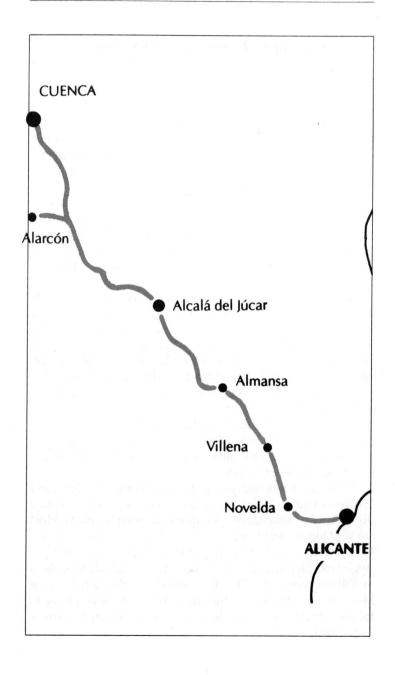

Villena's archaeological museum, in the town hall, includes a priceless collection of Bronze Age gold artefacts, which were found in a jar buried in a dried-up river bed. (Open daily morning and afternoon but with varying hours. Tel: 96-580 11 50 for information).

If you want to see more castles, two of the best are off-route. It's worth a 10km detour (along the A-210 from Villena) through the vineyards to see Biar (pop. 3,300), an attractive town of radiating steps and concentric streets policed by arched gateways which were closed off in the event of attack. The 13th-century fortress has a large dungeon and a hall covered by a Caliphate-style vault. Bañeres (pop.7,000), which has another restored castle, is further off route (23km from Villena on the C-3316 and then the C-3313).

Keep on the motorway (merging on to the N-430) to Almansa (pop. 22,300). Its castle, standing proud from the plain on the crest of a solitary rock, is a landmark and a witness to history. This was the scene of a pivotal battle in the War of the Spanish Succession. The far-reaching result of Felipe V's victory here - the subjection of the autonomous Kingdom of Valencia, which picked the losing side - wouldn't be undone until a new regional constitution was passed in 1982. According to a popular saying: "When evil comes from Almansa it affects everyone".

Head towards Albacete but after about 12km leave the motorway for Alpera (10km) on the AB-860 and carry straight on for Alcalá del Júcar. After 40 kilometres of rolling farmland, punctuated by pretty, flower-strewn slopes, the land suddenly drops away into the deep, spectacular gorge that the River Júcar carves across the plains of Albacete.

The road snakes down to the bottom of the canyon to reach Alcalá del Júcar (pop. 800). Brilliant white to match the rock, the village looks as if it had been glued precariously to the inner curve of a tight river meander. It spills down the steep slope from the walls of its castle - perched on a rocky pinnacle - to an old stone bridge that bounds across the river below.

Alcalá was once used to a make an eye-catching Christmas commercial shown on Spanish television. At the throw of a switch the village was illuminated in a long, bright zig-zag strip from the bridge to a star raised on the castle's battlements. Because of its situation, Alcalá has few streets and it is impossible for cars to enter the village. Instead, there are endless steps (some shoulder-wide), ramps, alleys and passage-ways decorated with colourful, old doors and flowerpots. Park either at the top or the bottom and plunge yourself into the labyrinth.

A good way to begin a visit is to climb to the top of the restored castle - just keep going uphill, you can't miss it - and get your bearings. You won't be disappointed by the panoramic view from the ramparts and turrets. Down below the still-flowing, olive-green Júcar forms almost three-quarters of a circle round the cliff. On the other side of the gorge is a curious wavy-edged bullring.

Underneath the castle, stranded by erosion and inhabited only by acrobatic choughs and swifts which wheel and squeal incessantly, is a column of rock, Boliche Manazas, named after a local skittle game.

Far more interesting than the few other public buildings (which include a 15th century church and a 16th-century granary) are the ordinary houses of the village. Some ramble in all directions, with uneven floors, narrow staircases, pigeon lofts and secret courtyards. Most houses are decorated with rustic artefacts and still contain their original antique furniture. While the former postmaster was showing us around his house he didn't forget to point out the spot in the patio where he slaughtered his fatted pig each autumn and, in the attic, last year's hams were hanging from the rafters for curing.

There is more to these houses than meets the eye. Those that back onto the soft chalk usually have extra rooms excavated at the back and quite a few have tunnels that pierce the meander and emerge up to 90 metres away, high above the river. Caves have their advantages. Before the first fridge reached the village in the 1960s, a subterranean cubby-hole kept provisions fresh. Many *alcalaleños* still prefer to have their bedrooms underground, where the temperature is equable all year round and noise doesn't penetrate. Two of the largest caves are open to the public. Cuevas del Diablo and Cuevas de Masagó both

contain bars at the end of long, illuminated tunnels - the latter even contains a discotheque in summer.

Las Ramblas, beside the bridge, is the place for the day's *paseo*. Tall poplars rustle in the breeze, adding an extra touch of beauty to the valley in spring as the leaves appear and then in the autumn when they change colour.

From here you can take a walk or boat-trip along the river, beside the neatly tilled fields that line its banks. The farmland is scarce but productive and is used to grow vines, fruit and saffron (harvested on freezing mornings in autumn).

From the other side of the meander you can look up at the windows and balconies set high in the cliff-face where industrious tunnelers have broken through to daylight. Later, for a view of the whole village and its spectacular natural setting, go up to the hamlet of Casas del Cerro, across the river on the lip of the gorge.

One of the best places to eat is the restaurant in the new camping site - known simply as El Camping - a short way down river from the village. It serves hearty *gazpacho manchego* (not to

117

be confused with the cold soup, *gazpacho andaluz*). In the village, several of the bars serve food including another of La mancha's specialities, *el ajo*, which is made of potato mashed with garlic. The village bakers meanwhile specialise in *torta de sardinas* - bread stuffed with sardines.

For overnight accommodation, Alcalá has only a one-star hostal, Hermanos Plaza (Tel: 967-47 30 29). Many visitors prefer to stay in comfort in the parador in **Albacete**, 45km away.

Although you now leave the Júcar behind you will meet it again in Cuenca. Pick up the other road out of Alcalá, the AB-863 to Casas Ibañez. Cross the N-322 and carry on across country through Villalpardo on the CU -820. When you meet the N-111, turn left. (Although, if you feel like making a detour to a beauty spot, turn right to the nearby Contreras Reservoir and have a drink at the bar on the dam).

Turn right in Motilla del Palancar (Pop. 4,800) at the end of the town on to the N-320. If you are hungry, stop to eat at Del Sol (on the Madrid road, almost opposite the Cuenca turning. Tel: 966-33 10 25. M). which also provides inexpensive roadside accommodation.

There's one more worthwhile detour before heading for Cuenca; it can even be an overnight stop. The stunning castle of Alarcón, 17km from Motilla hangs over another deep valley of the Júcar. To get there take the N-111 towards Madrid and turn off at the sign-posted turning after 14km. The Moors considered the castle to be impregnable, although in 1184 the Christians still managed to take it. According to legend, Fernán Martín de Ceballos scaled its walls at night using two daggers dug into the cement between the stones. Alarcón castle is now a Parador (Tel: 969-33 13 50). Another, much cheaper, place to stay in Alarcón is El Infante (Tel: 969-33 13 60).

From Alarcón you have to return to Motilla del Palancar to pick up the N-320 which takes you at last towards Cuenca through rich ploughed lands, holm oak scrub and pleasant pine woods, which provide shady places to stop and stroll.

The entrance to Cuenca (pop. 43,000), through an industrial zone, comes as something of an anticlimax after the memorable locations en route and belies the beauty of a city and a province worthy of a lengthy visit ❏

Excursion 21 - In the Steps of Don Quixote:

Alicante - Albacete - Lagunas de Ruidera - Argamasilla de
Alba - Puerto Lápice - Consuegra - Alcázar de San Juan -
Campo de Criptana - El Toboso - Mota del Cuervo -
Belmonte - Alicante
(740km round trip)

If the bulls and flamenco dancers of Andalucia comprise one
typical image of Spain, Don Quixote and his side-kick Sancho
Panza are the other. This route takes you around their stomping
ground, the high plains of La Mancha; an area which is largely
off the beaten tourist track.

Hard on the heels of the befuddled Knight of the Rueful
Countenance dressed in dented armour and a barber's bowl,
you'll discover there is more on the plains than windmills. As
a bonus, if you want to extend your trip La Mancha is on the
way to Madrid (you can, by the way, start this route just as
easily from Valencia and join it at Almansa).

Leave the coast on the N-330 motorway from Alicante to
Albacete (see Excursion 20). The imposing castles of Almansa
(pop. 22,300) and Chinchilla (pop. 3,800) mark the beginnings
of La Mancha, and of Castile, that vast central region of Spain,
named after the 500 or more castles built around it during the
times of strife between Christians and Moors.

At Albacete, follow the signs for Ciudad Real (the same
direction as Madrid to begin with) and take the N-430 which
runs straight and level across an intensively farmed plain to
Barrax.

As you leave the town there's a disused windmill on the hill
on the right - a foretaste of things to come. The road takes you
around the outskirts of Munera and Sotuélamos, and through
rolling country of vines and olives dotted with brilliant white
farmsteads.

When you reach Ossa de Montiel (pop. 2,900), go through
the town and turn left just before the tight bend at the end.
Follow the signs to Lagunas de Ruidera.

A backroad sets off through an unpromising area of flat,

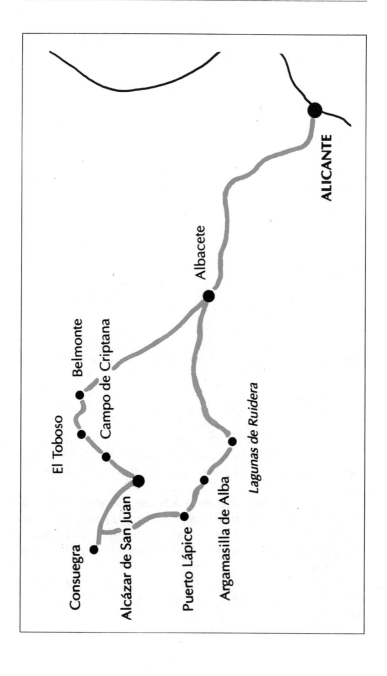

stony fields and vineyards. After 5km you pass a right turning to Lagunas de Ruidera, but don't take this: carry straight on. Immediately after the turning there's a wooden sign announcing "Parque Natural de las Lagunas de Ruidera" (Ruidera Lakes Nature Reserve). Behind it is a stone gateway leading to the first stop on the route of Don Quixote, the Cave of Montesinos. Park here. The cave is barely five minutes down a wide track between thickets of juniper, holm oak and rosemary.

Don Quixote had to be lowered into the cave, which had a mouth "choked with box thorn and wild fig-trees, brambles and briars". Although he spent no more than an hour inside, when he was hauled out he claimed to have spent three days conversing with the hapless Montesinos, who had been imprisoned in perpetuity by the magician Merlin. Sancho Panza considered that he was "talking the greatest nonsense imaginable." Since he was here a flight of steps has been built, which will lead you into pitch darkness. You can get well inside the cave if you have a torch.

Carry on down the road passing a left turning to the Castillo de Rochafrida. This is also mentioned in the book, although there is little to see as it was already in ruins when Cervantes passed this way. The little road now winds down past a white-washed hamlet and chapel and comes out by the side of the first lake, La Laguna de San Pedro. The best hotel in the area, the Albamanjón (Tel: 926-69 90 48, 3 stars) is on the right.

Follow the road around to the right after the small bridge and turn right on to the main road, the AB-650, which runs beside the main Ruidera lakes (and which can be choked with cars in the summer). A second choice of hotel, Entrelagos (Tel: 926-52 80 22, 2 stars) is on this road. It stands by the waterside and has a large open fire in winter.

The 16 Ruidera lakes, strung out over 28km and stepping down 120 metres on the way, are famous for their natural beauty and bird populations. In the parched plain they are a veritable oasis for coots, pochards, teals, grebes and marsh harriers. The colour of the water varies from hour to hour, day to day and season to season; from blue to turquoise to green. The lakes spill into each other by intermittent cascades which dry up when the water level drops. The noise - *ruido* - of falling water is said to give the lakes their name.

During his sojourn in the cave, Don Quixote was told by Montesinos that Merlin had turned a certain Mistress Ruidera, her seven daughters and two nieces into as many lakes (which leaves six unaccounted for). A knight's squire named Guadiana was converted into a river which rises here. The exact source of the River Guadiana is unknown. It disappears underground after a few kilometres to reappear 40km away near the Tablas de Daimiel National Park (worth visiting if you have time for a lengthy detour).

When you reach the N-430, turn right into Ruidera village. There's a National Park Reception Centre (Tel: 926- 52 81 16) opposite and to the left of this junction. Mesón de Juan (Avda. Castilla-La Mancha. Tel 926-52 80 56. No cards. B) is one of the best places to eat in Ruidera.

Turn left in the village on to the CR-151 for Argamasilla de Alba. This is a much faster road which heads up and away from the lakes. Eventually you come out at Peñarroya Castle (permanently open; marked on the map as a chapel) which is above a dam you can walk across. This castle is thought to have been the scene of Don Quixote's fight with a group of puppets which, in his madness, he took to be living Moorish warriors.

Carry on until you reach the junction with the N-310 and turn left into Argamasilla de Alba (pop. 6,600). Although this is a dull town, there is a reason to pass through: it was here that Cervantes was supposed to have begun writing Don Quixote while imprisoned for debt in the Cave of Medrano (Cervantes Street, 7; turn right just before the church.

Cervantes, a contemporary of Shakespeare (curiously, the two writers died on the same date), didn't even start the book until he was 56 years old. He repaid his debt to Argamasilla de Alba by beginning his novel, "In a certain place in La Mancha, whose name I do not want to remember..." The Knight of the Rueful Countenance may be modelled on a local hidalgo, Don Rodrigo de Pacheco.

Carry on along the N-310 through the town and turn on to the CR-133 (becoming the C-134). After 30km straight across country through Villarta de San Juan you strike the N-IV motorway. Head north.

Alternatively, from Argamasilla de Alba, you can keep on the N-310 for Manzanares (pop. 18,200), a wine town, where you can eat well and cheaply at Mesón Sancho (Jesús del Perdón, 26. Tel: 926-61 10 16. B-M) before taking the N-IV north to rejoin the route. Turn off the motorway for Puerto Lápice (pop. 1,000) where you'll find the Venta del Quijote beside a chapel. This is the scene of one of the early episodes of the book.

The story so far: with nothing to look at all day but these never-ending stony plains, Don Quixote escapes into a world of chivalrous epics. Soon he cannot distinguish between reality and his own fantasies. He dusts down the family suit of armour and sets off in pursuit of wrongs to right on his faithful steed, Rocinante. Only one thing is lacking: he has not yet been knighted.

Don Quixote mistook this inn for "a fortress with its four towers and pinnacles of shining silver, complete with a drawbridge and a deep moat," and asked its lord to knight him. The inn-keeper was happy to oblige. After all, it would bring bad luck not to humour a madman.

A castle it is not, but the inn is a beautiful old building in its own right, painted in bright blue and surrounding a rustic courtyard. It still serves meat and ale to the weary traveller (Tel: 926-57 61 10. Open 1-4.30pm and 8-11pm. Master, Visa, Diners. M). Specialities include Manchegan delicacies such as fried breadcrumbs, lamb stew and sponge cake. The bar, which has enormous three-metre-high wine vats, is open all day (8am-12pm). Sancho Panza, an accomplished trencherman, would feel at home here.

Puerto Lápice also has a hotel: El Aprisco (Tel: 926-57 61 50, 2 stars). The best place to stay in La Mancha, however, is the Parador in Almagro (Tel: 926-86 01 00), a little off route in an attractive old town, which itself is worth a visit.

Now for the windmills. Those that Don Quixote is presumed to have tilted at are at Campo de Criptana, which you will visit shortly. But there are better windmills a little way north at Consuegra. Take the N-IV motorway again and after 17km turn off on to the C-400 through Madridejos. You will know you are going in the right direction because Consuegra's windmills are arranged along the brow of a hill next to a castle making them a prominent landmark above the plains.

Go straight down the main street. The road to the castle (open 10am-6pm daily from spring to autumn but only on Saturday and Sunday in winter) and the windmills turns off left at the far end of town. Standing on the windy hilltop you have a vulture's-eye view of a level, phantasmagoric landscape receding to the horizon: of broad fields and vineyards interspersed with whitewashed, isolated farm buildings, artesian wells and stunted trees.

Consuegra's (pop. 10,000) other claim to fame is a Saffron Festival held every October. La Mancha produces around 70 per cent of the world's saffron. If you travel through it in autumn you may well see piles of discarded purple petals beside the road. The flower, a kind of crocus, is grown only for its tiny stigmas which are worth their weight in gold.

Returning to Madridejos, cross over the motorway on the C-400 for Alcázar de San Juan (pop. 24,500), one of the main cities of La Mancha. You can stay in reasonable comfort in the Hotel Don Quixote (Avda. Criptana, 5. Tel: 926-54 38 00, 2 stars) and eat well in Casa Paco (Avda Alvarez Guerra, 5. Near the railway station. Tel: 926-54 06 06 or 54 10 15. Open for lunch from 1.30pm and for dinner from 8.30pm. Closed Monday and October 1-15. Visa. M).

Take the N-420 to Campo de Criptana (pop. 12,500), home of the famous windmills which stand in a wasteland above the town (one of which is a tourist information office). To get to the windmills you have to negotiate a badly-signposted maze of little streets. Don Quixote confronted 30 or 40 of them, creakily turning in the bright sun. Now there are only a handful left, immobile and preserved as a tourist attraction. Although these venerable old machines seem to us to have been part of the landscape since time immemorial, in Cervantes' and Don Quixote's day they represented new technology imported from the Low Countries.

A few kilometres beyond Campo de Criptana, turn left on

to the little road to El Toboso.

A knight must have a lady love in whose honour to perform his daring deeds. Don Quixote chooses his, the fair and peerless Dulcinea, somewhat at random here in El Toboso. Sancho Panza remembers her differently: "she pitches rocks as well as the strongest lad in the whole village. She's a brawny girl, well built, and tall and sturdy ... what muscles she's got and what a pair of lungs!"

El Toboso is a seigneurial town grouped around a pretty square in which stand statues of Don Quixote and Dulcinea. It has been well cared for and has made the most of its slim claim to fame. Dulcinea's House (open weekdays 10am-2pm and 4-6.30pm; Sunday 10am-2pm. Closed Monday) is decorated in a local style. The Cervantes Centre, next to the church, has a collection of Don Quixote translated into 30 languages. All over the village you'll see quotations from the book stuck to the walls in iron letters.

From El Toboso take the TO-104, which quickly brings you to another old inn (no longer functioning), the Venta de Don Quijote, which is decorated with ceramic murals depicting scenes from the book. Turn right on to the N-301.

Mota del Cuervo (pop 5,700) also has windmills on a hill behind but it has something even more entertaining - a hotel celebrating the good knight's reputation in high-kitsch style. To begin with, the Meson de Don Quijote (Tel: 967-18 02 00. All cards. M) is preposterously located behind a petrol station, but don't let this - or its theatrical, Quixotic decorations - put you off. You can eat excellently here and this can be a useful overnight stop. Mota del Cuervo is also the place to stock up on Manchegan cheese (made from sheeps' milk) and wine.

There's one more stop to make before returning home. Take the Cuenca road, the N-420, to Belmonte (16km). This pretty, unspoilt village (pop. 2,900) has streets of white houses and a famous late-Gothic castle (open daily from 10am-2pm and 5-7pm; if it's closed, apply at the town hall) crowning a neighbouring hill. The castle is not in a defensible position; it is there to keep the aristocracy physically separated from the commoners below. It's built to a star-shaped plan, its six corners marked by round towers. Inside it has coffered ceilings. It was used as one of the sets for the 1960s film *El Cid* (starring Charlton Heston and Sofia Loren).

The hills around here were once forested and they provide the backdrop for Don Quixote's skirmish with the Knight of the Wood - one of the few battles he actually won (by luck, it should be added).

Take the CU-834 to El Pedernoso and turn left on to the N-301 for Albacete. If you want to make one more detour, San Clemente (9km out of your way) has several fine old buildings, including a 16th-century town hall and square.

When you get to Albacete, return to Alicante on the N-430 and the N-330 ❑

Excursion 22 - The White Island:

Denia - Ibiza - Denia (by ferry); Ibiza - Cova Santa - Cala
d'Hort - San Antonio Abad - Santa Inés - San Miguel - San
Lorenzo - Balafi - San Carlos - Santa Eulalia del Río - Ibiza
(98km)

Ibiza became a household name during the '60s and '70s - not
so much for its booming, package holiday trade but rather for
its singular, anything-goes life-style which has attracted film
and rock stars, jetsetters, exhibitionists, eccentrics, artists and
intellectuals ever since. Ibiza, they say, is more an attitude than
a place on the map.

Forty-five nautical miles (85km) southwest of Majorca and
80km from the coast of mainland Spain, Ibiza is known as the
White Island for its brilliant white cubist houses and churches.
Most of its land surface consists of thickly-wooded hills. Its
coast is carved into a myriad of secluded coves, some
unfrequented, a few inaccessible, except by sea.

The fastest boat from mainland Spain is the catamaran
which takes just two and a half hours to get from Denia to Ibiza
(this high-speed service operates only from June 15 to Sep 15).
It can be a rough voyage when seas run high. Flebasa Lines
offer a day- return ticket which gives you 10 hours on the island
- just long enough to drive this route. However, if you want to
get more than a superficial feel for Ibiza, and especially if you
want to visit Formentera (see Excursion 30), you'll need at least
two days.

Most ferries go to the capital, Ibiza (also known as Eivissa),
but some head for the island's third biggest town, San Antonio
- check to see where yours is going and phone ahead to have a
hire car (or moped or bicycle if you prefer) waiting for you.

There is a car ferry but it is only worth taking your car if you
plan to stay more than a week; otherwise it works out cheaper
to hire one. For more travel and car hire details see Ibiza in the
Town and City Guide at the end of the book.

Leaving Denia, you have a fine view of the town and its
castle, and the hump-shaped Mount Mongó which overlooks

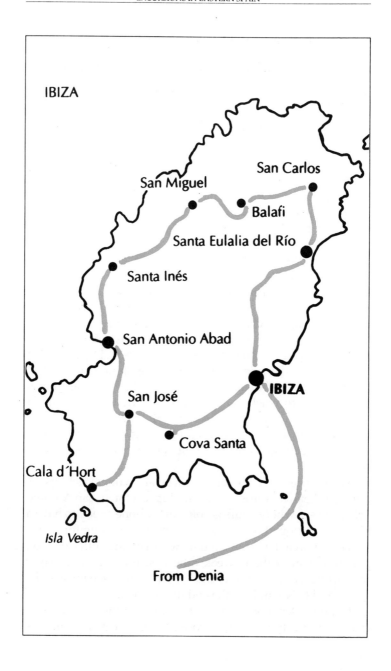

IBIZA

San Carlos

San Miguel

Balafi

Santa Eulalia del Río

Santa Inés

San Antonio Abad

IBIZA

San José

Cova Santa

Cala d´Hort

Isla Vedra

From Denia

it. As the boat picks up speed and heads out to sea you can see a long stretch of the coastline south: the tall cliffs beyond Las Rotas beach, the lighthouse of Cape San Antonio and the sweep of Jávea's Arenales beach. Travelling at such a high speed, you are only out of sight of land for around 50 minutes. Dolphins are sometimes spotted on the way but, although they will follow the slower ferries, they can't keep up with the catamaran.

After about an hour and a half, the south coast of Ibiza comes into sight. The first point visible is the immense craggy peak of Isla Vedra, which rises 382 metres out of the sea (you'll get a closer look at it later).

The boat rounds Cape Llentrisca and two more headlands: Punta de Sa Rama and Punta de Ses Portes, on which stands an old tower. Behind these you may see jets landing at Ibiza's airport. You get a good view of inland Ibiza, too, with its characteristic rolling, pine-clad hills. The Greeks knew it as Pitusa - the island of pine trees. Look out on the other side (starboard) and you will see the lighthouse on Isla Ahorcados (Hanged Men's Isle) and beyond that the low-lying landmass of Formentera.

The ferry now swings around sharply to port, towards the apartment blocks along the capital's two principal beaches, Figueretes and Bossa. Ibiza itself is prominently marked by its fortified old town (Dalt Villa), on a hill above the modern city, ringed by massive walls and crowned by the cathedral. Even if you don't have much time on Ibiza, a walk around the Dalt Villa is a must.

On arrival, you will first need to buy a map. Ibiza's intricate road network (which includes several good, but unsurfaced, tracks) is not shown in full on most maps. The Michelin 1:400,000 covering the island, for instance, omits some important roads. The tourist office doesn't have much to offer although there are a couple of locally-produced maps which, while not comprehensive, are the best available.

Sign-posting on the island leaves much to be desired; and just to make matters more difficult for the tourist, most villages have two names - one Spanish and another in the local language, a dialect of Catalan - but few sign-posts are bilingual. So, to get around Ibiza you'll need intuituion, a sense of adventure, and above all a sense of direction. At least, on an island measuring onky 41 by 20 kilometres you can't get very lost.

Most tourists go to Ibiza for the beaches, of which there is no shortage on the 210km coastline. This route round the island, however, keeps mainly inland. But, inevitably, you are never far from the coast and you can always break off sightseeing to have a dip.

Leave Ibiza (Eivissa) town and pick up the signs for San José on the ring road. To begin with this is the same road as the airport. Keep straight on for San José, on the PM-810, when the dual-carriageway comes to an end. After 5km or so the road enters the gentle, green, pine- clad hills of inland Ibiza. Look out for a left turning to Cova Santa (0.4km).

Alhough small, this cave (open 9.30am -1.30pm) is well worth stopping to see. It takes only 15 minutes to visit and it can be a great place to cool down in mid-summer. A short tunnel leads you into a large, illuminated chamber, which slopes downwards. Seventy steps bring you to the bottom, 27 metres below ground level, past stalactites, stalagmites and columns formed by the meeting of the two. A short passage connects with a smaller chamber. The cave was once used by smugglers and was the home of a priest in the last century.

Return to the main road and carry on for San José (Sant Josep, pop. 9,700) a modest tourist service centre. Ca Na Joana (Ctra. San José, km 10. Tel: 971-80 01 58. Closed mid-October to December, Sunday evening and Monday. Dinner only during summer. E) is one of the town's best restaurants.

Turn left at the crossroads after the public library for Els Cubells (6km) and you are heading towards the sea. This road skirts the southern slopes of the Sierra San José, a diminutive mountain range culminating in the island's highest peak, variously called Atalaya, Atalayassa and Sa Talaiassa (475m), the one with the radio masts.

Take the right turning to Cala d'Hort, a tiny beach with three or four restaurants. The main reason for coming here is to see the magnificent and mysterious-looking rock, Isla Vedra, from close quarters. It was used as the island of Bali Ha'i in the film *South Pacific*. Shearwaters, storm petrel and Eleonor's falcon nest in its cliffs. The surrounding underwater rocks were once a refuge for the monk seal, one of the world's most endangered species.

From Cala d'Hort you have a choice of route. You can either return to San José the way you came and carry on through the village for San Antonio (on the PM-803); or, if you want to see some pretty scenery and don't mind exploring along a stretch of (passable) dirt road, take the left turning at the top of the hill as you leave Cala D'Hort for Cala Vadella. If you follow the signs for Cala Vadella and then San José this windy track, which has several turnings and forks, will bring you to the other side of the Sierra San José. Turn right on to the surfaced road. Along here you'll get some good views of the south west corner of the island, taking in Sa Conillera island (said to be the birthplace of Hannibal) and the resort of San Antonio Abad. When you meet the PM-803, turn left for San Antonio.

Whichever variation you take, you will shortly drop down the hill into San Antonio Abad (pop. 14,000, also known as Sant Antoni de Portmany, echoing its Latin name of Portus Magnus), a thriving, package holiday centre. However, you needn't linger here if you don't want to. The road skirts the beach head and then comes to a junction. Turn left towards the town centre and right almost immediately for Santa Inés (sometimes sign-posted as Santa Agnès de Corona).

Near San Antonio is one of the most exclusive hotel-restaurants on the island, Pikes (Camino de Sa Vorera, Tel: 971 34 22 22. E-VE) which is frequented by jetsetters and showbiz personalities. Sa Capella (Ctra de Santa Inés, km 0.5. Tel: 971-34 00 57. Closed December-Easter Week and Monday and Tuesday in November. M-E) is a slightly cheaper alternative.

Keep following the signs towards Santa Inés/Santa Agnès de Corona. A short way out of San Antonio the road surface degenerates into a series of long-standing pot-holes. Turn left at the next crossroads, again for Santa Inés (0.8km). Like many villages on Ibiza, Santa Inés is really a hamlet comprising a few houses grouped around a bulky, whitewashed church - built for defence as well as for worship.

From here take the right turning beside the church (signposted "Cami de Santa Agnès a San Mateu"), which takes you through wooded scenery and past some ancient Ibizan houses. Bear right at the junction, poorly marked for San Mateo (Sant Mateu), another bright white hamlet. Turn left here for Sant Gertrudis and left again immediately for San Miguel. Turn right at the T- junction, still for San Miguel.

As you head from settlement to settlement across the northwest of the island, the uplands unofficially known as Els Amunts, you will get a glimpse of the contradictory nature of Ibiza. While the best beaches are built up and the whole island seems to be dedicated to tourism, traditional agricultural life still exists in these parts as it has done for thousands of years. Nowadays, however, many of the red-earthed terraces of almond, carob and olive trees are showing signs of neglect.

San Miguel de Balansat (Sant Miquel) is a much bigger village than the others you have passed through. It has bars, restaurants and even a supermarket. The prominent block-shaped building with a stubby belltower on top of the hill is the church-cum-town hall where every Thursday throughout the summer a colourful display of traditional Ibizan dancing is held on the patio.

Near San Miguel is one of the best hotels (also a restaurant) on the island. The exclusive La Hacienda Na Xamena (Tel: 971-33 45 00. Closed December-April. All cards. E-VE) is surrounded by crags and pinewoods and its terrace hangs over a spectacular, rocky cove accessible only by a scramble. To get there, take the road from San Miguel to the port. Just before you reach the beach, turn left onto the leafy lane (worth the drive itself) sign-posted to "La Hacienda."

From the crossroads in the centre of San Miguel, take the road for San Juan and turn off on to the badly-surfaced road to San Lorenzo de Balafia. When you come to a T-junction turn left.

San Lorenzo has a pretty church above the village. Continue for another kilometre until you meet the C-733 and turn left. There are several restaurants along this stretch of road. Es Pins (Ctra. San Juan km, 14.8. Tel: 971-33 32 16. Closed December and January B-M) is especially popular because of its terrace under a shady ficus. Another simple, country restaurant is Balafia (closed Friday. B).

Head towards San Juan, but watch out for a little dirt track sign-posted for Balafia (Balafi). This inconspicuous hamlet clusters around two stone towers a short way off the main road - an easy and pleasant walk. It will give you an idea of what Ibiza was like before the tourists arrived *en masse* - rural peace and quiet, broken only by the clucking of chickens. With its bright, white walls and shady, unpaved alleys, Balafia is stamped with the indelible mark of five centuries of Arab occupation.

If you have time, you may want to continue up the C-733 to explore the north-east corner of the island. You can take a short-cut from here by heading directly for Santa Eulalia del Río down the C-733. Otherwise, from the crossroads near the Balafia turn-off a lane leads through pleasant country to San Carlos (Sant Carles de Peralta 8km). This village was once important for its lead mines. It became moderately famous in the days when hippies used to gather in Anita's Bar (in the village centre). From San Carlos, take the PM-810 to Santa Eulalia.

Santa Eulalia del Río (Santa Eulària, pop. 16,000) sits beside the only river in the Balearic Islands. It has long been popular with artists and is now developing as a tourist resort. It also has one of the prettiest of all Ibizan villages attached to it.

Go through the town in the direction of Ibiza. After passing the petrol station (on your left) take the first turning to the right, which doubles back and climbs a small, evergreen hill to Puig de Missa.

If other villages on Ibiza seem small, Puig de Missa is minute. It gathers around a church with a cream-coloured dome, adjoined by a cool porch filled with arches under which countless swifts nest. The defensive tower was added shortly after the church was built (in the 16th century), as a gun emplacement from which to guard the surrounding countryside. The cemetery-cum- garden is also worth a stroll. The small art gallery behind the church houses a collection by the local impressionist painter, Laureano Barrau.

One of Santa Eulalia's better restaurants, La Posada (Tel: 971-33 00 17. Closed mid-January to mid-March and Tuesday. Local and Belgian cuisine. M), is housed in a 17th century farmhouse near the base of the hill.

From Santa Eulalia, take the main road to Ibiza, the PM-810, which crosses the river (look out for the old Roman bridge). It is 15km back to the capital this way. If you want to make one more detour, an alternative route (about the same distance, but on a slower road) is to take the left turning to Cala Llonga after crossing the river. This runs nearer the coast and passes through the village of Jesús, whose church contains the island's most valuable treasure, a 16th-century altarpiece.

Either way, you will quickly be back in Ibiza - in time to catch the evening ferry to Denia or, if you are staying on, to watch the last ferry leave and the sun go down from one of the viewpoints in the Dalt Villa before straying out to enjoy the capital's legendary nightlife ❑

Excursion 23 - Valencia's Lost Corner:

Valencia - Benisanó - Lliria - Chelva - Titaguas - Aras de
Alpuente - Ademuz - Teruel
(180km)

Although there is a more direct route to Teruel, this roundabout excursion, via the Rincón de Ademuz - a portion of Valencia stranded beyond the province's borders - will take you through some attractive scenery and offer the possibility of interesting detours.

Leave Valencia on the Pista de Ademuz (by the side of Nueva Centro shopping centre) which becomes the C-234 for Lliria and Ademuz.

Benisanó (pop. 1,700) has its own curious castle (private property not open to the public) which grew out of a Muslim farmstead. It was briefly the prison of Francis I of France after his defeat at the battle of Pavia in 1525. Although the rest of the town is undistinguished, Benisanó also has three old gateways still standing.

Valencia is "brass-brand country" and Lliria (pop. 13,400) - which styles itself "the music city" - is its capital. The first civic band in Spain, the Banda Primitiva, was formed here in 1819. It has since been joined by a rival, the Unión Musical.

The Convent of San Miguel, which overlooks the town from on high, used to contain an unusual relic - part of the wing of the Archangel Michael - but it disappeared during the Civil War. There is a good view from the courtyard of the pretty, painted chapel.

From Lliria to Casinos there are long stretches of straight road flanked by concrete irrigation channels. The dry country is planted with olives, artichokes, almonds and vines (mellowing into tones of yellow and red in autumn). Casinos (pop. 2,200) is renowned for its *peladillas* - sugared almonds - a tasty souvenir sold in several shops.

The first possible detour is to a lush green valley and the little village of Chulilla (pop. 800), surrounded by cliffs. To get there, take the Requena turning 9km after Casinos, through

135

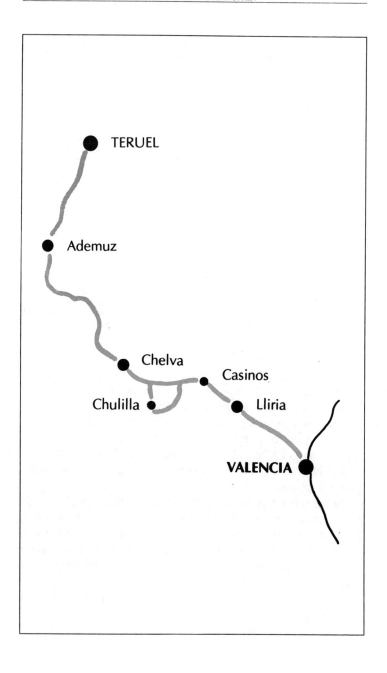

Vanadoig, a semi-abandoned village with a farm school. Leaving the fields behind, you enter an area of heavily-wooded hills. Turn right at the next junction into Chulilla. If you go down to the river from here you'll find the spa of Fuencaliente where there is a hotel-restaurant (Tel: 96-165 70 13. M).

Carry on through the village and stop after the last houses to look left at the view of dramatic, red cliffs pock-marked with caves. This lane now brings you back to the C-234 at Losa de Obispo.

The road to Ademuz has run more or less straight since Lliria but now it winds into attractive hills of bare rock, pine and carob trees.

Round a curve you suddenly come across Loriguilla reservoir, which has a waterfall at one end and the ghost village of Domeño at the other. The inhabitants of Domeño were forcibly rehoused elswhere to make way for the reservoir; but some of the houses have been rehabilitated by homeless people. As the water-level rises and falls it covers and uncovers the old bridge.

Chelva (pop. 2,600) is 6km further on. A 4-km detour out of town is Peña Cortada: a local beauty-spot near the ruins of a Roman aqueduct. To reach it, turn right off the main road in the town centre (as sign-posted). Turn right again on to the track (rough but passable), by the side of a white-washed bullring, which first heads for a Moorish tower. From here the signs are not so clear.

Fork left after the tower and right at the next junction. After a while the track enters a narrow river valley. The ruined arches of the aqueduct appear on the left. Peña Cortada is 1km further on but the track becomes badly eroded and it would be better to leave your car by the aqueduct and walk.

Another excursion from Chelva takes you up to Pico del Remedio, a 1000m-viewpoint. To get there, keep to the surfaced road by the bullring.

Continuing towards Ademuz on the C-234, there is another side-excursion after 5km. A left turning takes you along a scenic route to Benagéber dam (18km) and Serratilla nature reserve.

If you just want to stop for a picnic, the Nacimiento del Río Tuejar, a pretty spot by the river, is a short way off the road on the right, just after the Benagéber turning. Centro Altur, near here, is the departure point for treks around the rugged forests of the Alto Turia region. It also has a restaurant (Tel: 96-163 52 21).

The road now twists up to the Montalbana Pass (780m), through peaceful hills of pine trees, and descends to Titaguas (pop. 650), an excursion centre for hikers and campers, which sits at the side of a dry plain.

From Titaguas it is worth making a short detour to see Alpuente, a pretty village which was once the capital of a Moorish taifa or kingdom and briefly, in the 14th century, the seat of the Valencian parliament. The quaint town hall sits in cramped quarters over an ancient gateway. Outside the village is a medieval aqueduct.

Between Titaguas and Aras de Alpuente the road passes through vineyards and the pretty pine woods of the Dehesa del Rebollo. Aras de Alpuente (pop. 500) has a prominent tower. There are not many places to stop to eat around here, but Los Tornajos (Tel: 96-201 20 88. Open 2-4pm and 9-11pm. B) is clean and simple. It specialises in *morteruelo* (a rich game dish), trout with almonds, homemade sausages and roast leg of lamb.

The next part of the route is the most picturesque. The road traverses a large pine forest (slipping briefly into the province of Cuenca), and comes down into a deep gorge with the River Turia at the bottom, which you cross by a high bridge.

After a series of hairpin bends the road drops deeper down into the gorge and crosses back into the province of Valencia, more precisely into the Rincón de Ademuz. You pass through two villages before reaching Ademuz itself: Casa Bajas (pop. 430), by the river, which has some adobe houses, and Casas Altas (pop. 220).

Ademuz (pop. 1,450) is a decaying mountain town that has seen better days and which has still not fully entered the twentieth century. Many of the buildings are timber-framed and have wooden balconies. The eaves of the houses lean together over the narrow streets.

The only place to stay is Casa Domingo, an enormous rectangular, cream-coloured building, on the way out of town towards Teruel (Avda de Valencia 1. Tel: 978-78 20 30; 78 23 77 and 78 20 50. B) which also serves as a bar-cum-restaurant-cum-gift shop. If you stay there at the weekend, be warned: pigs are slaughtered outside every Sunday morning.

You are now on the N-330, a good road which takes you swiftly through Villel (with its ruined castle) towards *Teruel*, following the River Turia across a landscape of red earth.

At the end of the trip, the modern outskirts of Teruel appear ahead, quickly followed by the whole compact silhouette of this rose-coloured city full of romantic architecture ❏

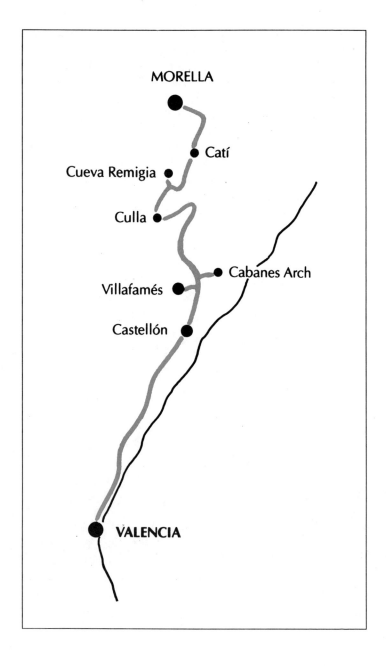

Excursion 24 - Gothic Palaces:

Valencia - Castellón - Villafamés - Culla - Benasal - Catí -
Morella
(224km)

If there is one town in eastern Spain you should not miss it is *Morella*, built around a massive rock rising to 1,000 metres out of the magnificent mountain landscape of the Maestrazgo. It retains its old city walls intact; the streets within have barely changed over the last four centuries.

The Maestrazgo, which straddles the mountainous border between the provinces of Castellón and Teruel, could occupy a whole book in itself. Not being on any major inter-city route, it is relatively remote yet easily accessible from the coast and imbued with natural charm. From the many pretty lanes and scenic landscapes, the historic towns and villages, we have compiled two routes (this one and Excursion 28).

Leave Valencia for Castellón on the road to Barcelona. You can either take the N-340 or the toll-motorway, the A-7, leaving it at Exit 47.

In the centre of Castellón turn left on to the C-238 for Villafamés (it is not well indicated). The road swings around the southern end of the Sierra de les Santes and crosses the plain to reach Borriol, watched over by a superbly-placed castle, now reduced to a ruin of reddish walls.

For 11km you follow a long, straight road north up a valley, punctuated with a wiggle of curves through wilder slopes. Almonds, carobs and olives gradually replace the orange trees which grow near the coast.

Turn left in Puebla Tornesa onto the C-300 for Villafamés (8km). After 2km turn left onto the C-814 for Villafamés (pop. 3,000), which climbs from a gentle plain of olive and almond trees along a rocky ridge to the restored ruins of its castle.

The bottom part of the town is modern with a large square to park in if you don't mind walking up the hill. There's a good restaurant, Meson Villafamés, in this square (Plaza la Fuente, 1. Tel: 964-32 90 08. Open 1-4pm and 8-11pm. Closed Thursday.

B) which specialises in seafood, lamb, rabbit and game. Outside main meal times it serves a variety of tasty tapas. There's another restaurant, El Rullo, (C/La Font, 34. Tel: 964-32 91 10. No cards. B) on the way up to the old town and a small hotel of the same name (C/la Font, 2. Tel: 964-32 93 84) nearby.

The upper part of Villafamés, around the 16th century church, is a warren of sloping, uneven streets filled with sturdy houses rich in architectural details, and decorated with plants and flowers. Here and there the living rock bulges into the street.

Long flights of steps lead you to the castle. There's not much left around its roofless, cylindrical keep but what remains is well preserved. There are also impressive views of the plains below and hills behind the town. You may be able to make out the peak of Peñagolosa (1,814m), the highest mountain in the Comunidad Valenciana, 30km to the north-west.

What has put Villafamés on the tourist map is something quite unexpected - the Museum of Contemporary Art (open daily 11am-1pm and 5-8pm; Saturday, Sunday and holidays 11am-2pm and 5-8pm), housed in the 15th century Palacio del Bayle behind the church.

Even if you definitely do not like art, this magnificent building is worth exploring. It is a lot bigger inside than it looks from the outside. It rambles over a variety of floors and levels; up and down staircases; through rooms of varying shapes, sizes and proportions which preserve beams, tiles and other original details.

The collection adds a bright splash of colour to this elegant old palace. Apart from the paintings, which are mainly figurative and date from 1959 to the present, there are sculptures and holograms. The roof-top terrace-garden, a setting for more sculptures, incorporates chunks of natural rock, a tower and a stretch of battlements.

From Villafamés, take the CS-814 back the way you came and turn left on to the CS-800 towards Albocácer on a long, straight road across the plain. After five or six kilometres look out for a small crossroads just before reaching the next village. The left turning is marked "La Barona"; take the unmarked turning to the right and turn right again at the next crossroads. Two and a half kilometres down the road a Roman arch - its voussoirs still skillfully suspended in the air after two millenia - stands in a dusty roundabout marking the Roman road of Via Augusta. Return along the same road to the CS-800 and turn north again for Albocácer.

The mountains converge and the valley narrows. The road climbs gently and descends again. There are several roadside restaurants along this stretch.

Three kilometres before Albocácer you come to the 16th century chapel of San Pablo overhung by leafy plane trees. Turn left immediately after it on to a little unsignposted road.

The next part of the route meanders through the mountains. If you want to reach Morella more quickly, stay on the main road. Fork left on to the CS-802 and take the left turning after 6.5km for Catí to rejoin the route.

The little lane rattles across the plain past olive and almond groves and then climbs through a small, dry valley to Torre de Embesora (pop. 270). When you enter the oblong square at the bottom of the village keep straight on, taking the lower road out which will bring you to a crossroads. Go straight over for Culla (12km).

Although this is certainly a roundabout way to reach Morella, it does offer magnificent views of the massive, flat-topped mountains of the Maestrazgo. Culla (pop. 1,000), at an altitude of 1,088 metres, gathers around a prominent rock which, from a distance, looks as if it is part of the town.

Continue down the road for Benasal and look back at Culla as you leave it. The tall, defensive walls on its northern flanks blend into houses at the top. Washing is now hung out to dry on the towers which were once used to look out for marauding enemies. As you round a corner some kilometres further on, the parched upland landscape changes abruptly into lush, grassy terraces: there is water near here. You are approaching the spring of Fuente en Segures.

On the left is an industrious restaurant, Novella (Ctra. Culla. Tel: 964-43 10 94. Open 12am-5pm and 9-11.30pm daily during the summer; weekends only the rest of the year, although you can get a meal on a weekday in winter if you order in advance. Visa. B). Amongst its specialities are *tombet* - rabbits and white snails in sauce (to order) - and homemade desserts including *cuajada* (curds).

Just before you reach the spa itself there's a right turning on to a small concrete road that climbs to an 18th century chapel, the Ermita de San Cristobal, perched on top of a blustery hill from which there are 360 degree views of the peaks, cliffs, hill-terraces and semi-wild slopes of the Maestrazgo. If you look over the rooftops of Benasal, in the distance you can see the dramatically located Ares del Maestre (visited in Excursion 28).

The town of Benasal (Benassal, pop. 1,500), below the spa, is disappointing but it does have a couple of old stone towers and a medieval arcade, which once served as a commodity exchange. The Palacio de Cutanda is a fine Gothic building, but in bad repair and difficult to find.

When you come to the CS-802 turn right. It is only a short detour, however, to the Cueva Remigia where there are cave paintings. Turn left instead to get there. Guided tours to the

cave are led from Bar Montalvana (Tel: 964-44 15 84), on the right of the road. The cave is 3km from here along a rough track. Only the first kilometre is manageable by car. Payment for the tour is left to your discretion. Snacks are available in the bar. The cave has been called the Mesolithic Sistine Chapel. The artist's favourite subject was himself. Altogether there are 200 human figures, mostly hunters and their prey: deer, goats, boars and bulls. One curious scene appears to depict an execution by a firing squad of archers. Return down the CS-802 the way you came to rejoin the route.

Turn left on to the CS-V-8022 to Catí. This road follows a line of rocky hills, to the left. On the way you pass a line of extremely large holm oak trees - it's unusual to see them grow to such a fulsome size.

Catí (pop. 1,000) is a pleasant little town which has a few arched doorways and coats of arm carved in stone. One of the town's best mansions has, unfortunately, been insensitively converted into a bar.

Continue until you strike the N-232, the main road which comes up from the coast. This passes by the shrine of Morella's patroness - the Virgin of Vallivana - and then climbs a magnificent valley cut into deep ravines and filled with trees and crags. You are entering the district of Els Ports - "the mountain passes". At the top, after crossing the Puerto de Querol (784 metres), the road runs over a plateau broken up by dry stone walls and *masías* - squat, ochre-coloured farmhouses with wooden balconies and pantiled roofs weighed down with stones.

Coming down from the plateau you have the best possible view of Morella (pop. 3,100) ahead. This ancient, walled town swarms around a huge rock which rises like a celestial vision high above the valley floor. An access road takes you the same way as many an itinerant medieval merchant to the gate of San Mateo, now left permanently open to receive the weary traveller ❑

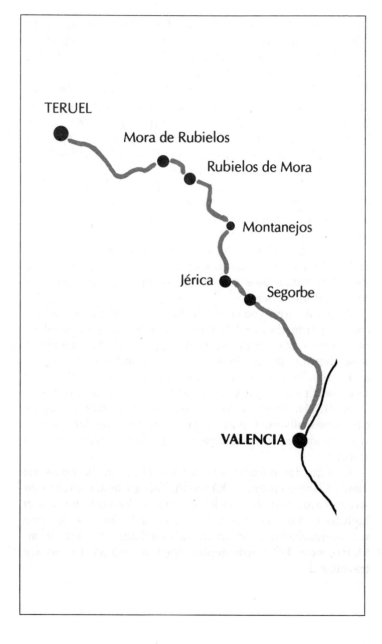

Excursion 25 - Stately Streets:

Valencia - Segorbe - Jérica - Montanejos - Embalse de Arenós
- Rubielos de Mora - Mora de Rubielos - Teruel
(180km)

This is an improvisation based on the main route to Teruel (the N-234), making a detour to see two historic towns.

From the centre of Valencia follow the signs for Barcelona on to the toll-free A-7 motorway. Leave this road at exit 5, before the toll booths, and take the N-340 towards Sagunto. Just before you reach the town, turn right on to the N-234 to Teruel. You don't notice the gradient at first but this road climbs steadily from sea-level to the inland *meseta* over 1,000 metres up.

First it passes through a succession of small towns: nuclei surrounded by Valencians' weekend homes. This is also good orange-growing country - from harvest-time (December and January) until the middle of summer you will see many roadside stalls selling bags of the fruit at bargain prices.

The road is lined with restaurants offering *paella a leña* - paella cooked on a wood fire. One of the best is El Pins (Camp de Morvedre, 16. Tel: 96-262 80 60. Open 1-4.30pm and 8-11pm. No cards. B), a large, family-run place just before you cross the bridge into Estivella (pop. 1,200). The restaurant's paellas are for the discerning: the cooks use specially selected carob tree wood for the fires and water from a local spring.

Torres Torres (pop. 110) has a fine ruined castle on the left above the road just before the town, and a handsome church tower.

The road now climbs through a series of 'S'-bends. Sot de Ferrer, over to the right, has a distinctive white, zig-zagging line of stations of the cross.

Segorbe (pop. 7,600) is by-passed but you may want to stop and visit the town's many monuments, including the Gothic cathedral and the palace of the Dukes of Medinaceli (now the town hall), with its 16th century coffered ceiling.

Passing Segorbe on the main road you'll notice a mini-

Mudejar brick tower in the cemetery on the right: an architectual sign that the Mediterranean region is yielding to Aragón. As you proceed towards Jérica, ever gaining height, Aragón exerts more of an influence. The land is less fertile and not so well irrigated as on the coast; the climate untempered by the proximity of the sea.

At Jérica (pop. 1,800), which is grouped around a tall Mudejar tower, turn off on to the C-223 (becoming the C-211) to Caudiel and Montanejos.

People from Valencia flock to Montanejos (pop.470) in the summer to drink from its numerous springs and bathe in the invitingly green pools of the River Mijares. Its handful of hotels serve standard holiday fare to non-residents. Typical is Hotel Xauen (Avda. Fuente de Baños, 26. Tel: 964-13 11 51. B).

Take the CS-200 for Olba and Puebla de Arenoso. One kilometre out of town you will come to the car-park of the Fuente de Baños, a mineral water spring in a handsome gorge which is recommended for digestive and skin disorders. There is also a popular river beach with sparkling clear water to swim in.

Continue up the gorge rimmed by tall cliffs and through three tunnels in quick succession to come face to face with a giant wall of stones - the Arenós dam. The road runs along the side of the reservoir behind, keeping its distance from the water's edge. On the left, overlooking the reservoir, stands the ruined castle of Los Angeles.

The lake gradually peters out around Puebla de Arenoso (pop. 230), which stands on a promontory over the water. You now follow the upper course of the River Mijares for a while. After passing La Monzona, the road surface degenerates into a series of deep pot-holes.

Just before Olba you reach a junction. Turn right for Fuentes de Rubielos (5.5km) on to a road not marked on the map. Fuentes de Rubielos is a typical village of Lower Aragon with its earth-coloured stones surmounted by time-worn pantiled roofs. The road by-passes it and brings you to a T-junction with the N- 232. Turn left for Rubielos de Mora (5.7km) along this quiet, main road, which passes through countryside dotted with holm oak, acacia, juniper and aromatic herbs.

Arriving above Rubielos de Mora (pop. 700), you come to a large, modern iron cross. Behind this is a viewpoint marked by a short stretch of battlement and some stone benches. It's the ideal place to begin a visit to this town full of solid stone mansions, grouped around a large church crowned by an octagonal finial.

Follow the road down to the T-junction. Turn left into the town and continue past the first gateway, the Portal del Carmen (on whose crenellations sits a carved owl) - one of the few parts of the town's 14th century walls that are still standing. Park in the square near the second gateway, the Portal de San Antonio.

Stepping through the archway you come to the main square, Plaza de Hispano America. The tourist office is in the town hall, a 16th century palace, on your right. To get to it you have to cross a large, low hall filled with columns. Look out for the small doorway which leads to what was once the prison. In the corner of the hall is a tiny, open courtyard with plant pots and a graceful flight of steps. The doorway at the bottom has a face carved on its jamb.

That Rubielos was once a prosperous place is evident from the large number of palaces, built from the 16th to the 18th

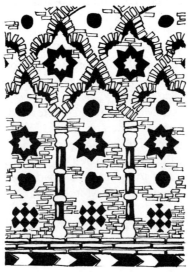

centuries, that you encounter in its stately streets. Most of them have semicircular Gothic doorways, lofts, wrought iron grilles over their windows and long eaves leaning towards each other as protection from the extremes of the weather.

From the town hall, take Calle San Antonio which brings you to the 17th century, Renaissance-style church. It was built to replace the town's original church (now incorporated into an Augustine monastery a short way out of town). One of the chapels has a vast, gilt 15th century Gothic altarpiece painted by an artist known simply as the Master of Rubielos.

From the church it is only a short step to the trickle of a river feeding ancient, well-tended terraced allotments. Find your way up to the top of the town again and to the Plaza del Carmen, where there is a neo-Gothic house. In the middle of the square is a monument to *el toro embolao*: a fiesta held here, popular with the locals though not with animal rights' campaigners, in which burning balls of pitch are placed on a bull's horns. The sculpture is by José Gonzalvo, an artist who was instrumental in the meticulous restoration of Rubielos de Mora.

Just off the square is a former Carmelite convent with a delightful patio, now a restaurant and hotel, Portal del Carmen (Glorieta 2, Tel: 978-80 41 53. Open 1.30-4pm and 8.30-10.30 pm. Amex, Master, Visa, Diners. M-E).

For drinks, try the lively Bar La Posada (C/San Antonio, 33. Tel: 978-80 43 86), next to the Portal de San Antonio. Bar Pichán (C/El Plano, 8. Tel 974-80 40 33), on the main road opposite the Portal de San Antonio, has two large showcases of enormous fossilized animals.

From Rubielos de Mora take the C-232 towards the seemingly palindromically named town of Mora de Rubielos (13km). If you want to explore off the route, from Rubielos de Mora you can climb to the Puerto de Linares, which, at 1,720 metres is amongst the highest in Spain. This road leads you into the Maestrazgo and eventually to Morella (see Excursions 24 and 28).

The C-232 crosses an arable plain and then rises through beautiful little hills covered with rocks and pinewoods. Coming down again to another plain it follows a line of hills with exposed sloping strata into Mora de Rubielos.

Mora de Rubielos (pop. 1,400) is dominated by its huge 13th-century castle built of worked stone. It was largely remade in the 15th century and for a time was the home of a Franciscan monastery.

Another imposing building is the Colegiate church. Although Romanesque in origin, it is more in the Mediterranean or Levante style of Gothic. Its chapels are decorated with ceramics from Manises, near Valencia.

The vernacular architecture is also unmistakeably "mountain" Gothic; with porticoes along the main street, big arched stone doorways, lofts for drying food, and windows divided into two lights by thin columns. Parts of the 14th- and 15th-century walls, punctuated by towers, are still standing.

From here it is only a short hop off route into the Sierra de Gúdar, which has a peak of over 2,000 metres. From spring to autumn this is a popular area for walking and ski-ing.

From Mora de Rubielos keep to the C-232 through Valbona to La Puebla de Valverde (20km) - a beautiful drive across good, ploughed land of pink earth dotted with holm oak and conifers, and farmhouses that seem a natural part of the landscape. At La Puebla de Valverde turn right for Teruel (23km) on to the N-234.

After the Puerto de Escandón (1,242 metres) you descend to the dry, red plateau around the rose-coloured Mudejar city of *Teruel* ❑

Excursion 26 - The Enchanted City:

Cuenca - La Ciudad Encantada - Uña - Tragacete -
Nacimiento del Río Cuervo - Villalba de la Sierra - Ventana
del Diablo - Cuenca
(160km)

This popular trip takes you through some of the most picturesque and varied scenery of the green and beautiful Serranía de Cuenca: past wondrous rock formations, through lush woods and along river banks to fairy-tale waterfalls.

To leave the city take Calle Colón over the bridge and turn right immediately for Ciudad Encantada. Follow the turquoise river through the gorge under cliffs of smoothly rounded rocks.

As it emerges from the gorge, the road passes under a bridge. Turn left after it on to the CU-912 for Valdecabras, crossing the same bridge you have just driven under. This road runs up a tree-filled valley which gradually narrows until it enters a small rocky gorge. You leave the village of rustic stone houses clustering around a monolithic church to the right and climb the side of the valley into the woods above.

After a while, large rock formations appear among the trees: a foretaste of what is to come. Without further warning you drive straight into the car-park of the Ciudad Encantada - the "Enchanted City" (open daily from sunrise to sunset). Although it's become a bustling tourist attraction, overrun with coach parties in season, there's still something awesome about this remarkable collection of naturally-sculpted rocks. There's a bar- restaurant-hotel here too, the Ciudad Encantada (Tel: 969-28 81 94. Open 1.30-5pm. Closed January 7-February 1. Visa. B).

The road ahead rises and falls through the woods, gradually dropping down to re-join the CU-921 along the Júcar valley. Turn right for Tragacete (40km).

If, on the other hand, it's time for lunch already, turn left and go down to Villalba de la Sierra, stopping at the Ventana del Diablo - a cave-balcony, framed by two natural arches, from where there are excellent views over the gorge. Mesón Nelia (Tel: 969-28 10 21. All cards. M), one of the best restaurants around here, is the low building of wood and stone on the right after crossing the bridge. Retrace your steps to continue the route.

The CU-921 runs along the lip of the gorge and descends to Uña (pop. 160), which has a small lake behind it and is the home of assorted waterfowl. There's an unassuming restaurant in the village.

After Uña you pass underneath lofty crags over which griffon vultures wheel, soaring on almost motionless wings. The road skirts around the reservoir of Embalse de la Toba and sticks close to the bank of the green-flowing Júcar as it winds through thick wildwood. Look out for a natural rock column on the left. The little red-roofed village of Huélamo, on the other side of the river, nestles at the base of a prominent rock.

Follow the road across the river, but keep straight on for Tragacete at the next junction. The right turning connects with Excursion 27 by way of the pass of El Cubillo (1,620 metres).

Tragacete (pop. 440) lies in a wide, remote upland valley. It has two hotels, El Gamo (Plaza de los Caídos. Tel: 969-28 90 08) and Júcar (Fernando Royuela, 1. Tel: 969-28 91 47).

The way out of the village is sign-posted for "Vega del Cordono". The road continues up the narrowing valley and plunges into gentle pine woods with grassy floors.

Eventually you come to a junction with a picnic area (Area Recreativa) and a stone hut beside it. Carry straight on. The road descends and shortly a wooden sign-post opposite a bar points to Nacimiento del Río Cuervo (the "Source of the River Cuervo").

Park in the car-park, and from here it's only a 300-metre walk to the moss-hung waterfalls which could have come straight out of a fairytale and are particularly impressive in winter when half-frozen. If you are in the mood for an hour's stroll, follow the marked footpath up the steps for a round trip, which takes you into the pine woods undergrown with box trees. The path follows the embryonic river - no more than a sparklingly clear brook - to the cleft in the rock at the base of the cliffs from which it springs. Another path leads you down the other bank of the river, past more waterfalls, to a tiny bridge by the car-park.

Restaurant "La Tía Paz" (opposite the car-park. Tel: 969-28 90 78. Open 1.30-5.00pm and 7.30-9.00pm. No cards. B) specialises in garlic soup, trout with ham and *morteruelo* (a rich mixture of pork liver, giblets, game and spices). It also has rooms.

Return along the road you came on and when you get to the junction by the stone hut and the picnic area, fork right on to good road for Cuenca (64km) through Las Majadas. This passes through the same gentle forest as before and then follows a steep-sided, thickly-wooded valley with rock outcrops. There is a little balcony of the left to stop and contemplate the landscape. The road forks twice but keep on the wider surface for Cuenca. After climbing through a small gorge, you are again in gentle, grassy woodland. Bear left at the stone monument.

The Serranía de Cuenca abounds in wildlife - including roe deer, wild boar, mouflon, vultures, birds of prey and otters. A turning along this stretch of road leads to El Hosquillo, a nature reserve where bears and wolves roam in semi-liberty. You can only visit the reserve by prior permission (Tel: 969-22 80 22).

After crossing an open area of scrubland, Las Majadas appears on a rise ahead. Don't go into the village but bear left around it, taking the road for Cuenca. Although there is a large hill to climb, you do have fine views over large distances. For a long time the road keeps its height through pine and holm oak woods. Finally it winds down to join the Júcar valley.

When you reach the main road, the CU-921, in Villalba de la Sierra, turn right for Cuenca (if you didn't see the Ventana del Diablo earlier, you have another chance to do so by turning left). From Villalba de la Sierra the CU-921 follows the arable fields of the Júcar valley. Finally, you re-enter the familiar gorge over which the old quarter of the capital city precariously dangles ❑

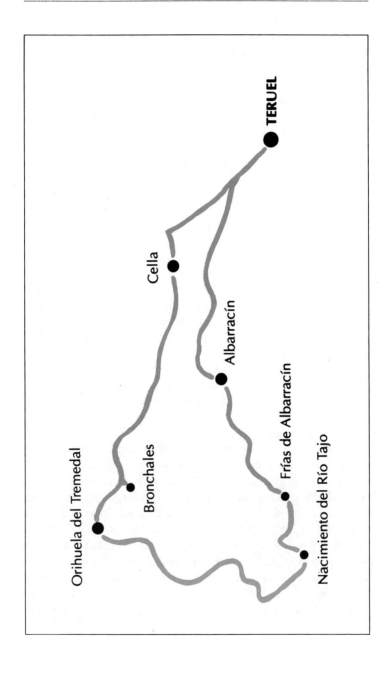

Excursion 27 - Juniper Hills:

Teruel - Albarracín - Nacimiento del Río Tajo - Puerto del
Portillo - Orihuela del Tremedal - Cella - Teruel
(180km)

This route is a long drive through the remote hills of the
Montes Universales, far away from the crowds. It begins by
visiting Albarracín, a town pervaded with the Middle Ages in
which you could almost spend the whole day.

Take the N-234 north from Teruel and after 5km turn off on
to the TE-901 for Albarracín (29km). The road runs dead
straight for 10km across a very dry upland plain but then
gradually curves into the hills.

The first town you come across is Gea de Albarracín, which
has stone buildings, wood framed houses and old pantiles
roofs: a taste of what is round the next few bends.

From here, the road follows a pretty valley. Soon you round
a corner and get a glimpse of a tower and the upper walls of the
historic town of *Albarracín,* (pop. 1,100), its narrow streets of
tall, reddish houses perfectly preserved over the centuries.

The excursion continues into the unpopulated mountains
of the Montes Universales. Before you set out it's wise to stock
up with fuel and provisions as there are no large settlements for
many miles. This is not, by the way, a route to do in mid-winter
when the small roads - especially over the pass of El Portillo -
can be blocked by snow.

Leave Albarracín on the TE-903 through the tunnel and
carry on up to the gorge alongside the river. After 2km there is
a restored, but inconspicuous, Roman bridge on the left.

The road climbs up into sparsely wooded hills and curves
down to a left turning to Frías de Albarracín (17km), the TE-911.
Cross the River Guadalaviar. At the fork before the small
bridge turn right on to an unclassified road for "Cuenca via
Frías de Albarracín".

The countryside opens up into a wide valley and the road
climbs into wild hills which, with their reddish *ródeno* rocks

157

and stands of savin (a kind of juniper - the leaves are aromatic when rubbed), are typical of the scenery of the Montes Universales. On the left side of the road there is a picnic area with a shady car-park. Further up, on the right, there is a natural rock arch.

Broad fields of red earth surround Calomarde, a hamlet of old stone houses. Just outside the village the road forks; take the one uphill, to the right, for Frías de Albarracín (pop. 240).

With its cobbled streets and little white houses, the village sits at the base of a prominent conical hill. There is a small hostal here, Frias, Egido 4, (Tel: 978-70 50 72). Turn right at the bottom of the village for Cuenca and the Nacimiento del Río Tajo (11.2km).

You are soon up in the hills again. The trees start thinning out and give way to gravelly slopes covered with dense, flat clumps of juniper. This whole area is gentle walking country with low rounded hills.

You can't miss the Nacimiento del Río Tajo - the source of the River Tagus, that mighty river which, as the Tejo, drains into the Atlantic at Lisbon 910km from here - because it's marked by an enormous metal statue. There is, however, no water to be seen. The actual source is a fountain, the Fuente de Garcia, 150 metres along a track behind the monument; but even this is unspectacular, as the water from it disappears into the ground.

Continue past the left turning for Cuenca, marked by a conical stone pillar (this road connects with Excursion 26, 10km away). Take the next right turning to Guadalaviar (8km). Immediately you set off on a steep climb to the pass of El Portillo (1,790 metres) along a road which can become perilously icy in winter.

Arriving in Guadalaviar, turn left to go round the village, above the semicircular bullring, and carry straight on for Griegos on a better road surface. After Griegos, head for Orihuela del Tremedal through mature pine woods scattered with small oaks. Turn left at the T- junction. The road rises through more delightful woods over the Puerto de Orihuela (1,650 metres). Orihuela del Tremedal (pop. 740) is dominated by its church of San Millán. You can get a reasonable, home-cooked meal at La Sierra (Plaza de Clavo Sotelo. Tel: 978-71 40 29. B). The house specialities are quail, rabbit and lamb.

A smart new, reclassified road, the A-1511 (marked as the TE-902 on older maps) takes you towards Bronchales (pop. 440) with its pretty white 16th century church on the top of a hill. Three kilometres after the Puerto de Bronchales (1,500 metres) take the right turning to Monterde and Teruel.

You now leave the Montes Universales behind and return to the dry, denuded plains of Lower Aragón. The road crosses a threadbare landscape of red earth. Monterde de Albarracín has a pretty church tower and old stone houses capped with pantile roofs. Afterwards, come high plains and large arable farms interspersed with clumps of holm oak.

The last stop on the route is Cella. Shortly after the bullring, on the left, you'll notice a small park marked by a clump of trees. These surround a quite unusual and beautiful artesian well known locally as the "Fuente". It was built by the Italian engineer Ferrari in 1729 and feeds the River Jiloca. The round stone pond is filled with a vivid green weed, forming an underwater forest. They say that when it snows on the sierras around Madrid the water level in the well rises.

Follow the road around the park. This side of the town seems to be flowing with water. An irrigation channel flows along the left hand side of the road to the fields; another flows into a tunnel beside the church. Also on the left, a Mudejar house stands in the middle of a fish-farm fed by the well.

Leaving Cella, fork left to Zaragoza. You pass between two factories and go over a level crossing to meet the N-234. Turn right back to Teruel (17km) ❏

Excursion 28 - Medieval Mountains:

Morella - La Balma - Forcall - La Mata de Morella -
Mirambel - Cantavieja - La Iglesuela del Cid - Villafranca del
Cid - Ares del Maestre - Morella
(150km).

There is too much of the Maestrazgo - that austere upland region punctuated by verdant oases and historic towns - to see in one day, but this route aims to include as much of it as possible. The itinerary itself is relatively short but the several detours mentioned are all worth including in your journey if you have the time.

Thankfully, the Maestrazgo has yet to be "discovered" by the majority of tourists who come to eastern Spain. Away from Morella, you will be one of the few outsiders to venture to the nearby towns and mountains. There are good lanes for cycling and endless countryside for hill-walking. Almost everywhere you go you will be met with interest and kindness from a people used to fending for themselves in a remote region and not yet corrupted by indiscriminate tourism.

Leave Morella on the CS-840 for Forcall, a road which follows a line of crags. Pass the Forcall turning on the left for now and follow the road along the Bergantes valley past Ortells and Zorita del Maestrazgo, two ancient towns with fine, but crumbling buildings gathered around defiant church towers.

Keep going up the valley and at last you will see the spectacular shrine of La Balma, which looks like half a church and a house stuck precariously to a vertical wall of rock. This has been a place of pilgrimage since a shepherd discovered the image of a black virgin here in the 14th century.

The shrine is in a cave halfway up the cliff; its ceiling a sloping bulk of black rock. Access is by a ledge - you have to duck in places. An ante-room contains a bizarre collection of *exvotos* - plastic effigies of arms, legs, stomachs and so on - given to the Virgin by devotees in gratitude for her miraculous cures. Next to the shrine is a guest house and bar in which you

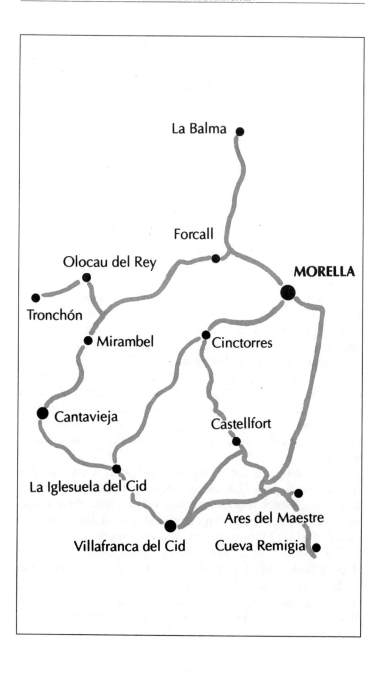

can eat paella made with mountain snails (Tel: 964-17 12 02. B).

Return down the valley to Forcall (pop. 740). The porticoed square has two 16th-century palaces, one of which has been converted into a hotel; the other has a restaurant in its basement, Mesón de la Vila (Plaza Mayor. Tel: 964-17 11 25. Visa. Open daily 1.30-4pm and 9-11pm. Closed 15 days in November. B). Here you can eat Forcall soup, rabbit cooked with snails and curds underneath ogival and semicircular arches.

From Forcall take the road to La Mata de Morella which runs along a wide, green agricultural valley. After crossing the bridge you can make a short detour up the hill to Todolella on the CS-V-8422 (right). Todolella (pop 160) is a pretty, one-horse place of timber, brick and stone walls. Its extremely tight streets are full of right angle bends and you will be better off parking outside the village or in the square, and exploring on foot. At the top of the village is a small, but well-restored castle - more a fortified house - with decorated windows and a tiny balcony. The owner is a foreigner who is rarely in residence.

Return to the main road in the valley. La Mata de Morella (pop. 220) is another well-kept village with some porticoes along its main street, neat houses and two mansions.

After another 5km or so you come to a bridge marking the boundary between the provinces of Castellón and Teruel. Here there is a longer detour (almost 30km) to two out- of-the-way villages.

Turn right onto the CS/TE-810 to Olocau del Rey (4.5km). This road leaves the green valley behind and climbs into bleaker scenery carved into thousands of terraces and fields by dry stone walls, some of them running vertically up and down the hills: boundary lines which, as farming is modernised and young people drift to the cities, are losing their *raison d'être*.

Olocau del Rey (pop. 180) is a reddish-coloured town. Old and crumbling, it is one of the poorer places in the Maestrazgo but it has some mansions with overhanging eaves of carved wood and once-proud doorways. There's a bar-restaurant in the basement of one of these mansions, which was formerly the home of the Marquises of Figueras. A fig leaf, from which the family name derives, is carved in stone over the main doorway.

El Temple (Tel: 964-178 401. No cards. B) serves a bargain menu of pork and lamb.

The church (ask for the key in El Temple) treasures a 13th century Romanesque carving of the Virgin and child. It also has a secret chapel: a small alcove with a vaulted ceiling of bare stone. It's hidden by a side-altar and can only be visited with permission from the bar-owner who will fetch a torch and take you crawling through a hole. The Marquises of Figueras are said to be buried under the flagstones of the chapel.

Leave Olocau del Rey the way you came and take the right fork to Tronchón (10km) at the entrance of the village. Soon after this there is another fork. Both roads lead to Tronchón and join up later. The right one goes up the hill, over a pass and curves along thickly-wooded slopes, affording magnificent views. You will have this road to yourself because the left fork is a newer, faster road up a pretty valley; it too has many curves but it is more direct. You can choose one or the other; or go up one and back down the other.

Tronchón (pop. 160) has been almost untouched by time, largely because it is at the end of the road. Many of its streets are unsurfaced and there are few cars. You enter through an old

gateway with balconies across it. There are two large old mountain palaces - one of which is being restored as the town hall. Near the church a rusty iron door leads into an improbably narrow building which was once the town prison. At the bottom of the village a small factory sells delicious goat's cheese.

Return to Olocau del Rey and turn right towards the main valley (the way you came up earlier). Turn right again on to the TE-810 for Mirambel (3.7km).

If you had approached Mirambel (pop. 170) 500 years ago it probably wouldn't have looked much different. Few places in Spain have been both preserved and restored as well as this walled medieval village, which was presented with a prize in 1981 by Queen Sofia for its outstanding beauty.

The cylindrical Torre de la Sacristía, with its tiny, pointed roof, stands proud of the walls beside the main gateway of the Portal de las Monjas. The cobbled streets are lined with tall Gothic mansions, their stonework meticulously cleaned and repointed. Each has a large wooden door, contained by an arched portal, small iron grilles over the windows, overhanging balconies enclosed in *celosías*, and a line of small windows under the overhanging eaves to aerate lofts once used for storing food. Behind the façade of Fonda Guimerá is a modernised bar-restaurant-hotel (C/Augustin Pastor, 28. Tel: 964-17 82 69. No cards. B). This is a simple, inexpensive place to stay or eat. After Mirambel the road has to pull away from the valley because the river carves through a series of small gorges. Instead, it crosses a rather desolate open landscape of fields, terraces and scrubland. All around are stark hills which are typical of the Maestrazgo. Suddenly you round a corner and Cantavieja appears high up ahead, spread out in a line above a cliff. The town looks as if it had grown straight out of the landscape. All the roofs lie in a long, flat line parallel to the ridge with only the church standing proud above them. It's difficult to say where the rock ends and the houses begin.

Although Cantavieja is now close, the road has to gain height to get there. It crosses the river and passes under the town, following a wooded valley, until it gets to another bridging point where it can double back on itself. Again it passes underneath the town but this time much higher up. Finally, it rounds the end of the ridge and enters the town from the other, walled side.

Cantavieja (pop. 650) preserves an arcaded square (with a viewpoint nearby) and a church tower which sits upon an archway over the main street. Leaving Cantavieja for La Iglesuela del Cid on the TE-800 you pass a clean, modern restaurant on the right, Baj (Avda. Maestrazgo, 6. Tel: 964-18 50 33. Open 1.30-3.30pm. Closed February. No cards. International cuisine. Menu changed daily. M). Accommodation in these parts is limited to the Hotel Balfagón (Avda. Maestrazgo, 20. Tel: 964-18 50 76), a modern block on the same side of the road a little way further up, or Fonda Julián (G.Valiño, 6. Tel: 964-18 50 05).

At first the road climbs even higher into the mountains and to the right you may see groups of vultures soaring effortlessly over the crags. The stretch of road is bordered by grassy banks rich in wild flowers.

Losing height again, you descend past thick conifer woods, and fields separated by dry stone walls. The ingenious design of the shepherds' cabins, with their simple domed roofs, dates from prehistoric times.

The old town centre of La Iglesuela del Cid (pop.600) includes a couple of old gateways, a fountain, a tower and two or three mountain palaces. An arch by the side of the church lets you underneath the town hall into a small, cobbled square with an arcaded commodity exchange along one side.

You can shorten the route here and return to Morella on the TE/CS-844 through Cinctorres (pop.700), a town of narrow streets (some of which change into steps without warning) and more old stone palaces.

To continue, take the CS-803 for Villafranca del Cid. Dropping down again in between mile upon mile of brownish walls you cross the Rambla de las Truchas(back into Castellón), where there is a lovely old bridge on the left. The CS-811, to the right, takes you over the picturesque Puerto de Linares to connect with Excursion 25 at Rubielos de Mora (70km).

Nearing Villafranca del Cid (pop. 2,850) you pass the shrine of the Virgen de Losar, linked to the town by a pilgrims' footpath. This town is fairly large, with plenty of shops and bars but not many sights worth seeing. The streets of the older part are narrow and stepped. The town hall (next to the church) is a Gothic palace but the most of the original stonework has been plastered over.

Leave Villafranca for Castellón on the CS-802. You can now keep straight on for Ares del Maestre or take another detour. For the latter option, turn left on to the road for Castellfort (11km) at the end of the town, just after the petrol station. This passes a mass of dry-stone walls then follows a pretty valley of grassy slopes, conifers and holm oaks.

When the valley finishes, the road comes out high above the landscape and runs across a plateau divided up by hundreds of stone walls. Near and far every line of contour seems to be higlighted by a natural stratum of rock or by an ancient hill-terrace.

Turn left at the T-junction for Castellfort (pop. 300), which is built on top of a rock. The buildings preserve a few noble details - the odd balcony, arch and shield. There is a good view of the village's emplacement from the road towards Cinctorres.

Turn round and leave Castellfort in the direction of Castellón; it's the same road you came in on but carry straight on past the T-junction. The boundless, bare landscape of dry-stone walls and panoramic views is left behind as you descend into a secluded, tree-filled valley, which hides the somewhat neglected shrine to the Virgen de la Fuente, which crosses the road in a rectangular arch. If you ask in the incongruous bar next to the church you will be taken up to a pilgrims' dining room, the walls of which have been completely covered with black and white drawings of Biblical scenes. According to a legend, a mysterious visitor created this work of art in a single night.

The valley widens and you then come to a sign-post indicating Morella and Cinctorres to the left (you'll be coming back to this turning later, but for now keep straight on to the T-junction with the CS-802). Turn left for Albocácer.

Turn left off this road by the Mesón El Coll (Ctra. Villafranca. Tel: 964-44 16 85. B) for Ares de Maestre, snuggly wrapped around the base of a 1,318m rock. Arguably this is the most spectacularly situated of all villages in the Maestrazgo.

Park in the main square and go through the archway into a *lonja*, where bustling markets were held in medieval times. The church is unusual as it rises above its own belltower (erected 500 years before the rest of the building). The façade is short of one column which was destroyed by a bolt of lightning during last century. Opposite is the old prison.

A path behind the church sets off for the summit of the round rock. All that's left of what was once an important Moorish castle is a lump of stone and a hole in the ground over which, according to local folklore, the Saracens used to cut the throats of their Christian captives. Supposedly, when it rains the water that gathers here is tinted red.

From Ares del Maestre you can make a detour to see the cave paintings of Cueva Remigia. To get to Bar Montalvana where tours start (see Excursion 24 for details) follow the CS-802 which snakes down into a wooded valley, fringed with white cliffs. To return to Morella, retrace your steps along the CS-802 and take the right turing for Castellfort, which will bring you back to that junction marked for Morella that you passed not long ago. This is a scenic backroad which brings you out on the N-332. Turn left and you will see the unmistakeable silhouette of Morella ahead ❏

Excursion 29 - The Flowering Slopes:

Alcoy - Cocentaina - Agres - Bocairente - Alcoy
(61km)

The Sierra Mariola behind Alcoy is one of the prettiest and most interesting mountain ranges in eastern Spain. Although this is a side-trip from Alcoy you could do this tour from the coast with an early start (take the C-3311 from Denia, the C-3313 from Benidorm or the N-340 from Alicante).

Leave Alcoy on the N-340 dual carriageway in the direction of Valencia. On your right is a renowned restaurant, Venta de Pilar (see Town and City Guide). The Sierra Mariola goes with you, on the left.

Concentaina (pop. 10,500), on the site of an ancient settlement, is overlooked by the stranded stump of its castle, which is a landmark for miles around. But the town's best-known building is the Gothic-style palace (open Monday-Friday 11am-1pm and 5-10pm; Saturday 10am-1pm. Closed Sunday) with an imposing tower at each corner. It was built by the Duke of Cocentaina, of the Medinaceli family, and now houses a public library and museum. The town also has a very good restaurant, L'Escaleta (see under Alcoy in Town and City Guide).

When you reach Muro de Alcoy, turn off for Agres on the A-203 (sign-posted as the C-3311). The road follows a small valley planted with olives, almonds and pines. On the left, the Sierra de Mariola is carved into impressive crags.

Turn off left for Agres (2km. pop. 720) which tumbles down the mountainside in steep, narrow streets. Head up the hill to the shrine, a pretty spot with a bar-restaurant. Above the shrine is the walled-in ruins of a castle (kept permanently locked).

Having reached this far, it's tempting to carry on further up the slope on foot towards the summit of Montcabrer, which has an unusual ruin close by (a minimum of one hour's climbing). The footpath sets off from the bottom of the car-park, passing a spring. It starts as a paved track but quickly becomes a dusty path, steep in places, which climbs in zig-zags through

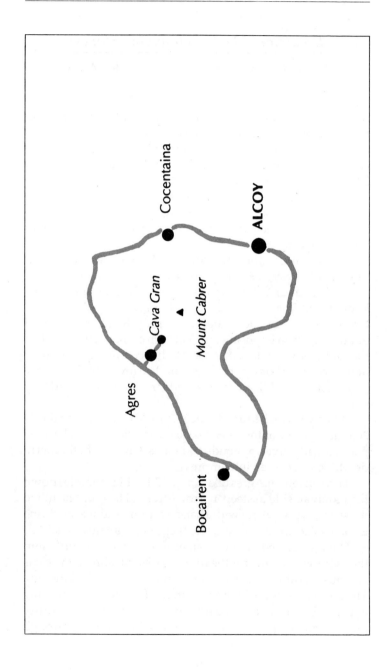

the woods.

The Sierra Mariola is famous for its flora and this path, first through the woods and then up shrub-clad slopes, will be a joy for any plant lover. Medicinal and culinary herbs - thyme, rosemary, sage, lavender, mint, marjoram, lemon balm - abound as well as rock roses and orchids. The aromatic herbs are used to flavour a local liqueur, *herbero*, the ingredients of which are an open secret. The flowers in turn attract multitudes of butterflies.

The path leads to a mountain refuge belonging to Alcoy Mountaineering Club. The summit of Mount Cabrer (1,390m) is in front, about another half hour's climb. You can even walk right across the Sierra Mariola from here to Alcoy.

Near the mountain refuge are two *neveras* - ice storage pits stones and covered by domes.

Ice-pits were built high up on north facing slopes and packed with snow during the winter. Later in the year, when the snow had turned into ice, it was brought down to villages on mule-back (insulated with rice husks) where it was put into smaller ice-pits for preserving fish and meat.

From the mountain refuge there's a wider and gentler (though much less enjoyable) track for the descent if you prefer. Turn right at the first juction you come to and you will come out at the top of the village. Pensión Mariola (San Antonio, 4 - at the bottom of the village. Tel: 96-551 00 17. Open for lunch and dinner. Closed Monday and from September 15-Oct 15. M) is the place to eat in Agres.

Returning to the main road, turn left for Bocairent through green and grassy countryside, where the lush fields of wheat are dotted with walnut trees.

Turn left at the T-junction into Bocairent (1.6km. pop 5,000). The medieval quarter of the town clusters around a hill above a ravine which once provided a natural moat. The unusual location for the town has determined its construction: nothing is on the same level and the bullring has had to be carved out of the rock. Outside the town you can see some ancient caves, Les Covetes dels Moros, which, despite their name, have nothing to do with the Moors, whom they long pre-date. They

171

were probably Iberian cave tombs later used as dwellings by Christian ascetics.

Bocairent's railway station has been converted into a small hotel. L'Estació de Bocairent (Parque de la Estació. Tel: 96-290 52 11.)

Leaving Bocairent, turn right towards Alcoy and after 2km take the left turning, again to Alcoy (27km). This small unclassified road climbs quickly into the soft heart of the Sierra Mariola and rolls through pleasant woodlands punctuated with wheat fields, pasture and the odd villa.

Finally, you start to come down high above the deep valley containing Alcoy. If you look ahead, high on the hill you will see the large, white statue of the Virgin Mary standing proudly on top of the old hotel in Font Roja (see Excursion 10). Turn left when you meet the C-3313 to descend into Alcoy ❏

Excursion 30 - The Last Mediterranean Paradise:

Ibiza - La Savina - Ibiza (by ferry); La Savina - Es Pujols
- San Fernando - Nuestra Señora del Pilar - La Mola
- San Fernando - San Francisco Javier - Cap Barberia
- Cala Sahona - La Savina
(58km)

Formentera's long and often-empty beaches, with their clean sand and clear waters, have been described as the best in the Mediterranean. Although the island's agricultural and fishing community has turned to tourism as its principal source of income, it still preserves much of its calm, traditional way of life. Because there is no airport and because fresh water is scarce, the tourist hordes have been kept away from what has been dubbed "the last Mediterranean paradise." Several of Ibiza's famous visitors like to escape from the limelight to Formentera.

During the hot, dry months of July and August the ferries are extremely busy when Formentera's resident population of 5,000 quadruples. The island is much more peaceful in the winter months but the ferries are far less frequent and many hotels and restaurants are closed.

There is a fast and a slow way to get there. The catamaran and hydrofoil take about 20 to 25 minutes to cover the 11 miles from Ibiza port to La Savina. The conventional -- and cheaper -- ferry services take about an hour. The three companies covering the Formentera route are Flebasa (Tel: 971-31 20 71); Maritima de Formentera (Tel: 971- 31 11 57) and Umafisa (Tel: 971-31 44 86). All three companies have offices in the ferry station in Ibiza harbour. During the summer, the first ferry departs around 7.30am and the last one leaves Formentera at 8pm, but sailing times vary from month to month and it's best to check beforehand. You may want to reserve transport on Formentera in advance (see below).

To get to Formentera the boat passes through a chain of islets, or *freus*: the remnants of an isthmus which once joined the islands to each other. Espalmador is said to have been a

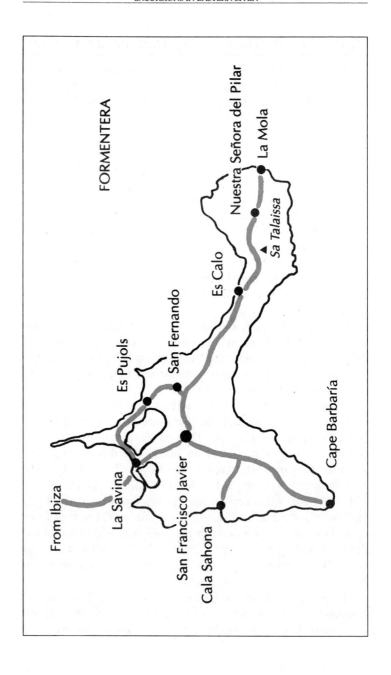

contender for "Never-Never Land" in Walt Disney's version of *Peter Pan*: only the lack of coconut palms distinguishes it from a tropical island. Its white beaches are popular with day trippers and it is close enough to the tip of the Trocadors peninsula on Formentera to swim between the two.

Your point of arrival is the port of La Savina (La Sabina), which stands between two big lagoons: Estany d'es Peix and the unfortunately named Estany Pudent - "Stinking Lake".

There is a tourist information office here (Tel: 971-32 20 57) as well as hostals and restaurants. From one restaurant, Bahia (Tel: 971-32 21 42. B-M) you can watch the boats coming and going by the waterside. More importantly, this is where you can hire transport. There is a bus service from La Savina to San Francisco Javier and La Mola but it will not allow you to see much of the island.

You can get around Formentera either by car (Avis, Tel: 971-32 21 23; Isla Blanca Tel: 971-32 25 58/9), moped or bicycle (Mijorn Tel: 971-32 23 06 or 32 86 11), all of which are for hire in La Savina. Another alternative is to take a taxi (Tel: 971-32 20 02). However, considering the size of the island (32 square miles or 82 square kilometres), the climate, as well as the absence of contours (you will only have to climb one hill), it is no wonder that cycling is the most popular way to get around.

If you haven't stopped for breakfast, head up the road to San Francisco Javier (see below). Otherwise, take the left turning out of La Savina which leads you round the northern edge of the Estany Pudent, past the salt-flats, which attract a variety of the base of the Trocadors peninsula, which is flanked by Formentera's two official nudist beaches, Illetas and Llevant. In reality, however, nude sunbathing is tolerated almost everywhere on Formentera.

This road brings you into Es Pujols, the tourist centre of the island, which has the greatest concentration of bars, restaurants and hotels. El Capri, also a one-star hostal, specialises in fish and lobster (Tel: 971-32 83 52. B-M) as does Fonoll Mari (C/ Fonoll Mari, Tel: 971-32 81 84). There are two small hotels: Sa Volta (Tel: 971-32 81 25. Three star. Unusually for Formentera it is open all year and heated in winter) and Cala Es Pujols (Tel:

175

971-32 82 27). Es Pujols even has a discotheque.

Continuing along the road you reach San Fernando (Sant Ferran)after 1.5km. Near here (if you want to look for it - it isn't marked on the maps) is Can na Costa, a megalithic sepulchre, estimated to have been built in 1,600 BC. To eat in San Fernando try Las Ranas (on the road to Cala en Baste, Tel: 971-32 81 95. Dinner only. Closed January to April, and Tuesday. M).

From San Fernando take the road for Nuestra Señora del Pilar and La Mola, which heads south east with hardly a gradient or curve towards the island's highest point. It follows the longest beach on Formentera, Mijorn (on your right). After 5km this road brings you to the beautiful natural port and fishing village of Es Calo.

Just after Es Calo there's a right turning to the best (and most expensive) hotel on the island, Club La Mola (Playa de Mitjorn. Tel: 971-32 80 69. Closed between November and April). The road now begins to climb steeply on to the mini-plateau of La Mola surrounding the peak of Sa Talaissa (192m). Near the top of the slope you will come to Bar El Mirador, which has a terrace offering panoramic views of the island and is just the place to get your breath back.

This is one of the few areas of Formentera which retains its original tree cover, a mix of Aleppo pines and sabina (a kind of juniper which is slow growing but survives hostile conditions). The only other trees you are likely to see are figs, almonds and carobs. Most of the woods on the island were cut down between the 18th and 20th century to clear land for cultivation - not that Formentera was ever thickly wooded. It is thought that it may have been an important cereal producer in classical times and that its name derives from the Latin Frumentum ("forment" in the island dialect) for wheat.

In the middle of the plateau lies Nuestra Señora del Pilar (El Pilar for short) around its 18th century church. There is a thriving arts and crafts community and a crafts market is held every Sunday. Bar La Mola in El Pilar serves tapas. There's also a one star hostal, Entrepinos (Tel: 971-32 70 18).

Just over 2km further on, the road comes to an abrupt halt at La Mola lighthouse which stands above 100m cliffs. Jules

Verne is said to have found inspiration here for his "Journey Round the Solar System". The African coast is just 250km south.

There's nothing for it now but to retrace your steps to San Fernando. From there, take the road to San Francisco Javier (Sant Francesç Xavier), a white hamlet gathered around an 18th century fortified church, which formerly afforded protection for the islanders against attacks by Barbary pirates. Formentera had to be abandoned in the Middle Ages because of such raids and was only re-populated at the end of the 17th century. With just short of 800 inhabitants, San Francisco passes for the capital of the island. Cafe Matinal (Tel: 971-32 25 47) is the place to have breakfast.

Another long, straight road takes you from San Francisco up to the wilder and less scenic cape, Cap de Barbaria, from which, on a clear day, you can see the coast of Alicante. Nearby stands one of the five defensive towers built on Formentera to keep a lookout for the aforementioned pirates.

On the way back from the cape turn off for Cala Sahona (Saona) where you'll find a family hotel, Cala Sahona (Playa de Cala Sahona. Tel: 971-32 20 30. Open May-October) and a restaurant specialising in French cusine, Es Plá (Tel: 971-32 27 09. M). From here it is an easy run (6km) back to San Francisco. Three kilometres further on is the ferry terminal of La Savina ❑

■ SEVEN-DAY TOUR ■

Although each excursion is complete in itself, the longer routes can be combined as follows to make the most of a week's holiday in Eastern Spain.

Day One: Alicante - Alcalá del Jucar - Cuenca *(Excursion 20).**

Day Two: Cuenca - La Ciudad Encantada - Nacimiento del Río Cuervo *(Excursion 26)* - returing to cross the Puerto de El Cubillo - Frías de Albarrcín to Albarracín *(Excursion 27).*

Day Three: Albarracín - Teruel - Mora de Rubielos - Rubielos de Mora *(Excursion 25).*

Day Four: Rubielos de Mora - Linares de Mora - then to Morella via either Ares del Maestre or Mirambel *(Excursion 28).*

Day Five: Sightseeing in Morella, then to Peñíscola by the N-232 and N-340.

Day Six: Peñíscola - Valencia visiting the Desierto de las Palmas *(Excursion 17),* Vall de Uxó caves and Sagunto *(Excursion 16)* on the way.

Day Seven: Sightseeing in Valencia and return to Alicante via Játiva *(Excursion 18)* or the coast *(parts of Excursions 4,5, 6 and 7).*

*An alternative itinerary, taking an extra day, is:
1st day: Alicante - Lagunas de Ruidera *(Excursion 21);*
2nd day: Lagunas de Ruidera - Puerto Lápice - Consuegra - Toboso - Belmonte *(Excursion 21)* - Cuenca.

■ TOWN AND CITY GUIDE ■

Distances
Road distances between the major towns and cities vary according to which book or map you consult. Those given follow the latest information available from tourist authorities.

Telephones
Each Spanish province has its own telephone code which has to be used when dialling between provinces. When dialling within a province no code is necessary. When dialling into Spain from another country omit the digit 9 from the area code.

Some public telephones take phone cards, which saves having to feed them with loose change. However, phone boxes tend to be in noisy pavement locations and, in major cities, you will be better off seeking out a Telefónica cabin. Here, you make your call from a semi-soundproofed booth which metres your call in units. You pay afterwards. The private *locutorios* that you will see in tourist resorts provide the same service but charge more.

Addresses
Addresses are given in their Spanish form in case you have to show them to a local to get directions. The number comes after the name of the street. A second number separated by a dash refers to the storey of the building: eg 4-3° means No 4, third floor.

Standard abbreviations are as follows:

C/ *(calle)*, street

Ctra. (Nal.), *(Carretera Nacional)*, main road or highway. It is normal for places to be identified by the nearest kilometre post.

Pl. *(Plaza)*, square

P° *(Paseo)*, a wide avenue with space to walk in the middle.

s/n *(sin número)*, not numbered (usually for important buildings, such as railway stations or where there are few buildings in a street).

Many street names were changed in the transition from dictatorship to democracy and some streets are known locally by more than one name. The main square of Valencia, for instance, has had three names in the last 15 years.

Emergencies

In most major cities the National Police can be contacted urgently by dialling 091. In smaller towns and villages, contact the Civil Guard or Municipal/Local police.

Opening Times

The opening times of monuments and museums are sometimes changed and you are advised to check by phoning the nearest tourist office wherever possible before making a long journey to see something special.

Note that the Spanish lunchtime is usually around 2-4pm and that the majority of public buildings close on Mondays.

Every village, town and city in Spain celebrates one or more holiday of its own when monuments are usually closed, in addition to regional and national holidays. To complicate the calendar further, every profession - including that of musuem curator and tourist information officer - can also enjoy an annual day off. As it is not possible to list all these, check beforehand if you can.

Shops are normally open from 10am-1.30pm and 5-8pm (except hypermarkets, which are usually open from 10am-10pm). Post offices and banks are open only between 9am and 2pm.

Eating Out

As in the Excursion sections, the letters B, M and E are used to give an indication of the price of a three-course meal, not including wine.

B (budget) = under 1,500 pesetas;

M (moderate) = 1,500-3,000 pesetas;

E (expensive) = more than 3,500 pesetas.

Unless otherwise stated, you can expect meals to be served approximately between 1-4pm and 8-10pm.

Hotels

No prices or price guides are given. See introduction for an idea of what you can expect to pay. For the most recent information, consult the official *Guía de Hoteles* (see Further Reading).

Tourist Information

The Comunidad Valenciana operates tourist information phone lines from 9am-2pm and 5-7pm:

Alicante province Tel: 96-520 00 00

Castellón province Tel: 964-22 10 00

Valencia province Tel: 96-352 40 00

The Comunidad also operates a central reservation service for hotels, called "Sorolla". Tel: 96-362 22 11.

● ● ● ● ● ● ● ● ● ● ● ● ● ● ● ●

ALBACETE, provincial capital (Pop.126,000). Alicante 171km, Valencia 191km, Madrid 251km. Telephone area code: 967. A modern and functional city, famous for the manufacture of knives and capital of a flat, arid cereal producing province.

Albacete is en route between the Costa Blanca and Madrid and a useful base for excursions to Alcalá del Júcar (Excursion 20) and the Sierra de Alcaraz.

DON'T MISS

Archaeological Museum, Parque de Abelardo Sánchez. Its Iberian and Roman finds include a collection of third century dolls carved in ivory and amber found in a necropolis in Ontur. Open: 10am-2pm and 4-7pm. Closed Sunday afternoon, Monday and holidays.

PLACES TO STAY

Parador Nacional de La Mancha, Ctra. Nal. 301, km 260, Hondo de la Morena. Tel: 50 93 43. Three stars. 5km from centre. Popular with hunters. Typical Manchegan cuisine.

Gran Hotel, Marqués de Molins, 1. Tel: 21 37 87. Three stars.

Castilla, Pº de la Cuba, 3. Tel: 21 42 88. Two stars.

Albar, Isaac Peral, 3. Tel: 21 68 61. Two stars. A cheaper alternative to the above.

EATING OUT

Mesón Las Rejas, Dionisio Guardiola, 9. Tel: 22 72 42. Closed Sunday night and August. Serves local wines. All cards. (M-E)

Nuestro Bar, Alcalde Conangla, 102. Tel: 22 72 15. Closed Sunday night and July. All cards. One of the city's best restaurants. Manchegan cuisine. Specialises in desserts. (M-E)

SERVICES

Tourist Office, C/Virrey Morcillo, 1. Tel: 21 56 11.
Taxis, Tel: 50 00 01.
Post Office, C/Dionisio Guardiola, s/n. Tel: 23 06 13.
Bus Station, C/Federico García Lorca, s/n. Tel: 21 60 12.
Railway Station, Avda. de la Estación, s/n. Tel: 21 20 96.

EMERGENCIES

National Police, Tel: 091.
Municipal Police, Tel: 21 60 45.
First Aid, Tel: 24 00 00.
Red Cross, San Antonio, 23. Tel: 21 90 50.

• • • • • • • • • • • • • • • •

ALBARRACÍN, in Teruel province (pop. 1,100). Teruel 37km, Cuenca 105km, Zaragoza 191km, Madrid 315km. Telephone area code: 978. Historic, walled medieval town designated a National Monument.

DON'T MISS

The whole town: a place to stroll leisurely around. Sights include Juliana's House (not open to the public), the walls and the cathedral.

Cave paintings (4km) on the road to Bezas.
Sierra de Albarracín (see Excursion 27).

PLACES TO STAY

Casa de Santiago Subida a las Torres II. Tel: 700316. Exquisite interior decoration

Montes Universales, Ctra. Teruel s/n. Tel: 71 01 58. One star. On main road just outside the town. Clean and serviceable.

El Gallo, Los Puentes, 1. Tel: 71 00 32. One star. Attached to a renowned restaurant.

EATING OUT

Albarracín, Azagra s/n Tel: 71 00 11. Master, Amex, Diners, Visa. Specialises in trout, lamb and garlic soup. (M)

El Gallo, Los Puentes, 1. Tel: 71 00 32. Open all year, lunch and dinner. No cards. Specialities include ham with green beans, quails, garlic soup, lamb and trout. (B-M)

BARS

La Covacha, C/ del Chorro. Bar-cum-craftshop-cum-delicatessen.

La Taberna, on main square.

SERVICES

Tourist Office, Plaza Mayor, 1. Tel: 71 02 51. Open weekdays in winter 10am-2pm; Saturday and holidays in winter 10am-2pm and 5-8pm. Summer 10.30am-2pm and 5-8pm.

Buses, Tel: 60 26 80.

EMERGENCIES

Red Cross, Tel: 71 00 62.

Civil Guard, Ronda del Pintor Garate s/n Tel: 81 20 02

● ● ● ● ● ● ● ● ● ● ● ● ● ● ●

ALCOY, in Alicante province (pop. 62,300). Alicante 55km, Valencia 110km, Murcia 136km, Madrid 400km. Telephone area code: 96.

An industrial city picturesquely sited at the confluence of three rivers and surrounded by high mountains. Famous for its Moors and Christians festival (see below) and its *peladillas,* almonds coated in sugar.

DON'T MISS

Moors and Christians Museum, San Miguel, 60. Tel: 554 05 80. Open: 10am-1.30pm and 5.30-8pm. Closed Saturday.

Font Roja Nature Park, a short way out of Alcoy (see Excursion 10)

Toy museum, Casa Gran, Plaça de l'Esglesia (next to the church), Ibi (18km from Alcoy). Open Tuesday-Saturday 10am-1pm, 4-7pm. More than 400 rare and antique items from the beginning of the century to the 1950s, housed in an 18th-century mansion. Ibi still has an important modern toy industry.

Museo Arqueológico, Camilo Visedo, San Miguel, 29. Open: 8am-1pm. Closed Sunday.

Art Nouveau houses, especially on Calle San Nicolás. There are more on Juan Cantó, San Lorenzo and Avenida del País Valenciano. See also the Unión del Trabajo building and the old fire station.

Fiesta: Moors and Christians, Apr 22-24. Day One features massive costumed parades; day three is dedicated to noisy symbolic battles.

PLACES TO STAY

Reconquista, Puente San Jorge, 1 Tel: 533 09 00. Three stars.

San Jorge, San Juan de Ribera, 11. Tel: 554 32 77.

EATING OUT

Venta del Pilar, Ctra. Valencia, km 2.5. Tel: 559 23 25. Closed Sunday, August and Easter Week. Eighteenth-century inn converted into a restaurant. (E)

L'Escaleta, Ctra. Valencia, Cocentaina (6km). Tel: 559 21 00 or 559 03 36. Specialities include salmon, pigeon, kid, steak, venison and excellent desserts. (M-E)

SERVICES

Alcoy doesn't have a tourist office. Ask for a city plan in the town hall. For tourist information Tel: 554 52 11.

Taxis, Tel: 554 28 29 and 533 93 72.

Post Office, Plaza Emilio Sala, s/n. Tel: 554 02 41.

Bus Station, Anselm Aracil, 30. Tel: 533 09 05.

EMERGENCIES
National Police, C/ Peru, 10. Tel: 533 04 28.
Municipal Police, Tel: 554 05 48
Ambulances, Tel: 552 18 45.
First Aid, Tel: 533 08 83.
Red Cross, Tel: 533 22 40.
Civil Guard, Tel: 533 03 18.

● ● ● ● ● ● ● ● ● ● ● ● ● ● ● ●

ALICANTE (ALACANT), provincial capital (pop.265,500). Murcia 75km, Valencia 166km, Albacete 171km, Madrid 422km. Telephone area code: 96.

Situated on a natural harbour with large beaches nearby, Alicante is both a busy commercial port and the tourist capital of the Costa Blanca. It's sunny climate has made it famous for centuries. The Greeks called it Akra Leuka - the white citadel - from which the title Costa Blanca derives and the Romans, Lucentum - the city of light. There are ferries from here to Tabarca (see Excursion 1), Ibiza (see Excursion 22) and Orán in Algeria.

DON'T MISS
Castillo de Santa Bárbara, on the 166m summit of Mount Benacantil. Panoramic views over Alicante and its bay, including the Isle of Tabarca. You can get there on foot (a long walk), by road or by lift from Postiguet beach. The fortification dates from the times of the Carthaginians and was invulnerable for 2,000 years until the French army blew up part of it in the Peninsular War.

Castillo de San Fernando, a smaller castle on the other side of town which provides a view of Santa Bárbara.

Town hall. Seventeenth-century Baroque building. At the foot of the stairs is a marker used to guage sea level throughout Spain.

La Explanada de España. Palm lined promenade by the waterfront.

Iglesia de Sta María. Built on the site of a mosque in 1265, rebuilt in the 14th and 16th century, Baroque façade from 1721.

Museum of Twentieth Century Art. Casa de la Asegurada. C/ Villavieja. Open October-April 10am-1pm and 5-8pm. November-March 10.30-1.30 and 6-9pm. Closed Monday and Sunday afternoon. Eighteenth-century palace housing the collection of Alicante painter Eusebio Sempere. Includes works by Chagall, Dali, Miro, Picasso, Saura, Tàpies and Sempere himself.

Cathedral de San Nicolás de Bari. Incorporates work by Juan de Herrera, who also designed the Escorial in Madrid.

Coin and Stamp market. For collectors. Sunday mornings in the Plaza del Ayuntamiento.

Fiesta: Las Hogueras de San Juan. Papier-maché sculptures are burnt in the streets on June 24.

PLACES TO STAY
Meliá, Playa del Postiguet s/n. Tel: 520 50 00. Four stars.

Hotel Palas, Calle Cervantes, 5 (on Explanada near port). Tel: 520 9210. Closed November. Three stars. Fading turn-of-the-century grandeur. Its restaurant is renowned for pasta dishes.

Sol Alicante, Gravina 9. Tel: 521 07 00. Three stars. Waterfront tower block.

Almirante, Avda de Niza, 38, San Juan beach. Tel: 565 0112. Three stars.

EATING OUT
Delfín, Explanada de España, 12. Tel: 521 49 11. Amex, Diners, Master, Visa. (M-E)

Dársena, Muela del Puerto (next to yacht club). Tel: 520 75 89. Closed Sunday night and Monday. Amex, Diners, Visa. Magnificent selection of rice dishes as well as fish and seafood. Try the *turrón* ice-cream. (M-E)

La Piel de Oso, Complejo Vistahermosa, Ctra. de Valencia, Avda. de Denia. Tel: 526 06 01. Closed Sunday night and Monday. Amex, Master, Visa.

Auberge de France, Flora de España, 36, La Albufereta. Tel: 526 06 02. All major cards. Well stocked wine cellar. (E-VE)

BARS

Quo Vadis, Plaza de Santísima Faz, 3. Tel: 521 66 60. Tapas bar with terrace for open-air dining in summer. Local cuisine.

Salón Italia, Rambla 14. Outdoor terrace. Eleven kinds of *tortilla* and 40 varieties of ice cream available.

Bodegas Las Garrafas, Calle Mayor 33. Tapas bar with more standing room than chairs.

SERVICES

Tourist Offices: Explanada de España, 2. Tel: 521 22 85; Plaza del Ayuntamiento, 1. Tel: 521 78 35; Avenida de Niza, (summer only), San Juan. Tourist line, Tel: 520 00 00.

Taxis, Tel: 525 25 11 and 510 16 11.

Post Office, Plaza General Miró, s/n.

Bus Station, C/Portugal, s/n. Tel: 522 07 00.

Railway Stations: Renfe intercity services, Avda. Salamanca. Tel:522 68 40; FGV narrow-gauge line to Benidorm and Denia, Estación de la Marina, Avda. Villajoyosa, 2. Tel: 526 27 31.

Airport, El Altet (11 km from city centre). Tel: 528 50 11; Iberia information, Tel: 520 60 00.

Port (Transmediterránea passenger lines), Tel: 520 60 11.

Foreigners' Office (for residency permits etc.), C/San Fernando,18.

CONSULATES

Belgium, Avda del Catedratico Soler, 8. Entresuelo B. Tel: 522 31 47/522 31 48. Open Monday-Friday 9am-2pm.

Denmark, Plaza Calvo Sotelo 4-7° C. Tel: 520 79 38. Open Monday-Friday 10am-1pm.

Germany, C/ San Francisco 67-4. Tel: 521 70 60.

France, C/ Virgen del Socorro, 39. Tel: 526 66 00 or 526 45 23.

Netherlands, C/ Castaños, 29. Tel: 521 21 75.

Norway, Avda, Dr Rámon y Cajal, 3. Tel: 521 83 00.

Sweden, Avda. Dr Ramon y Cajal, 3. Tel: 521 83 00.

United Kingdom, Plaza Calvo Sotelo, 1. Tel: 521 60 22 and 521 61 90. Open Monday-Friday 8.30am-2pm.

EMERGENCIES

National Police, Tel: 091 and 514 22 22.

Municipal Police, Tel: 510 47 11.

Ambulances, Tel: 511 46 76.
First Aid, Tel: 590 80 00.
Red Cross, Tel: 523 07 02.
Civil Guard, Tel: 521 66 11.

● ● ● ● ● ● ● ● ● ● ● ● ● ● ● ●

ALTEA, in Alicante province (pop. 12,300). Benidorm 9km, Alicante 50km. Telephone area code: 96.

A fishing village named Atalaya by the Moors, meaning "Health for All", which has rapidly developed into a tourist resort. The attractive streets of the old town, popular with artists, cluster around a hill crowned by a blue-domed church. The local game *pelota*, in which a ball is struck with bare hands, is played in the streets on Sundays and fiestas.

DON'T MISS
The old town, a labyrinth of alleys, steps (over 250 from the modern town to the square at the top) and white houses.

Street market: Tuesday on Paseo Marítimo by the seaside.

PLACES TO STAY
Cap Negret, Ctra. Valencia-Alicante, km 159. Tel: 584 12 00. Three stars.

Altaya, La Mar, 115. Tel: 584 08 00. Closed January 1-March 1. Two stars.

San Miguel, Generalísimo, 65. Tel: 584 04 00. One star.

EATING OUT
Studio Klaus, Conde de Altea, 6. Tel: 584 12 26. Open Friday-Sunday from November to Easter. Closed Thursday in summer. All major cards. British couple serving exquisite dishes at budget prices. Sometimes impromptu live music. (B)

Bodegón de Pepe, Conde de Altea. Busy bar decorated with bric-a-brac, which serves only three dishes (enough to make a meal of): broad beans, fried fish and mussels. A bucket is provided to toss the detritus in. Get there early before the mussels run out. (B)

Mister X, Partida El Planet, 136. Tel: 584 28 81. For gourmets.

Out of town down a little lane. (E)

La Costera, Costera Mestre de Música, 8. Tel: 584 02 30. Swiss food. (M-E)

El Negro. Santa Bárbara, 4. Tel: 584 18 26. Closed Monday in winter.

BARS

Miramar, C/La Mar. An otherwise undistinguished bar which has a library of foreign books, many in English, and a terrace with a sea view.

Café dels Artistes, Plaza de la Iglesia. In the old town, near the church.

SERVICES

Tourist Office, Paseo de San Pedro, s/n. Tel: 584 23 01.

Taxis, Tel: 584 02 36.

Post Office, Avda Fermín. Tel: 584 01 74.

Buses, Tel: 585 02 71 (Benidorm-Madrid); Tel: 585 14 85 (Alicante-Valencia).

Railway station. On the main road out of town towards Benidorm.

Port, Tel: 584 08 28.

EMERGENCIES

Municipal Police, Tel: 584 14 00.

First Aid, Tel: 584 14 00.

Red Cross, Tel: 585 56 74 or 584 15 91 (sea rescue).

Civil Guard, Tel: 584 05 25 or 585 42 72 (traffic).

● ● ● ● ● ● ● ● ● ● ● ● ● ● ● ●

BENIDORM, in Alicante province (pop. 42,400). Alicante 42km, Valencia 142km, Denia 50 km, Madrid 453km. Telephone area code: 96.

Package-holiday resort which, with its clusters of skyscrapers, today resembles Manhattan rather than the tiny fishing village it was in the early '50s. Benidorm has more accommodation than any other resort on the Mediterranean. It became infamous for its licentious lager-louts in the '70s and

'80s. Since then the town has made an effort to clean up its act, for example by paying attention to ecological problems and cutting down on noise, in order to attract a more sober class of visitor.

Nowadays you are as likely to see elderly holidaymakers from the northern provinces of Spain as youths from the north of England. Even with its changing clientele, Benidorm continues to be a concrete playground for adults where everyone is on holiday.

Love it or hate it, you don't meet many people who are indifferent to Benidorm. If the town appeals to you, with its numerous inexpensive hotels, bars, good-value restaurants and international newsagents, it can make an ideal base for excursions to prettier parts of the Costa Blanca.

DON'T MISS
The *"castle"* and *Balcón de Mediterraneo*, a small park and viewpoint from where you can see both Benidorm's beaches (Levante and Poniente - ending in the headland of La Cala), the Isle (shaped like a submerging slice of cake), and a giant off-shore waterspout. You can get a different view by taking the road up to the Sierra Helada from the Rincón de Loix.

The Isle. Although badly cared for and overrun by imported hens and peacocks, the Isle is still home to a number of sea birds and has a certain charm. The waters around it are good for scuba- diving and snorkelling. There are plans to deport the misplaced fowl and turn the Isle into a nature reserve. Boats leave hourly from the harbour (from about 10am-3pm) and the trip takes 20 minutes.

Parque de l'Aigüera. Extravagant public park and open air auditorium with monumental decorations and palm trees.

Castell de Guadalest (25km; see Excursion 3). There are frequent private coach trips from Benidorm if you don't have your own transport.

PLACES TO STAY
Among Benidorms' 140-odd hotels are:
Delfín, Playa de Poniente, La Cala. Tel: 585 34 00. Four stars.

Cimbel, Avda. Europa, s/n. Tel: 585 21 00. Four stars.

Don Pancho, Avda Mediterraneo, 39. Tel: 585 29 50. Four stars.

Poseidón, C/ Esperanto, 9. Tel: 585 02 00. Three stars.

Alameda, Calle Alameda, 36. Tel: 58 55 650. Three stars.

Outside Benidorm:

Bermudas, Estocolmo 17. Tel: 586 59 24.

El Molí, Alfaz del Pi (5km). Tel: 588 82 44. Small hotel in expanding town a short way inland. One star.

EATING OUT

Sorrento, C/ Estocolmo, 36. Tel: 585 94 13. Family-run Italian restaurant with outdoor dining.

Tiffany's. Avda de Mediterraneo, 51 (Edif Coblanca, 3). Tel: 585 44 68. Closed midday and from January 7-February 7. Amex, Diners, Master, Visa. Reputedly one of Benidorm's best restaurants for food and atmosphere.(E)

El Molino, Ctra. Alicante-Valencia, km 123. Tel: 585 71 81. Amex, Diners, Master, Visa. Pseudo-rustic decoration with wine museum. (M-E)El

Vesubio, Avda. Mediterraneo, 12. Tel: 585 45 35. Closed Tuesday. Sea bass cooked in salt is a house speciality. (M-E)

Magic Roundabout, Edificio Gemelos IV, C/ Ibiza. Tel: 585 18 39. Open noon-1am. Satellite TV, "pub grub" and traditional three-course Sunday lunch. (B-M)

Oryca, Avenida de la Marina Española, La Cala. Tel: 585 71 87. At the other end of Poniente beach from the town centre. Good value menu of the day. (B)

The Taste of India, C/Esperanto (close to Plaza Triangular). Open daily from 6pm. Authentic Indian food. Take-away service available.

Restaurant Enrique, C/ Ricardo, 3. Tel: 585 09 35 . Regarded as one of Benidorm's best fish restaurants and inexpensive to boot. (B)

BARS AND CAFES

Most are in the old town and the streets immediately behind Levante beach. Along the beach itself there are a number of large cafés with live music where you can dance throughout the afternoon.

Valor, Lepanto, s/n. Tel: 585 22 20. A *chocolatería* for chocaholics.

Mesón del Jamón, Calle de Gerona. Specialises in ham.

Teremar, Almendros, 23. Tel: 585 35 16. Cafeteria.

AFTER DARK

Benidorm Palace, Rincón de Loix. Tel: 585 16 60. Varied programme of entertainment.

Penelope and *Star Garden,* Ctra. Alicante-Valencia, are two of the largest discotheques, next door to each other on the ring road on the edge of town (going towards the main road from Benidorm towards Altea and Valencia). You can't miss them - Star Garden is shaped like a flying saucer and has a helicopter parked on its roof.

Nabab, Avenida de Carrero Blanco, s/n. Another popular disco.

Black Sunset, C/Lepanto. Discotheque mainly for over-thirty swingers.

Casino Costa Blanca, Ctra. N-332, km 115, Villajoyosa (5km). Roulette, blackjack and other games. Also has an art gallery.

SERVICES

Tourist offices, Avda. Martínez Alejos, 16. Tel: 585 32 24 and 585 13 11; and in foyer of town hall, Plaza Torrejó, s/n. Tel: 585 02 68. Summer only: Avda. Marina Española, s/n, La Cala (at the far end of Poniente Beach). Tel: 585 30 75 and Avda. Europa. Tel: 586 00 95.

Taxis Tel: 586 18 18, 586 26 22 and 585 30 63.

Post Office, C/ Herrerias.

Bus stations: for Valencia and Alicante, Ubesa, Ctra Alicante-Valencia (opp La Isleta petrol station), Tel: 585 01 51; for other cities, Enatcar, C/ de Gerona, Tel: 522 06 73 and 585 14 85.

Railway Station, C/Estacion s/n (off road to Callosa). Tel: 585 18 95 and 585 29 60.

Airport, Alicante (53 km), Tel: 528 50 11. Iberian Airlines, Tel: 520 60 00.

CONSULATES
Finland, C/ Vikingos, 4. Tel: 585 35 99.
Edificio Cervantes, Avenida de Europa, s/n. Tel:
585 70 12.
Norway, Edificio Aurea, 6° A & B, Calle Pal, 1. Tel: 585 21 07.
Sweden, C/ Gambo, 6-2°, 6th floor. Tel: 585 20 00.

EMERGENCIES
National Police, C/ Apolo XI, s/n. Tel: 091.
Municipal Police, C/ Del Forn, s/n. Tel: 092 and 585 02 22.
First Aid, Tel: 585 74 13.
Red Cross, Tel: 585 56 74 and 585 39 38 (sea).
Civil Guard, Tel: 585 03 30 and 585 42 72 (traffic).

● ● ● ● ● ● ● ● ● ● ● ● ● ● ● ●

CALPE, in Alicante province (pop. 11,000). Benidorm 24km, Alicante 63km, Denia 33km, Valencia 120km, Madrid 471km. Telephone area code: 96.

Holiday resort and fishing port dominated by a distinctive rocky peak, the Peñón de Ifach, which rises 382m abruptly out of the sea. The port and beach are a long way from the old town centre on a steep hill gathered around the inclined main street of Avenida Gabriel Miró and the Plaza de la Constitución.

In 1637 Berber pirates conquered the town and carried the entire population with them to Algiers where they were held prisoner for five years.

DON'T MISS
The Peñón de Ifach Nature Reserve. The visitors' centre is above the harbour (see Excursion 4).

Old quarter. At the top of the hill in the town centre. A maze of small, stepped streets and squares. Look out for a series of enormous pastel coloured murals depicting dreamily ascending staircases, floating cubes and a trompe-l'oeil plaza.

Parish Church. 14th-century, Gothic-Mudejar church with 15th century altarpiece.

Cruises around the bay and Peñón. From the harbour.

Street market: Saturday.

PLACES TO STAY
Galetamar, La Galeta, 28. Tel: 583 23 11. Three stars.

Venta La Chata, Ctra. de Valencia (between Calpe and Benissa). Tel: 583 03 08. Old inn next to main road. Pleasant gardens and porch. Two stars.

Paradero de Ifach, Explanada del Puerto, 50. Tel: 583 03 00. Small, conveniently located for the beach but sadly rundown. Two stars.

Swiss Hotel, Urbanización Club Moraira. Tel: 574 71 04 (12 km). Small luxurious four-star hotel in a quiet location.

El Parque, Portalet, 4. Tel: 583 07 70. Central and inexpensive one star hostal.

EATING OUT
Casa de Maco, Partida Pou Roiq-Lleus, s/n, Benisa. Tel: 597 31 21. French food in 18th-century country house setting. (M-E)

Capri, Avda. Gabriel Miró. Playa del Arenal. Tel: 583 06 14. Closed November. Master, Amex, Diners, Visa. Fish and rice. (E)

El Carro II, Esplanada del Puerto Pesquero. Tel: 583 02 34. By the fishing harbour. (B)

El Girasol, Ctra de Moraira-Calpe, km 1.5, Moraira (12km). Tel: 574 43 73. Closed January and February, Monday (in winter) and lunchtimes (in summer). Master, Amex, Diners, Visa. A restaurant for gourmets. (E-VE)

Club Naútico (Yacht Club), Calpe port. Tel: 583 56 48. Quayside restaurant. (B-M)

SERVICES
Tourist Office, Ejércitos Espanoles, 66 (near the port). Tel: 583 69 20.

Taxis, Tel: 583 00 43 and 583 17 16.

Consumer Information Office, Tel: 583 36 00.

Post Office, Avda. Ifach. Tel: 583 08 84.

Bus Station, Tel: 583 07 00. Bus stop is on the main road, the N-332.

Railway Station, Tel: 522 68 40.

EMERGENCIES

Municipal Police, Tel: 583 08 12.
Ambulances, Tel: 583 08 12.
First Aid, Tel: 583 11 16 and 583 22 00.
Red Cross, Tel: 583 16 16.

Civil Guard, C/ Purisima. Tel: 583 00 80.

• • • • • • • • • • • • • • • •

CARTAGENA, in Murcia province (pop. 171,000) Murcia 48km, Torrevieja 59km, Alicante 109km, Madrid 439km. Telephone area code: 968

Ancient port founded by the Carthaginians, after whom Cartagena is named, in Spain in 223BC. An important naval base as well as a commercial port.

DON'T MISS

National Underwater Archaelogy Museum, next to Faro de Navidad. Open: 10am-3pm Tuesday to Sunday. Closed Monday and holidays.

Naval Museum, C/Menéndez Pelayo 6. Open Tuesday-Friday 10am-1pm and 4-6pm. Sat 10am-12.30pm. Closed Sunday and Monday.

Castillo de la Concepción. An ancient fort set in public gardens from which there is a good view of the harbour. Nearby are the ruins of the old Romanesque cathderal destroyed in the Civil War.

Isaac Peral's Submarine. Near the harbour. An early craft which was launched in 1888, just too late to make it a first.

Byzantine wall, C/Nueva, Esquina calle Soledad. Open: Tuesday-Saturday 11am-1pm and 5.30-9pm. Closed Sunday and Monday. A metal catwalk leads you across the top of this gargantuan sixth century sandstone wall. A Roman mosaic is also on display.

Fiesta: Holy Week processions.

PLACES TO STAY

Los Habaneros, San Diego, 60. Tel: 50 52 50. Two stars.

Husa Alfonso XIII, Paseo Alfonso XIII, 30. Tel: 52 00 00. Two stars.

Manolo, Avda Juan Carlos I, 7. Tel: 53 69 12. Two stars.

EATING OUT

Artés, Plaza de José Maria Artés, 9. Tel: 52 70 64. Closed Sunday. All major cards. Regional cuisine including seafood and fish. (M-E)

Los Habaneros, San Diego, 60. Tel: 50 52 50. All major cards. Closed Sunday night. Fish and seafood from the Mar Menor and homemade desserts. Popular for business lunches. (E)

Los Sauces, Ctra. de La Palma-Cartagena, km 4.5. Tel: 53 07 58. Closed Sunday. Master, Visa. (E)

SERVICES

Tourist Office, Plaza del Ayuntamiento. Tel: 50 64 83.

Taxis, Tel: 52 04 04/8, 10 04 04 and 51 00 05.

Post Office Glorieta de San Francisco, s/n. Tel: 50 15 27.

Telephones, C/ Aire y C/Sagasta, s/n.

Railway Station, Avda. America, s/n. Tel: 50 17 96.

Airport, San Javier. Tel: 57 05 50.

CONSULATES

Denmark, Finland, Norway and Sweden: Muralla del Lar, 11. Tel: 50 70 00.

France: C/ Carmen, 59. Tel: 52 16 88.

EMERGENCIES

National Police, Tel: 091.

Municipal Police, Tel: 092 and 51 51 51.

Ambulances, Tel: 50 17 27.

Red Cross, Tel: 50 27 50 and 50 36 97.

Civil Guard, Tel: 50 11 17.

• • • • • • • • • • • • • • •

CASTELLÓN DE LA PLANA (CASTELLÓ DE LA PLANA),

provincial capital (pop. 134,200). Valencia 65km, Alicante 231km, Tarragona 186km, Madrid 417km. Telephone area code: 964.

Castellón was originally founded on a cliff inland. It was moved to its present site, on the plain, in the 13th century. Since then, the land all around has been intensively planted with oranges. The port, El Grao, is 5km from the city centre.

DON'T MISS

Fine Arts Museum. C/Cavallers (Caballeros), 25. Open 10am-2pm and 4-6pm. Saturday 10am-12.30pm. Closed Sunday and holidays. Interesting collection of ceramics.

Cathedral. Totally reconstructed after the Civil War but still retains its original 14th-century Gothic doorways.

Fadrí's Tower or *El Campanar.* 58-metre landmark erected in the 1590s.

Town Hall. 17th-18th century building containing a small collection of paintings by Ribalta and others.

Planetarium. Paseo Marítimo, 1. Tel: 28 25 84. Open Tuesday-Saturday 10am-2pm and 5-8pm. Sunday 10am-2pm. Closed Monday.

Columbretes Isles. Semi-circular group of islands now a nature reserve. Day trips are organised by Sematur, Avda. del Puerto, 10-6°. Tel: 908 28 51 83.

Fiesta: La Magdalena. Pilgrimage on the third Sunday of Lent, followed by a noctural procession with illuminated floats or *gaiates.*

PLACES TO STAY

Mindoro, C/ Moyano, 4. Tel: 22 23 00. Four stars.

Del Golf, Avda. Fernández Salvador. Tel: 28 01 80. Three stars. On Pinar beach.

Aloha, Avda. Mediterraneo, 75, Burriana (20 km). Tel: 58 50 00. Quiet beach setting up coast. Two stars.

EATING OUT

Castellón's port, El Grao, is the place to eat fresh fish and seafood.

Rafael, C/ Churruca 26, El Grao. Tel: 28 21 85. Master, Diners, Amex, Visa. Closed Sunday, holidays, September 1-15 and December 23-January 8. Famed for its seafood and rice dishes. (E-VE)

Eleazar, C/ Xímenez, 14. Tel: 23 48 61. Closed last two weeks of August. Major cards. Carefully prepared dishes. (M-E)

Casa Juanito, Paseo de Buenavista 11, El Grao. Tel: 28 20 57. Amex, Diners, Master, Visa. Closed November and Wednesday (except in summer). Terrace. Valencian seafood. (M)

BARS

Como-Como, just off Plaza de Santa Clara. Large selection of inexpensive sandwiches.

Carlos, C/ Segorbe. Specialises in fish.

CONSULATES

France, Avda. Almazora, s/n. Tel: 21 17 77.
Sweden, Avda. Virgen Lidón, 44. Tel: 23 07 98.

SERVICES

Tourist office, C/ María Agustina, 5. Tel: 22 10 00.
Taxis, Tel: 23 74 74.
Post Office, Plaza Tetuán. Tel: 21 47 73 and 22 20 00.
Telephones, C/ Ruiz Zorrilla, 45.
Buses, Tel: 20 03 89.
Railway Station, Estación, s/n. Tel: 20 32 40 and 25 02 02.

EMERGENCIES

National Police, Tel: 25 36 00.
Municipal Police, Tel: 35 51 00.
First Aid, Tel: 21 19 04 and 21 12 53.
Red Cross, Tel: 22 48 50.
Civil Guard, Tel: 22 46 00.

CUENCA, provincial capital (pop. 43,000). Teruel 153km, Madrid 167km, Albacete 142km, Alicante 313km, Valencia 220km. Telephone area code: 969.

A small city in a beautiful inland province of forests, crags and rivers. Cuenca is divided into the old and the new; the older, higher part of the city overhangs the spectacular gorge of the River Huécar.

DON'T MISS

Casas Colgadas ("Hanging Houses"). The city's trademark and now Museum of Abstract Art. Open Tuesday-Friday 11am-2pm and 4-6pm. Saturday 11am-2pm and 4-8pm. Sunday 11am-2pm. Closed Monday. For a good view of the Casas Colgadas cross the nearby Puente San Pablo. No one knows who built them but it is thought they were there in some form in the 15th century.

Cathedral. Open 9am-1.30pm and 4.30 to 7.30pm (6.30pm in winter). 12th and 13th century.

The Cuenca countryside. Especially the Ciudad Encantada (35km) and the source of the River Cuervo (80 km - for both of these see Excursion 26).

Cuenca's Easter celebrations are also a tourist attraction, especially the now notorious "Drunkards' Procession" (see Fiestas).

Castles of Belmonte (70km - Excursion 21) and Alarcón (85 km - Excursion 20).

PLACES TO STAY

Parador de Cuenca, Paseo Hoz del Huécar s/n, Tel: 23 23 20. Converted Gothic monastery on the Huécar gorge with good views of the town.

Leonor de Aquitania, C/ San Pedro, 60. Tel: 23 10 00. Three stars. The up-market place to stay in the old town.

Cueva del Fraile, Ctra. Cuenca-Buenache Sierra, km 7. Tel: 21 15 71. Three stars. Some way out of town.

Posada de San José, C/ Julian Romero, 4. Tel: 21 13 00. Two stars. Charming hotel rambling through historic building. A favourite.

EATING OUT
Figón de Pedro, C/ Cervantes 13. Tel: 22 68 21 or 22 45 11. Closed Sunday night and Monday. Amex, Diners, Master, Visa. Central, in new part of city. Also a hotel. (E)

Mesón Casas Colgadas, C/ Canónigos, s/n. Tel: 22 35 09. Closed Tuesday night. Amex, Diners, Master, Visa. Next to famous hanging houses, and with equally spectacular view of the gorge. (M-E)

Rincón de Paco, C/ Hurtado de Mendoza. Open from 9pm. (M)

BARS
Cafetería Gran Vía, C/ Fermín Caballero.

La Ponderosa, C/ San Francisco, 20. Tel: 21 32 14. Open 11am-4pm and 7pm- midnight. Tapas bar without tables. Bars and cafés in Cuenca open late in the mornings. If nowhere else is open, try the café at the bus station on C/ Fermín Caballero.

SERVICES
Tourist office, C/ Dalmacio García Izcara, 8, 1°. Tel: 22 22 31.
Consumer's phone line, Tel: 21 20 08.
Taxis, Tel: 21 36 66.
Post office, C/ Parque de San Julián, 18. Tel: 22 40 16.
Telephones, C/ Cervantes, 2.
Bus station, C/ Fermín Caballero.
Railway station, Tel: 22 07 20.

EMERGENCIES
Civil Guard, Tel: 22 11 00.
National Police, Tel: 091 and 21 20 51.
Municipal Police, Tel: 22 48 59 and 22 48 65.
First Aid, Tel: 21 19 52.
Red Cross, Tel: 22 22 00.

● ● ● ● ● ● ● ● ● ● ● ● ● ● ●

DENIA, in Alicante province (pop. 24,800). Alicante 92 km, Valencia 99 km, Madrid 447 km. Telephone area code: 96.

Originally a Greek colony, Denia is named after the Goddess

Diana - a Roman temple to her honour was excavated here. In the Middle Ages it became the capital of a Muslim kingdom. Denia castle was occupied by French forces in the Pensinsular War (called the War of Independence in Spain) and blockaded for most of 1813. In the last century it had an important grape and raisin export trade and there was a significant British community working for the Co-operative Wholesale Society. Many of the larger houses of the "huerta" were built for British merchants and there is still a little-known British cemetery in Denia. The modern town is both a fishing and ferry port (with daily services to Ibiza in the summer; see Excursion 22), and a bustling holiday resort.

DON'T MISS

Castle and Archaeological Museum. Open 10am-1pm, 4-7.30pm. Closed Thursday.

Folk Museum, Cavallers, S/n. Open Tuesday to Saturday 10.30am-1pm and 4- 7pm. Sun 10.30am-1pm.

Town Hall. Neo-classical façade and bell tower.

Fiesta: During the town's main celebrations in the first fortnight of July a bullring is set up by the waterside and young men chase bulls trying to force them to jump into the sea. More often it is the humans who get a dunking.

PLACES TO STAY

Denia, Partida Suertes del Mar, s/n. Tel: 578 12 12. Three stars. Closed November 1-March 31. Modern and comfortable.

Rosa, Las Marinas, 98. Tel: 578 15 73. Two stars. Well-equipped and hospitable modern hotel.

EATING OUT

El Trampolí, Playa Les Rotes. Tel: 578 12 96. Open all year. Visa. Closed Sunday evening. Set menu of rice and fresh, succulent seafood. (E)

Mesón Troya, Ctra. Les Rotes. Tel: 578 14 31. Visa Closed Monday and February.

El Poblet, Ctra. Las Marinas, Km 2. Tel: 578 41 79. Closed Monday except in summer. All cards. Modern international cuisine. (E-VE)

Port, C/ Explanada Bellavista, 12. Tel: 578 49 73. Open 10am-4pm and 6-12pm. Closed Tuesday from October to June. All cards. Fish and seafood. Terrace. (B-M)

La Parrilla, Sanduga, 50-52. Tel: 578 20 92. Closed Wednesday in winter. French and Italian cooking, grills and seafood. (M)

Jo Roland, Explanada Bellavista, 10. Tel: 578 50 97. All cards. Open 12.30am-3.30pm and 7-11.30pm. Closed Wednesday in winter. Run by Swiss pop singer. Extensive *menúdel día* and *tapas*. Terrace. (B-M)

Trópico, Pare Pere, 1. Tel: 578 10 47. No cards. A simple bar-restaurant which enjoys the unusual distinction of having been mentioned in Who's Who. (B)

BARS

Caudeli "El Rochet", Plaza Fontanella, Bellavista, 1. Tel: 578 10 54. Across the road from the harbour. Good choice of *tapas*.

SERVICES

Tourist office, Patricio Ferrándiz, s/n. Tel: 578 09 57 and Plaza Oculista Buigues, 9. Tel: 578 01 00.

Ferries to Ibiza, Flebasa Lines, Estación Marítima, s/n. Tel: 578 42 00

Taxis, Tel: 578 34 98.

Post office, Patricio Ferrándiz. Open 9am-2pm. Sat 9am-1.30pm.

Telephones, Plaza Jorge Juan.

Railway station (services to Benidorm and Alicante), Calderón. Tel: 578 04 45.

Bus station, Plaza Archiduque Carlos. Tel: 578 05 64.

Yacht Club, Suertes del Mar, 2. Tel: 578 08 50.

EMERGENCIES

National Police, Castell d'Olimbroi, 5. Tel: 578 38 51.
Municipal Police, Plaza Constitució. Tel: 578 01 90.
Civil Guard, Avda. de Gandía s/n. Tel: 578 00 36.
Ambulances, Avda de Valencia, 15. Tel: 578 02 69.

Red Cross, Castell d'Omlimbroi. Tel: 578 13 58.
First Aid, Marqués de Campo, 52. Tel: 578 23 10.

● ● ● ● ● ● ● ● ● ● ● ● ● ● ● ●

ELCHE (ELX), in Alicante province (pop. 188,000) Alicante 22km, Murcia 65km, Madrid 409km. Telephone area code: 96.
A city famous for its forest of palm trees (the largest in Europe) planted by the Carthaginians around 300BC and watered by an irrigation system laid out in the 10th century, drawing water from the River Vinalopó. The Romans called the town Colonia Julia Ilici Augusta - hence the present name for the inhabitants, "Ilicitanos". It is said that in the 18th century, Elche had a million palm trees; now there are just over half that number. As well as being shady and ornamental, the palms have their uses. Elche is Europe's only date-producer, although the harvest is declining in economic importance. You'll notice some of the palm branches have been wrapped tightly together in plastic sheeting. This is to bleach the new shoots and make them supple for the craft of palm weaving. The palm decoration carried by the Queen of Spain on Palm Sunday is made in Elche. Palm fronds are also tied to balconies to ward off lightening. Modern Elche, however, relies for a living more on its shoe industry than its palm trees.

DON'T MISS
The Palm Groves. These dominate the part of the city on the left bank of the River Vinalopó.
Huerto del Cura (Priest's Garden). Open 9am-8.30pm. An enclosed palm grove also planted with citrus, carob, pomegranate trees, exotic plants and cacti. Some of the palms are more than 200 years old. The star attraction is the seven-branched Imperial Palm named after the Empress Elizabeth of Austria who visited the garden in 1894. Most of the other trees in the Huerto de Cura bear the names of famous people, crudely pinned on to them as if by afterthought. There is one each for King Juan Carlos and Queen Sofía: these trees provide fruit for the royal household. There is a copy of the bust of La

Dama de Elche on display by a pond in the garden. It's still something of a mystery because the face, its expression and the costume defy exact identification. The original was found in nearby La Alcudia in 1897 and is now in Madrid's archaeological museum.

Basílica de Santa María. 17th century Baroque church built to accomodate the Misterio de Elche (see below).

La Alcudia. Ctra. Elche-Dolores, (2km). Open winter 10am-2pm and 4-6pm. Summer: 10am-8pm. Closed Monday. Archaeological museum on the site where the Dama de Elche was found.

Museum of Contemporary Art, Plaza Raval s/n. Open 10am-1.30pm and 5-8pm. Closed Monday.

Municipal Park. Filled with palm trees. Also duck ponds, a large dovecot and a palm museum. Open 8am-1pm and 3-6.30pm. Closed weekends.

Archaeology Museum, Palacio de Altamira. Open 10am-1pm and 4- 7pm. Closed Sunday afternoon and Monday. Housed in 15th century palace.

Bed of the River Vinalopó, beside the Municipal Park and Archaeology Museum. In 1991 artists from around the world painted the world's longest mural along the walls and bed of the river. The results are still visible.

City Hall. Look up at the roof and you'll see a small tower, the Torre del Concejo, with a clock in which two figures, Calendura and Calendureta, ring the hours and half hours. They have been the faithful timekeepers of Elche since the mid-18th century.

La Calahorra. Next to the church. A 15th century Gothic tower. The last remaining part of the city's extensive defenses.

Fiestas: El Misterio de Elche. August 14-15. Five days of fiesta culminate in this spectacularly-staged liturgical drama dating from 1462. It's the only event of its kind in a Catholic Church, which is performed by an all male, all amateur cast (see section on Fiestas). Elche's Palm Sunday procession is also worth seeing.

PLACES TO STAY

Huerto del Cura, Porta de la Morera, 14. Tel: 545 80 40. Luxurious four-star hotel, clustered around swimming pool and shaded by palm fronds.

Don Jaime, Avda Primo de Rivera, 5-7. Tel. 545 38 40. Two stars.

Hostal María, C/ Llibertat. Tel: 546 02 83. One star. Inexpensive and simple accommodation for a night.

EATING OUT

Els Capellans. The restaurant of the Huerto del Cura Hotel-see above. Tel: 545 80 40. All major cards. (M-E)

Mesón el Granaíno, C/José María Buch, 40. Tel: 546 01 47. Closed Sunday, Easter Week and August 9-23. Master, Amex, Visa, Diners. Regional and Andalucian cuisine. (M-E)

SERVICES

Tourist office, Passeig de l'Estació, Parc. Tel: 545 27 47.

Taxis, Tel: 545 50 19.

Post office, Parc Projecte, s/n. Tel: 544 69 11.

Bus Station, Avinguda de la Libertad, s/n. Tel: 545 58 58 and 545 98 43.

Railway Station, Avinguda de la Llibertat, s/n. Tel: 545 62 54.

Airport, El Altet. Tel: 528 50 11.

EMERGENCIES

National Police, Miguel de Unamuno, 38. Tel: 091.

Municipal Police, Antiga Fàbrica Messalina, (Altabix). Tel: 542 25 00.

First Aid, Tel: 544 44 45.

Red Cross, Tel: 545 90 90.

Civil Guard, Fra Pere Balaguer, 13. Tel: 545 10 02.

● ● ● ● ● ● ● ● ● ● ● ● ● ● ●

GANDIA, in Valencia province (pop. 51,800). Denia 33km, Valencia 65km, Madrid 418km. Telephone area code: 96.

Standing at the mouth of the River Serpis, Gandía is a commercial city with a growing tourist industry. The port (El

Grao) ships large quantities of oranges produced in the vast groves that stretch inland. Gandía was the home of the notorious Borgia family. The founder of the clan was Rodrigo, who became Pope Alexander VI in 1492 and is remembered for his scandalous private life. His son Cesare, Machivalli's model for the Prince, had his brother-in-law murdered for political reasons. Lucretia, Alexander's illegimate daughter was beautiful, treacherous and, like her father and brother, debauched. Alexander VI's great grandson, however, born in Gandía, redeemed the family name when he was canonised as St Francis Borja in 1671. After his wife died he renounced worldy pleasures and joined the Jesuit order. The medieval writers Ausias March and Joanot Martorell (author of Tirant lo Blanc, one of the few books on chivalry that Cervantes admired) were born in Gandía. The town's typical dish is *fideuà* - a paella made with thick noodles instead of rice.

DON'T MISS

Palacio Ducal (The Duke's Palace), C/Santo Duque, 1. Tel: 287 12 03. Guided tours at 11am, 12am, and at 6pm and 7pm (summer); 5pm and 6pm (winter). Closed Sunday and holidays. The mansion in which St Francis was born in the 16th century, now a school run by the Jesuits. The tour includes the Gothic courtyard, richly decorated chambers and the Duke's private chapel.

Santa María Colegiate Church. A 14th-century building, expanded in the 16th century.

Town Hall. Carlos III Neoclassical façade.

Hospital de Sant Marc. A 14th-century pilgrims's hostal with separate halls for men and women.

Real Monasterio de Santa Clara. Gothic church with Romanesque doorway.

Universidad, C/Mayor. 18th century façade.

International Festival of Classical Music, July and August.

PLACES TO STAY

Bayren I, Paseo Neptuno, s/n. Tel: 284 03 00. Four stars.
Mengual, Plaza del Mediterráneo, 4. Tel: 284 21 02. One star.

EATING OUT

Gamba, Ctra. Nazaret-Oliva ,s/n. Tel: 284 13 10. Closed Monday, November and evenings in winter. All major cards. High-class restaurant with distinguished wine cellar. Seafood, fish and rice. (VE)

As de Oros, Paseo Neptuno, 26. Tel: 284 02 39. Closed Monday and January 15-31. All major cards. Near the beach. (E)

Celler del Duc, Plaza del Castell 1. Tel: 284 20 82. All major cards. Paella, other rice dishes, seafood. (M-E)

BARS

In the summer the nightlife is found around Paseo Marítimo Neptuno.

SERVICES

Tourist office, Avda. Marqués de Campo, s/n (opposite railway station). Tel: 287 77 88. Open weekdays 10am-2pm and 5-9pm. Saturday 10am-2pm. Summer only: Paseo Neptuno (Passeig Maritim Neptú), s/n. Tel: 284 24 07. On the beach near the port.

Taxis, Avda. Marqués Campo, 3. Tel: 287 21 20.

Post office, Plaza Rey Jaume I, s/n.

Railway Station, Plaza Parc de l'Estació, s/n. Tel: 286 54 70.

EMERGENCIES

National Police, Plaza Sant Roc s/n. Tel: 287 19 35.

Municipal Police, Ayuntamiento (town hall), Plaza de la Constitución, 1. Tel: 287 16 00.

Ambulances, Tel: 286 25 59.

First Aid, C/ Hospital, 20. Tel: 287 19 70.

Civil Guard, Avda. del Mar, 10. Tel: 287 14 44.

• • • • • • • • • • • • • • •

IBIZA (Eivissa), capital of the third largest Balearic island, in Baleares Province (pop. 33,500). Telephone area code: 971.

The town of Ibiza is divided into two parts: the old Dalt Vila

(D'Alt Villa) on the hill and the modern centre and suburbs below. Ibiza is well known for its nightlife and free living which has attracted such famous names as Niki Lauda, Roman Polanski, Nina Hagen, Grace Jones, Boris Becker, Björn Borg and Freddy Mercury.

DON'T MISS

Dalt Vila (the old town). A 16th century Catalan Gothic labyrinth enclosed by gigantic ramparts. Enter it through Las Tablas gateway or Portal Nou if you are on foot. From the watchtower of Baluarte de Santa Lucia there are views over sea and harbour.

Museo Dalt Vila (closed for reform). Half of Ibiza's archaeology museum containing important Punic relics.

Puig des Molins, C/Via Romana. Open 4pm-7pm. The other half of Ibiza's archaeology museum is on the site of a necropolis to which the Carthaginians brought their venerated dead.

Cathedral. In the old town. 13th century with a viewpoint beside it.

Formentera (4km from Ibiza). See Excursion 30.

HOW TO GET THERE (see also Excursion 22)

The fastest journey is by Flebasa's catamaran from Denia which sails daily at 7.30pm and takes two and a half hours. The catamaran returns from Ibiza at 8pm. There is a special price for a day return ticket. Flebasa also operates a daily car ferry from Denia to San Antonio, and an Alicante-Ibiza fast service two days a week. All these ferries operate only between June 15 and September 15. For the rest of the year there is a daily ferry from Denia to San Antonio at 10pm which takes five hours. For prices, reservations and other information about Flebasa Lines, Tel: 96-578 40 11 (Denia) or in Ibiza Tel: 34 28 71. Trasmediterranea operates a Valencia-Ibiza service two or three days per week depending on the time of year. It leaves Valencia at 11.30pm and takes nine hours. Tel: 96-367 07 04 (Valencia) or in Ibiza Tel: 31 51 50. There is also a daily flight to Ibiza from Valencia. Tel: 96-351 96 37 (Valencia).

CAR AND MOPED HIRE

Avis, Tel: 900-13 57 90 (central reservation service).

Autos Unión, Tel: 33 19 34.

Autos Ibiza, Tel: 31 09 66.

Isla Blanca, Tel: 30 44 31 and 30 63 25 (also mopeds)

Moto Sud, Tel: 30 24 42 (for mopeds and motorbikes). Run by a young Scot.

PLACES TO STAY

Los Molinos, Playa de Figueretes. Tel: 30 22 50. Four stars. The town's top hotel.

El Corsario, Poniente, 5. Tel: 30 12 48. Three-star hotel in a 16th-century house in Dalt Vila.

El Palacio, C/ de la Conquista, 2. Tel: 30 14 78. An hotel especially for movie buffs. Each room is named after a famous film star and has a view of the Dalt Villa.

Montesol, Vara del Rey, 2. Tel: 31 01 61. One star. On the main square.

EATING OUT

El Corsario, Poniente, 5. Tel: 30 12 48. Open April-October, for dinner only (8pm-midnight). Visa, Amex. International, French and Basque cuisine. Views over old town. (M-E)

Foc i Fum, C/ de la Virgen, 55. Tel: 31 33 80. Open mid-April to mid-October. Small restaurant in old town with tables outside. (M)

S'Oficina, Avda. España, 6. Tel: 30 00 16. Closed Sunday and Christmas. All major cards. (E)Mesón de Paco, Avda Bartolomé de Rosselló, 15. Tel: 31 72 27. Closed Wednesday. All major cards. Seafood and fish. (M)

La Masia d'en Sord, Ctra. San Miguel (near Santa Eulalia turn off). Tel: 31 02 28. Open Easter-October dinner only 7.30-midnight. Converted farmhouse with tables on terrace. (E)

Ama Lur, Ctra. Ibiza-San Miguel, km 5. Tel: 31 45 54. Dinner only 8pm-midnight. Closed Wednesday (except in summer) and December 1-March 1. Restaurant in an 18th-century country house. (VE)

BARS

Montesol, Paseo Vara del Rey. A sober, classic café.

Teatro Pereyra, Conde Rosellón 3. Plays classical music during the day and has live music at night. Chairs and tables on the street.

La Maravilla, Plaza de la Constitución. Opens early.

AFTER DARK

This is when Ibiza comes alive, especially around the Avda. de Ardenes, beside the harbour, and the neighbouring Sa Penya quarter. This is the place to see and be seen. Try Marisol, Zoe or El Mono Desnudo (C/ Garijo, 16). The island has 85 discotheques, including the "macrodiscotheques" Amnesia and Ku. Others include Space and Kiss.

SERVICES

Tourist Office, Vara del Rey, 13. Tel: 30 19 00.

Taxis, Tel: 30 17 94.

Post Office, C/ Madrid, 25.

Telephones, C/ Felipe II.

Bus Station (local buses), Avda. Isidro Macabich, 42. Tel: 31 20 75.

Airport, Tel: 30 22 00. Iberia, Tel: 30 09 54.

Port: see above for shipping lines

CONSULATES

United Kingdom, Avda. Isidoro Machebich, 45. Tel: 30 18 18.

EMERGENCIES

National Police, Avda. Paz. Tel: 091.

Municipal Police, Vicente Serra, 25. Tel: 31 58 61.

First Aid, Tel: 30 12 14.

Red Cross, Tel: 30 12 14.

Civil Guard, Ctra. Aeropuerto, Can Xifre. Tel: 30 58 61, 30 05 21 and 30 11 00.

• • • • • • • • • • • • • • • •

JÁTIVA (XÀTIVA), in Valencia province (pop. 24, 400). Valencia 58 km, Alicante 102km, Madrid 380km. Telephone area code: 96.

An historic town founded by the Phoenicians. Its magnificent ruined castle running along a high ridge was once the most important fortress under the Crown of Aragón. Játiva took the losing side in the War of the Spanish Succession - that of Archduke Charles of Austria. The victor, Felipe V, burnt the town and renamed it San Felipe. So it was called until the 19th century, when it reclaimed its Moorish name and exacted its revenge by hanging Felipe's portrait upside down. Several ancient churches and numerous stately buildings have been preserved of the Játiva of old. The modern part of the city has a pleasant avenue and gardens to stroll in. The Iberians established a linen weaving industry. Later, in the 11th century, Europe's first paper was made here out of rice and straw. The painter José de Ribera and two infamous popes (founders of the Borgia clan; see Gandía) were born in Játiva.

DON'T MISS (see also Excursion 18)

Castle. Sprawling ruins with fortifications from all ages of Spain's history. Open winter: 10am-2pm and 3.30-6pm. Summer 10am-2pm and 5-8pm. Closed Monday and the day after public holidays.

Colegiate Basilica of Santa María, known for short as La Seu or Seo. Open 6.30-8pm.

Chapel of Saint Felix, on the road up to the castle . Open winter 10am-1pm and 3-6pm. Summer 10am-1pm and 4-7pm. Nearby is the chapel of Saint Joseph which has a viewpoint outside.

Medieval Gothic fountain. Plaça de la Trinitat.

Municipal Museum, Carrer de la Corretgeria. Open Tuesday-Friday 11am-2pm and 4-6pm. Saturday and Sunday 11am-2pm. Closed Monday. The upside down portrait of Felipe V hangs in the art gallery upstairs.

The old town. From the museum follow Carrer de la Corretgeria to La Seo. Then take Calle Abad Pla, Calle San Vicente, Calle de Bruns and Calle de Segurana. This brings you to the Fuente de los 25 Caños - the Fountain of 25 spouts. Return along Calle de San Pedro, Carrer de l'Angel and Calle de Moncada.

PLACES TO STAY

Residencia Vernisa, C/ Acadèmic Maravall, 1. Tel: 227 10 11. Two stars. The city's best equipped hotel.

Hotel Murta, C/ Angel Lacalle, s/n. Tel: 227 66 11. One star.

El Margallonero, Plaça del Mercat, 42. Tel: 227 66 77. Rooms above restaurant. Central.

EATING OUT

Casa la Abuela, C/ Reina, 17. Tel: 227 05 25. Closed Sunday and second half of July. Valencian cuisine. (E)

Mesón Simón, C/ Corretgeria, 5. Tel: 227 53 04. Open 1.30-3.30pm and 8.30-11pm. Clean and cool. Just off market place and close to monuments. (B)

El Margallonero, Plaça del Mercat, 42. Tel: 227 66 77. Straightforward and central. (B)

Floro, Plaça del Mercat. Central and unpretentious. B.

SERVICES

Tourist Office, Noguera, 10. Tel: 227 33 46. Open 9am-2pm and 4- 6pm. Saturday and Sunday 10am-2pm. Closed Monday and May 22.

Taxis, Tel: 227 16 81 and 227 34 37.

Post Office, Albereda Jaume 1, 33. Tel: 227 51 68.

Bus Station, Avinguda del Cavaller Ximen de Trovia.

Railway Station, C/ Estacion, s/n. Tel: 227 16 64.

EMERGENCIES

National Police, C/ Sant Agusti, 17. Tel: 227 37 61.

Municipal Police, C/ Baixada del Carme, s/n. Tel: 227 55 61.

Ambulances, Tel: 227 10 95 or 227 20 82.

First Aid, C/ Espanyoleto, 13. Tel: 227 30 44.

Red Cross, C/ Sant Domènec, 13. Tel: 227 44 31.

Civil Guard, C/ Acadèmic Maravall, s/n. Tel: 227 41 30.

● ● ● ● ● ● ● ● ● ● ● ● ● ● ●

JÁVEA (XÁBIA), in Alicante province (pop. 16,500). Alicante 91km, Valencia 110 km, Madrid 461 km. Telephone area code: 96.

Jávea is situated between the two capes of San Antonio and de la Nao, and separated from Denia by Mount Mongó. The World Health Organisation found it to be, climatically and environmentally, one of the healthiest places on earth in which to live. The town centre is a short way inland from the modern port and the beach. In the 70s the council wisely imposed a ban on buildings of more than three storeys and there are only three high-rise blocks along the Arenales beach. More characteristic of Jávea are the sprawling estates of bright white villas, popular with foreigners. Much of the old town is built of *tosca* sandstone, which is also incorporated into many modern houses, especially in the form of *nayas* - wide, arcaded terraces, covered over to give areas of well-aired shade which were traditionally used to dry grapes into raisins.

DON'T MISS

The old town. Its houses built of *tosca*, their windows covered by elegant pot-bellied grilles.

Church of San Bartolomé. 16th century. Fortified against attack with machiolations over the door from which boiling oil could be tipped over attackers.

Nuestra Señora de Loreto church. In the port. A modern building inspired by the ribs of a ship's hull.

Cape San Antonio and Cape de la Nao, both points from which to view the coast.

Cala Granadella, a cove amongst pine woods discreetly distanced from the main tourist areas.

PLACES TO STAY

Parador Costa Blanca, Playa del Arenal, 2. Tel: 579 02 00. Modern hotel set on a low promontory into the sea.

Bahía Vista. Crta. Cabo de la Nao, km 7.5, Portichol, 76. Tel: 577 04 61. One star. English-run hotel with gardens, pool and bowling green.

EATING OUT

Bar Paco, C/ Historiador Palau, 30 (between the town and the port). Tel: 579 42 33. Open 1-4pm and 7-10.30pm. Closed Saturday afternoon, Sunday morning and August. Family-run bar-restaurant, serving tasty home-made food.*Tapas* served all day. (B)

La Estrella, El Arenal, 4. Tel: 579 08 02. Closed Wednesday. French cuisine. (M-E)

Lázaro, Ctra. Benitachell, Partida Capsals, 19. Tel: 579 01 74. (M)

Tosalet Casino Club, Urbanización Tosalet, Algarrobos s/n. Tel: 577 09 58. (E-VE)

BARS

Bar Paco, C/ Historiador Palau, 30 (see above).

Casa de Cultura, C/ Mayor. Bar on one side of a pretty patio.

International, Avda. Juan Carlos I, 63 (between the town and the port). The place to play snooker. Also a restaurant.

SERVICES

Tourist Office, Plaza Almirante Bastarreche. Tel: 579 07 36.

Taxis, Tel: 579 10 60 (town) and 579 10 15 (port).

Post Office, C/ La Coma.

Consumer Information Office, Tel: 579 34 99.

Bus Station, Principe de Asturias, Tel: 579 08 54.

Telephones, C/ La Coma.

EMERGENCIES

Municipal Police, Tel: 579 00 81.

Ambulances, Tel: 579 19 61.

First Aid, Tel: 579 25 00.

Red Cross, Tel: 579 19 61.

Civil Guard, Tel: 579 10 85.

● ● ● ● ● ● ● ● ● ● ● ● ● ● ● ●

LORCA in Murcia province (pop. 68,200). Murcia 62km, Madrid 449km. Telephone area code: 968.

Lorca, something of an oasis amongst sierras which are some of the most arid areas in Europe, was a frontier town in the time of the Romans and the Moors. It enjoyed a hey-day in the 17th century. Lorca's numerous fine baroque buildings, some of which are in a bad state of repair, date from this period. In the late 18th century a British traveller, the Rev. Joseph Townsend, was still able to compare its public spaces to Oxford.

DON'T MISS

Plaza Mayor (also called Plaza de España). Buildings with Baroque façades, notably the town hall.

Colegiata de San Patricio, Plaza Mayor. 16th century, but the interior is later, mainly Baroque. The only church in Spain dedicated to the Irish saint, Patrick.

Palacio de los Guevara; splendid carved doorway of 1694 and fine inner courtyard.

Castle. Of the original 35 towers of this 13th-century castle, only the Torre Alfonsina and the ruins of Torre del Espolón remain. The main reason to make the ascent is for the view of the surrounding countryside.

Columna Milinaria (Roman milepost). On the corner between Calle Corredera and Plaza San Vicente, marking the distance between Lorca and Cartagena on the Via Heraclea.

Porche de San Antonio, the last surviving gateway from the city walls.

Fiesta: Holy Week. Lorca is know for its spectacular processions of costumed Biblical characters.

PLACES TO STAY

Parador de Puerto Lumbreras, Avda. de Juan Carlos I. Tel: 30890.

Alameda, C/ Musso Valiente, 8. Tel: 46 75 00. Three stars.

La Hoya, Ctra. N-340, km 607. Tel: 48 18 06. Two stars.

EATING OUT

El Teatro, Plaza de Colón, 12. Tel: 46 99 09. Closed Sunday and August. (M-E)

Cándido, C/ Santo Domingo, 13. Tel: 46 69 07. Closed Sun in summer. Master, Visa. (M)

BARS
Alameda - hotel cafeteria, see above.

SERVICES
Tourist Office, C/ Lopez Gisbert (Palacio de Guevara). Tel: 46 61 57.

EMERGENCIES
National Police, Tel: 091.
Municipal Police, Tel: 092.
Ambulances, Tel: 46 84 00.
Red Cross, Tel: 46 79 57.
Civil Guard, Tel: 062.

● ● ● ● ● ● ● ● ● ● ● ● ● ● ● ●

MORELLA, in Castellón province (pop. 3,100). Castellón 106km, Valencia 175km, Teruel 150km, Madrid 442 km. Telephone area code: 964.

A thousand metres up, surging out of the landscape on its own rock outcrop, and protected by an unbroken ring of medieval walls, Morella cuts a dramatic profile. It is a town steeped in history and is thought to be one of the earliest settled sites in Spain. Pope Luna, Saint Vicent Ferrer and King Ferdinand of Antequera met here in 1414 to try and end the Great Schism that split Christianity. Well preserved, Morella still has the aura of a prosperous, fortified medieval town at a strategic location for both war and trade. It has an ancient tradition of craft weaving and brightly-coloured rugs and jumpers are on sale in several shops. As the main town in the beautiful Maestrazgo region, Morella makes a convenient centre for excursions. Some of the more interesting places to visit are covered in Excursions 24 and 28.

DON'T MISS
The town itself. A fan-shaped maze of steep, narrow streets, tapering alleys and a myriad steps. There are many timber-framed houses -- sometimes sloping towards each other, their

eaves almost touching -- and 15th- and 16th-century mansions.

Calle Don Blasco of Aragón. The narrow main street of Morella, named after one of the town's many proud owners, is lined with tall old buildings and could be straight out of a history book illustration. It is dominated by the Gothic mansion which was the residence of Cardenal Ram but has since been converted into a hotel. Each house, shop or bar has a porch in front of it supported on stone columns. These sheltered public areas, used to trade goods in medieval times, join together to form shady porticoes running the length of the street.

The plaque on the wall of Calle de la Virgen (behind the main street). This marks the house in which St Vicent Ferrer performed a bizarre miracle. A distraught housewife had no meat to offer the saint for supper so she cut up her son and put him in the cooking pot. When he discovered what had happened, St Vicent reconstituted the boy except for one little finger, which his mother had eaten to see if he was well-salted.

The walls. 14th century, two metres thick and pierced by six handsome gates.

Basílica of Santa María la Mayor. The church has a unique, raised choirloft, which is reached by a magnificently carved stone spiral staircase. Also three 14th-century stained glass windows.

The Royal Monastery of San Francisco. The peaceful and picturesque ruined cloister gives access to the castle. Open daily 11am-2pm and 3-7pm.

The Castle. Reached by a brisk walk from the monastery (not to be attempted at midday in summer). This impregnable fortress exploits numerous caves as extra chambers. One was once the infamous dungeon of *El Cacho,* where both Moorish and Christian noblemen were held awaiting ransom. From the battlements there is a fine view of the closely-packed red rooftops of Morella.

Aqueduct. 15th century. A short way out of town on the road towards Alcañiz. Impressive ruins in two parts.

Cave paintings, Morella la Vella (8km). Take the road to Chiva and turn left on to an unsurfaced track after 4km. The people who live nearby in the farmhouse will show you them if they have time. The most well-known of the paintings, The Fight or Dance of the Archers, is now difficult to discern.

Museum, Torre de San Miguel (near tourist office). Open 11am-2pm and 4-8pm. On various floors of old tower. Specimens of carved Gothic stone, dinosaur fossils, and textile craft display.

Fiestas: Classical Music Festival, August. Baroque music on church's 18th-century organ. Tourist's Day, August 15. The Sexenales is held every six years, the last being in in 1994.

PLACES TO STAY

Cardenal Ram, Cuesta Suñer 1. Tel: 17 30 85. Converted 16th century Gothic palace on main street. Two stars. Good restaurant serving local dishes.

Rey Don Jaime, C/ Juan Giner, 6. Tel: 16 09 11. Three stars.

Hostal Elías, C/ Colomer, 7. Tel: 16 00 92. Two star hostal. Centrally located (between church and main street). Good value but lacks a dining room.

El Cid, Puerta San Mateo, 2. Tel: 16 01 25. One star. Basic.

La Muralla, Muralla, 12. Tel: 16 02 43. Two star pension.

EATING OUT

Mesón del Pastor. Cuesta Jovani, 3-5. Tel: 16 02 49. Closed Wednesday. Master, Visa. Local mountain cuisine including Morella

Cardenal Ram (see above). Casa Roque, Segura Barreda. Tel: 16 03 36. Master, Amex, Visa. Owned by the same people as Cardenal Ram and slightly cheaper than the hotel's restaurant though serving a similar menu. Try the succulent specialities of Morella - broth with dumplings and *cordero trufado* - lamb stuffed with truffles. (M)

Rey Don Jaime (see above). Croquetas, perdices, rabbit. (M)

Moreno, San Nicolás 12. Tel: 16 01 05. Closed Sunday night. No cards. (B)

BARS

Vinatea, C/ Blasco de Alagón, 17. Tel: 16 07 44. Also a restaurant.

Casa Borras, C/ Segura Barreda. Tel: 16 02 44. Family-run bar.

SHOPPING

This is wool country and you'll probably be tempted to come away with one of the brightly coloured woollen jumpers on sale - knitting is a thousand year old art of the Maestrazgo. You may need one if you visit Morella between early autumn and late spring because the mountain nights can be chilly.

SERVICES

Tourist Office, Torre de San Miguel. Tel: 17 30 32.
Post Office, C/San Nicolás, 33.

EMERGENCIES

Municipal Police, Tel: 16 00 34.
Ambulances and First Aid, Tel: 16 00 72.
Red Cross, N-232, km 63.8. Tel: 16 03 80.
Civil Guard, Pl. Ramón Querol, 31. Tel: 16 00 11.

● ● ● ● ● ● ● ● ● ● ● ● ● ● ● ● ●

MURCIA, provincial and regional capital (pop. 305.200). Alicante 75km, Torrevieja 55km, Albacete 150km, Valencia 241km, Madrid 401km. Telephone area code: 968.

Founded in the 9th century by the Moors as Mursiyah, Murcia is now the capital of a province which is also a region - *comunidad autónoma.* It took over from Cartagena in importance during the 13th century, when the coast was plagued by pirate attacks. In Moorish times, Murcia was important for its silk industry and agriculture. Murcia's most famous sons are sculptor Francisco Salzillo and the statesman Count of Floridablanca, who helped stabilise the Spanish economy in the late 18th century.

DON'T MISS

Cathedral. Originally 14th century, but with a largely Renaissance and Baroque exterior. The Capilla de los Vélez is sumptuously late-Gothic. The tomb of Alfonso the Wise is in the Capilla Mayor. There is a museum (open 10am-1pm and 5-7pm), containing a splendid Gothic altarpiece; and a belfry giving a view of the city and the surrounding farmland.

Casino, C/ de la Trapería. Open 9am-11pm. Closed July and August. Not a place for gambling but a gentlemen's club. Lavishly decorated with Moorish and Art Nouveau influences. See especially the Arab Patio, the ladies' cloakroom (which has a painted ceiling) and the romantic ballroom.

Salzillo Museum, C/ San Andrés, 1. Open 9.30am-1pm and 4-7pm (3-6pm in winter). Sunday 11m-1pm. Closed Monday. Francisco Salzillo, acclaimed as one of Spain's greatest sculptors, turned out numerous polychromed religious images.

Museo de la Huerta and waterwheel, Alcantarilla (7km). Open weekdays 9am-1pm (holidays 10am-2pm) and 4-6pm. Closed Monday. Folk museum.

El Valle Nature Reserve and Sanctuario de la Fuensanta (5 km). Open 9am-1pm and 4-6pm. Take N-301 for Cartagena and turn off for La Alberca then follow the signs.

Fiesta: Easter Week processions, especially on Good Friday.

PLACES TO STAY

Conde de Floridablanca, C/Corbalán, 7. Tel: 21 46 26. In the old quarter, El Camen, across the river from the centre. Four stars.

Arco de San Juan, Plaza de Ceballos, 10. Tel: 21 04 55. Probably the city's best-equipped hotel. Central. Four stars.

Rincón de Pepe, C/ Apóstoles, 34. Tel: 21 22 39. Four stars.

EATING OUT

Rincón de Pepe, C/ Apóstoles, 34. Tel: 21 22 49. All major cards. Restaurant of national fame. (VE)

Conde de Floridablanca, C/ Corbalán, 7. Tel: 21 46 26. All major cards. Good value menu of the day. (B-M)

BARS

Casino, C/ de la Trapería. (see above). Has tables in what amounts to an enclosed private "street". There are numerous cafés with tables outside (in the summer) on Avda. Alfonso X El Sabio.

SERVICES

Tourist Office, Alejandro Seiquer, 4. Tel: 36 20 00 ext. 1134.
Taxis, Tel: 29 77 00 and 24 88 00.
Post Office, Plaza Ceballos.
Telephones, C/ de Saavedra Fajardo.
Bus Station, C/San Andres, s/n. Tel: 29 22 11.
Railway Station, C/Industria, Barrio del Carmen. Tel: 25 21 54.
Airport, San Javier (50km). Tel: 57 00 73. Iberia Tel: 24 00 50.

EMERGENCIES

National Police, Tel: 091.
Municipal Police, Tel: 25 60 11.
Ambulances, Tel: 22 22 22.
First Aid, Tel: 23 75 50.
Red Cross, Tel: 21 77 62.
Civil Guard, Tel: 062

● ● ● ● ● ● ● ● ● ● ● ● ● ● ●

ORIHUELA, in Alicante province (pop. 49,500). Murcia 24km, Alicante 57 km, Madrid 416km. Telephone area code: 96.

Orihuela, the capital of the Veja Baja district, was once a rich and prosperous city. In 1488 the "Catholic Kings", Ferdinand and Isabel, stopped here to collect men and money for the final struggle against the Moors defending Granada. It enjoyed its heyday in the 18th century. In 1829 an earthquake badly damaged the city. These days it has an air of faded grandeur - although, happily, there are moves to restore its palaces, churches and other elegant old buildings. Two famous Spanish poets were inspired by Orihuela: Miguel Hernández, who was born here and died in prison after the Civil War; and the Alicantine writer Gabriel Miró who poetically refers to it as "Oleza" in his works.

DON'T MISS

The cathedral. It has three doors: two Gothic (Cadenas and Loreto) and one Renaissance (Anunciación). There is some

221

ornamental grille work and a fine choir by Juan Bautista Borja. The peaceful and picturesque Romanesque cloister outside was moved here from a convent that suffered damage in the Civil War. In the cathedral museum you can see one of Velazquez's most well-known paintings, "The Temptation of St Thomas Aquinas".

Colegio de Santo Domingo. This stately building, now a school, was formerly a Dominican monastery and housed a university until the 18th century. There's an interesting cloister and a refectory with 18th-century ornamental tiles from Manises (you have to ask at the door for permission to visit these). Nearby you can still see one of the old city gates, the Puerta de la Olma.

Casa Museo de Miguel Hernández (in front of Colegio de Santo Domingo). Open 10am-1pm, 5-7pm. Closed Saturday and Sunday. Museum in memory of the poet.

Iglesia de Santiago. This Gothic-style church, built for the knights of the Order of Santiago on the site of a mosque, contains a Baroque organ and Salzillo's "La Sagrada Familia".

Palm groves. Best seen from the N-340 heading north out of the city.

Museo de Semana Santa (Easter Week Museum), Plaza de la Merced. Open 10am-1pm and 4.30-7pm. Tuesday and Sunday 10am-1pm. Among the grand gilded floats (by Salzillo and other artists) built for the Easter Week parades you'll find The "Diablesa", the image of a she-devil, which was carved in 1688 by Fray Nicolás de Bussi. Until the museum was opened it had to be kept in the public library because no church wanted to have such a profane object.

PLACES TO STAY

Casa Corro, Palmeral de San Anton, 1. Tel. 530 29 63. Two star hostal. Inexpensive.

Montepiedra, Rosalía de Castro, s/n, Dehesa de Campoamor (32 km). Tel: 532 03 00. Three stars. Overlooks the beach.

EATING OUT

Casa Corro, Palmeral de San Antón, s/n. Tel. 530 29 63. Closed Monday night and August 16-September 3. Master, Visa. (M)

SERVICES

Tourist Office, Francisco Die, 25 (Palacio Rubalcava). Tel: 530 27 47.

Taxis, Tel: 674 02 02 and 530 10 20.

Post Office, Avda. José Antonio, 21. Tel: 530 07 95.

Buses, Tel: 530 15 67 or 530 02 87.

Railway Station, C/ Estación Ferrocarril, s/n. Tel: 530 02 84.

Consumers' Information Office, Tel: 530 20 56.

EMERGENCIES

National Police, Tel: 091 and 530 00 82.

Municipal Police, Tel: 530 02 04.

First Aid, Tel: 530 01 65.

Red Cross, N-340, Km 24. Tel: 560 11 61.

Ambulances, Tel: 530 51 51.

Civil Guard, Tel: 530 01 39.

● ● ● ● ● ● ● ● ● ● ● ● ● ● ● ●

PEÑÍSCOLA, in Castellón province (pop. 3,200). Castellón 76km, Madrid 494 km. Telephone area code: 964.

The old town of Peñíscola clusters around the base of an impregnable castle on a promintory surrounded on three sides by the sea. This fortress was once the residence of the rebellious Pope Benedict XIII, also known as Pope Luna. Modern Peñíscola is a fishing port and tourist resort. Part of the film El Cid was shot on the long beach to the north with the castle in the background. Peñíscola stages an annual film festival. The coast to the south, dominated by the still unspoilt Sierra de Irta, has many relatively inaccessible coves.

DON'T MISS (see Excursion 17)

Old town. A maze of narrow streets of white houses enclosed by cliff-top ramparts, and entered by three gates.

Bufador. A blow-hole beside a house in the old town into which the waves rush with a chilling, subterranean booming sound.

Castillo del Papa Luna. Built in the 13th century, supposedly by the Knights Templar, and now well-restored. Inside there are vaulted rooms and Gothic windows. Pope Luna's study is in one tower. There are impressive views from the top battlements.

Boat trips. From the harbour. If you want to see Peñíscola from the sea.

PLACES TO STAY

Hostería del Mar, Ctra. Benicarló-Peñíscola, km 6. Tel: 48 06 00. Four stars. On the beach. Hosts Medieval banquets.

Peñíscola-Palace, Avda. Papa Luna, 34. Tel: 48 09 12. Four stars.

Benedicto XIII, Las Atalayas. Tel: 48 08 01. Three stars. On a private estate, some way out of Peñíscola, with a view of the town.

Papa Luna, Avda. Papa Luna, 6. Tel: 48 07 60. Three stars.

Del Duc, C/ Fulladosa, 10. Tel: 48 07 68. One-star hostal in the old town. Some rooms look out on the harbour.

EATING OUT

Peñíscola specialises in seafood, especially date mussels and lobsters.

Casa Severino, Urbanización Atalayas. Tel: 48 07 03. Closed Wednesday in winter, and during November. All major cards. Seafood, including *paella marinera.* (E)

Casa Jaime, Avda. del Papa Luna, 5. Tel: 48 00 30. Closed Wednesday in winter, and during November. Master, Amex, Visa. Local cuisine and seafood. (M-E)

Casa Joan, Plaza del Caudillo, 1. Tel: 48 03 50. Fish and seafood restaurant run by a couple from fishing families. (M)

Marisquería Casa Vicent, C/ Santos Mártires, 15. Tel: 48 06 82. (E)

SERVICES

Tourist office, Paseo Marítimo, s/n. Tel: 48 02 08.

Taxis, Tel: 48 00 44.
Post Office, C/ Pescadores, s/n.

EMERGENCIES
Municipal Police, ayuntamiento (town hall). Tel: 48 01 21.
Ambulances, Tel: 47 22 94 and 47 17 28.
Red Cross, Tel: 48 02 08.
Civil Guard, Tel: 48 00 46.

● ● ● ● ● ● ● ● ● ● ● ● ● ● ● ●

TERUEL, provincial capital (pop. 27,200). Valencia 145km, Zaragoza Madrid 300km. Telephone area code: 978.

An inland city almost 1,000m up on the *meseta,* famed for its Mudejar brick architecture (for which it has been named the Pink City), its cured hams (jamón serrano) and for its ill-fated, legendary lovers (see below), the Spanish equivalent of Romeo and Juliet. The immediate surrounding landscape is dry and ochre- coloured but the province of Teruel has some attractive mountains, including the Montes Universales around Albarracín (see Excursion 27), the Maestrazgo (see Excursion 28) and the sierras around Rubielos de Mora (see Excursion 25). Teruel was the site of an important battle in the Civil War during which freezing winter temperatures contributed to heavy casualties on both sides.

DON'T MISS
Cathedral. Combines Romanesque and Islamic elements. Coffered ceiling decorated with Gothic paintings. 13th-century tower.

The Lovers Mausoleum, C/ Matías Abad (beside the Church of San Pedro). Two mummified bodies, found in 1555, assumed to be those of the famous Lovers of Teruel, lie on display below marble statues (designed by Juan de Ávalos), the hands of which reach out for each other but do not quite meet. The story goes like this: Isabel de Segura, a beautiful girl from a wealthy family, falls in love with Diego de Marcilla, a young man from humble origins and a second son to boot - ie he doesn't stand to inherit. Isabel's father opposes the marriage but Diego begs for five years to make his fortune. In the meantime, however, Isabel is betrothed to another. Diego, rich but mortally wounded in battle, arrives back in Teruel as Isabel's wedding bells ring out. That night he steals into the house in which the newlyweds are asleep, wakes Isabel and asks her for a last kiss. She refuses him and he collapses and dies. The next day, as the mourners gather around Diego's bier, Isabel flings herself on Diego's body and dies of despair.

Mudejar towers. Five towers of ornamental brickwork decorated with white and green tiles, and arches at street level built between the 12th and 16th centuries. The two most interesting are San Martín (Plaza Perez Prado) and San Salvador (Calle el Salvador), to which another legend of forlorn love is attached. The two architects who built them, Omar and Abdalá, were said to be competing for the love of the same lady, Zoraida. He who built the finest tower would win her hand. But when the scaffolding was taken down, Omar's tower of St Martin's was seen to be twisted and its creator hurled himself from the top.

Aqueduct. Built by a French engineer in the 16th century. Now used as a footbridge.

Provincial Museum, Plaza Fray Anselmo Polanco, s/n. Open weekdays 10am-2pm and 4-7pm, weekends 10am-2pm. Closed Monday and holidays. Displays on rural life, an 18th-century chemist's shop, a Roman mosaic and archaeological finds housed in a 16th-century building.

Plaza del Torico. The main square has a statue of a tiny bull mounted on a column, a symbol of the city.

PLACES TO STAY

Parador de Teruel, Ctra. Teruel-Zaragoza. Tel: 60 18 00. Purpose-built Parador a short way out of the city.

Reina Cristina, Paseo del Óvalo, 1, Tel: 60 68 60. Three stars.

Civera, Avda. Sagunto, 37. Tel: 60 23 00. Two stars.

Goya, C/ Tomás Nogués, 4. Tel: 60 14 50. One star.

Oriente, Avda. Sagunto, 5. Tel: 60 15 50. One star.

EATING OUT

La Menta, C/ Bartolomé Estaban, 10. Tel: 60 75 32. Amex, Master, Visa. (E)

Mesón Óvalo, Paseo del Óvalo, 8. (M)

Milagro. Ctra. Sagunto-Burgos, km 124. Tel: 60 30 95. Visa. Enormous roadside building designed for coach parties. Also a bar serving sandwiches of Teruel cured ham, *jamón serrano.* (B-M)

BARS

Mesón Óvalo (see above).

Mi Cachirulico, Plaza de la Judería.

SERVICES

Tourist Office, C/ Tomás Nogués, 1. Tel: 60 22 79.

Taxis, Tel: 60 96 97.

Post Office, C/ Yagüe de Salas, 19. Tel: 60 11 92.

Telephones, C/ San Andrés, 13. Open 9am-1pm and 5-9.30pm.

Buses, Tel: 60 34 50 (for Madrid and Valencia); 60 20 04 (for Barcelona); 60 26 80 (for Albarracín); and 60 10 14 (for Zaragoza).

Railway Station, Estación, s/n. Tel: 60 26 49.

EMERGENCIES

National Police, Tel: 091 and 60 11 00.

Municipal Police, Tel: 60 21 78.

Ambulances, Tel: 60 26 09.

First Aid, Tel: 60 53 68.

Red Cross, San Miguel, 3. Tel: 60 52 16.

Civil Guard, Tel: 062.

• • • • • • • • • • • • • • •

TORREVIEJA, in Alicante province (pop. 25,000). Alicante 50km, Murcia 54km, Madrid 445km. Telephone area code: 96.

Not so long ago Torrevieja was an insignificant fishing village. Now it's one of the fastest-growing towns in Spain. Between 1981 and 1991 it doubled in size. Nearly a fifth of the population are foreigners, especially Britons. Apart from tourism, Torrevieja is also important for its salt works, considered the most important salt pans in Europe and the second most important in the world. Torrevieja has a traditional craft industry of modelling in salt and you can buy fragile miniature saline ships in souvenir shops.

DON'T MISS

Salt pans. Producing 75% of Spain's salt. You can visit them on Tuesday and Thursday evenings at 5pm by arrangement with Nueva Compañía Arrendataria de las Salinas de Torrevieja at the southern end of the square by the harbour. The salt pans are also important for their bird populations: flamingoes, amongst others, stop and feed here.

Cervera and La Mata Towers. Built as lookouts for pirate attack.

Street market: Fridays.

National Habaneras Competition. August 12-15. The *habanera* is a melodic form of song which was brought back from the Cuban capital by 19th-century salt exporters.

PLACES TO STAY

Fontana, Rambla Juan Mateo, 19. Tel: 670 11 25. Three stars.

Mar Bella, Avda. Alfredo Nobel, 8. Tel: 571 08 28. Two stars.

Masa Internacional, Avda. Alfredo Nobel, 150. Tel: 692 15 37. Two stars.

EATING OUT

Because of its international community, Torrevieja has a wide variety of restaurants apart from those serving traditional fare of fish and seafood.

Bosna Grill, San Gabriel, 3 (near Hotel Fontana). Tel: 571 34 77. Open 12am-2.30pm and 6.30pm until late. All cards. Central, family run restaurant serving Balkan and German food. (M)

La Vikinga, Avda. Gregorio Marañón. Open 7.30pm until late. British-run restaurant. (B-M)

Telmo, Torrevejenses Ausentes, 5. Tel: 571 54 74. All cards. Air- conditioned. Seafood. (M)

Cap Roig, Urbanización Cabo Roig. (7km on the road to

Cartagena) Tel: 676 02 90. All cards. On a promontory into the sea. Marvellous views, fish and seafood. (M-E)

Miramar, Paseo Vista Alegre, 6. Tel: 571 07 65. All cards. An elegant restaurant with a seaside terrace serving fish and seafood. (M-E)

SERVICES

Tourist Office, Plaza de Capdepont, s/n. Tel: 571 59 36.
Taxis, Pl. Waldo Calero, s/n. Tel: 571 10 26 and 571 22 77.
Bus Station, María Parodi, 29. Tel: 571 01 46.
Post Office, Caballero de Rodas, 59. Tel: 571 06 79.
Royal Yacht Club, Tel: 571 01 08.

CONSULATES

Sweden, Chapaprieta, 1 Tel: 571 09 85.

EMERGENCIES

Municipal Police, Tel: 571 01 54.
Ambulances, Tel: 571 01 50.
First Aid, Tel: 571 47 14.
Red Cross, Ctra. Cartagena, km 2. Tel: 571 18 18.
Civil Guard, Paseo Vista Alegre, 11. Tel: 571 01 13.

● ● ● ● ● ● ● ● ● ● ● ● ● ● ●

VALENCIA, Provincial and regional capital (pop. 753,000). Castellón 65km, Alicante 166km, Madrid 352km. Telephone area code: 96.

Spain's third largest city, a prosperous cosmopolitan Mediterranean sea port, a centre for manufacturing (notably ceramics) and export, and for international trade fairs. It's surrounded by a fertile plain, the *huerta*, which is famous for its rice (paella originated here) and oranges. Ferries to the Balearics leave from here. Valencia was founded by the Romans in 137 BC. It enjoyed a period of cultural and economic splendour in

The 15th century when it was equal in prestige to the great Italian and Mediterranean cities. The first book in Spain was printed here in 1474. It was the last refuge of the defeated Republican Goverment in 1939 and one of the last two cities of Spain to fall to Franco (the other was Madrid). More recently, in the ill-fated coup d,état of 23rd February 1981 it was in Valencia that a rebel general ordered his tanks to rumble along the streets to frighten the populace into submission. Valencia is the birth-place of the impressionist painter Joaquín Sorolla, who painted a famous series of canvases on El Cabañal beach. The novelist Vicente Blasco Ibañez was also born here.

The modern city is divided in half by the dry bed of the River Turia (the river was diverted to avert flooding). Despite its maritime traditions, it is often said that Valencia was built with its back to the sea: the port is some distance from the city-centre.

GETTING AROUND

The city centre is small enough to explore on foot. An alternative, in a city without a single hill, is to cycle. Valencia has Spain's first network of cycle lanes (painted green and with their own traffic lights) between the centre and the university areas. But beware: motorists do not have much respect for cyclists here, on or off cycle lanes. For longer journeys there is a good bus system. Buy a bargain *bonobús* from an *estanco* if you are going to make ten journeys. The metro network is rather confined to the side of the city centre bounded by the Gran Vía Fernando el Católico, along which there are frequent stations, but you can use it to get into the surrounding countryside. Again, there are special season tickets for 10 journeys. For metro information Tel: 347 37 50.

DON'T MISS

River Turia Gardens. In the dry bed of the diverted river which once flowed past the city centre. A 9km strip, including a giant Gulliver children's playground, near Angel Custodio bridge (open Tuesday-Sunday 10am-8pm. Closed Monday. Closed for lunch (2-5pm) from mid-July to mid-September.

Cathedral. Built in a mixture of styles so that it has one Gothic, one Baroque and one Romanesque doorway. Inside it houses a couple of Goyas, the withered arm of Saint Vicent the Martyr and a gold and agate cup said to be the Holy Grail. The cathedral's octagonal tower, the Miguelete, is a landmark of Valencia and offers fine views from the top (open daily 10am-1pm and 4-6pm).

Water Tribunal. Every Thursday at noon the solemn Water Tribunal meets in public under the cathedral's Apostles' Doorway (that's the one leading onto Plaza de la Virgen) to supervise the use of water in the *huerta*, as it has done for the past one-thousand years.

The Lonja. An exquisite Gothic building, once the city's silk exchange. It is decorated with curious gargoyles outside and inside has stellate-vaulting supported on gracefully spiralling columns. Open Tuesday to Saturday 10am-2pm and 5-9pm. Sunday 10am-2pm. Closed Monday.

National Ceramics Museum, C/ Poeta Querol, 2, (currently closed for restoration). Probably the best of Valencia's many museums. It is housed in the Churrigueresque (rococo) Palace of the Marques de dos Aguas, an 18th-century fantasy of coloured plaster and alabaster, which is almost as fascinating as the collection of 5,000 items inside. The designer of the extravagant portal died insane. One look at it and you find that easy to believe. The museum includes prehistoric, Greek and Roman ceramics; works by Picasso, a complete tiled Valencian kitchen, the Marques' Cinderella-style carriages and a collection of Ex Libris labels.

Palau de la Generalitat. Open 9am-2pm by prior appointment. Tel: 386 34 61. The seat of the regional government and is a magnificent Gothic building. The adjacent Calle de Caballeros has fine Gothic palaces with courtyards hidden behind enormous doors.

The Fine Arts Museum, C/ San Pío, 5. Open Tuesday-Saturday 9am-3pm. Sunday 10am-2pm. Closed Monday. Display of 15th-century altarpieces. Paintings by Van Dyck, Bosch and Goya. Also Velazquez's famous self-portrait.

Valencian Insititute of Modern Art (IVAM), C/Guillem de Castro, 118.Tel: 386 30 00. Open Tuesday-Sunday 11am-8pm. Closed Monday.

Free admission on Sundays. Highly-regarded gallery which houses major exhibitions.

Central Market. To see the daily life of the city, go along to the art nouveau Central Market in the morning where 1,300 stalls sell a colourful assortment of fruit, vegetables and seafood.

Torres de Serrano. This is all that's left of the city's old walls, which were pulled down last century, apart from the Torres de Quart. Houses a maritime museum (open Tuesday-Friday 10am-2pm. Saturday 10am-1pm. Closed Sunday and Monday).

Estación del Norte. The Art Nouveau foyer of the railway station is decorated with beautiful ceramic mosaics and stained glass.

Monforte Gardens, C/Monforte. Open Monday-Friday 10.30am-6pm. Saturday and holidays 10.30am-2.30pm and 4.30-6pm. Shady, secluded and romantic.

Botanic Gardens. C/ Beato Gaspar Bono. Open Tuesday-Sunday 10am-9pm. Closed Monday. The oldest garden in city, created in 1802 by the botanist Antonio José Cavanilles. Now has 7,000 species of shrubs and trees.

Street Market: Flea market around Plaza de Nápoles y Sicilia every Sunday morning.

Fiestas: The Fallas. Held in March, this is one of the showiest and most cathartic festivals in Spain. A week-long paroxysm of noise and fire in which 360 enormous papier-maché monuments are displayed in the streets and then burnt (see section on Fiestas).

La Huerta. A maze of intensively farmed fields sprinkled with *alquerías,* often exotic and palacial farmhouses.

La Albufera, a short way south of the city, is one of Europe's prime wetlands and has recently been declared a Natural Park to protect its abundant birdlife, especially egrets and herons (see Excursion 7).

PLACES TO STAY

Monte Picayo, Urbanización Monte Picayo (take Exit 7 off Autopista del Mediterraneo A-7), Puzol. (15km) Tel: 142 01 00. Five star hotel with its own bull ring and casino.

Sidi Saler Palace, Playa del Saler, s/n. (9km) Tel: 161 04 11. Five stars. By the beach.

Parador Luis Vives, Ctra. Saler, km 16. (11km) Tel: 161 11 86.

Surrounded by a golf course.

Reina Victoria, C/ Barcas 4. Tel: 352 04 87. Four stars. Central. Art Nouveau building with modern interior.

Excelsior, C/ Barcelonina, 5. Tel: 351 46 12. Three stars. Central.

Inglés, C/ Marqués de Dos Aguas, 6. Tel: 351 64 26. Three stars. Central.

La Marcelina, Paseo de Neptuno, 72. Tel: 371 31 51. Two stars. Simple accommodation on the beach near the port.

La Pepica, Paseo de Neptuno, 2. Tel: 371 41 11. One star. On the beach near the port.

For cheaper accommodation there are several hostals in the streets beside the main railway station.

EATING OUT

The city's favourite dish is paella. The traditional variety is *paella valenciana,* made with chicken, rabbit and snails, although there is an alternative seafood version, *paella de mariscos,* as well as the hybrid *paella mixta.* There are many other rice dishes to try, including *arroz a banda* - rice cooked in fish stock - and *arroz al horno,* a baked rice dish with chick peas, potato and sausage.

There are several restaurants specialising in paella on the Paseo de Neptuno along Las Arenas beach including La Marcelina (Tel:371 31 51), La Rosa (Tel: 371 20 76) and La Pepica (Tel. 371 41 11). All M-E.

Eladio, C/ Chiva 40. Tel: 384 22 44. Closed Sunday. All cards. (VE)

La Lluna de Valencia, Camino del Mar, 56, Almasserra. (5 km) Tel: 185 10 86. All cards. Closed Sunday and Saturday lunchtime. In country house. (E-VE)

Marisquería Civera, C/ Lérida 11. Tel: 347 59 17. Closed Monday and August. All cards. The leading seafood restaurant. (VE)

La Hacienda, Navarro Reverter, 12. Tel: 373 18 59. Closed Saturday lunchtime, Sunday and Easter Week. All cards. (VE)

Les Graelles, C/ Arquitecto Mora 2 Tel: 360 47 00. Various rice dishes. (E)

Mesón Manchego, Avda. de Madrid, Sedavi (1km). Tapas bar- restaurant. Reserve a table in advance at weekends. (B-M)

BARS

While bar-hopping, you'll almost certainly come across *Agua de Valencia* - a cocktail of champagne, orange juice and vodka which slips down all too easily.

In summer, bars and cafés serve an unusual, non-alcoholic thirst-quencher called *horchata*, a sweet, milky drink made from a vegetable root. The place to drink it is in the many *horchaterias* of nearby Alboraya (3 km), especially Daniel. In the centre you can drink *horchata* in Santa Catalina and El Siglo, off Plaza de la Reina.

Cervecería Madrid, C/Abadia de San Martin, 10. Decorated with naïve paintings. The home of *Agua de Valencia*. A quiet place to chat with plenty of intimate corners.

Juan Sebastían Bach, C/ de la Mar, 31. Tel: 332 04 02. In a 15th century palace. As preposterously kitsch and decadent as it is expensive but worth dropping in to have a look at. A pride of lions lives in a cage in the patio. The entrance ticket includes a drink.

Cervecería Serranos, C/ Blanquerías, 5. (behind Serranos Towers). Tel: 391 70 61. Famous for its tapas. Gets crowded.

AFTER DARK

Valencia has a legendary nightlife - the *luna de Valencia* - which doesn't get going until midnight. Most of the action is in what Spaniards call "pubs" - fashionable bars with loud music and few seats. You'll find the brash young Valencia around Plaza de Xuquer (just off Avenida Blasco Ibañez, in *Copa Litro*) and in Avenida de Aragón. Other areas to head for are Plaza Canovas (on Gran Vía Marqués del Turia), La Malvarrosa (the beach) and, right in the centre, the crumbling but atmospheric Barrio del Carmen - try *Calcatta* (C/ Reloj Viejo), an old house on several levels converted into a lively bar.

Monte Picayo Casino, see above, under hotels.

Perdido, Sueca 17. Bar with live jazz.

ENTERTAINMENT

For details of what's on see the weekly listings magazine *Cartelera Turia*.

Original language films. Filmoteca, Plaza del Ayuntamiento, 17. Tel: 351 23 36; and Albatros, Plaza Fray Luis Colomer, 4. Tel: 369 45 30.

Palau de la Musica, Alameda s/n. Tel: 360 33 56. Classical concerts with international orchestras and soloists.

ENGLISH BOOKS AND PRESS

Soriano, C/ Játiva, 15 (opposite the railway station). Tel: 351 03 78.

SGEL, C/Ruzafa, 23. Tel: 352 79 58.

English Book Centre, C/ Pascual y Genis, 16. Tel: 351 92 88.

Librería Inglesa, C/ Conde Trénor, 4. Tel: 331 21 51.

Foreign newspapers and magazines are available from newsstands in the Plaza del Ayuntamiento and from Soriano (see above)

SHOPPING

Manises (near the airport) is famous for its ceramic industry and you will see its colourful wares for sale everywhere. The successful porcelain manufacturer Lladró has its factory in Tavernes Blanques. Traditional fans are made in Aldaya. Paella dishes are sold in a range of sizes from tiny to enormous - specify the number of people it is for - outside the central market.

MAPS

Regolf, C/ de la Mar, 22. Tel: 392 23 62. Stocks the latest 1:50,000 army maps of the provinces of Valencia, Castellón and Alicante which are useful for walking.

SERVICES

Tourist Offices (for the city), Plaza del Ayuntamiento, 1. Tel: 351 04 17; and in the foyer of the Railway Station (Estación del Norte). Tel: 352 28 82.

Offices of the Regional Tourist Board (for the provinces of Valencia, Alicante and Castellón): C/ de la Paz, 48. Tel: 352 28 97; Avda. de Cataluña, 1. Tel: 369 79 32; and Manises Airport. Tel: 153 03 25. Tourist information telephone line: 352 40 00.

Traffic information, Tel: 331 81 15.

Taxis, Tel: 374 02 02, 357 13 13 or 370 32 04.

Post Office, Plaza del Ayuntamiento, 24.

Telephones, Plaza del Ayuntamiento. Open 9am-1pm and 5-9pm.

Bus Station, Avda. Menéndez Pidal, 3. Tel: 349 72 22.

Railway Station (for inter-city services), Estación del Norte, C/Játiva. Tel: 351 36 12. Metro/local narrow-gauge rail network, C/ Cronista Rivelles. Tel: 347 37 50.

Airport, Manises, (8km from the city centre). Tel: 370 95 00.

Iberia information, Tel: 351 96 37.

Port passenger terminal (4 km from the city centre). Tel: 323 75 80. Transmediterránea (Balearic ferries), Tel: 367 65 12.

CONSULATES

Austria, Francisco Cubells, 43. Tel: 367 16 58.

Belgium, Gran Via Ramon y Cajal, 33. Tel: 325 32 48.

Denmark, Cirilo Amoras, 68. Tel: 351 36 06.

Finland, Paz, 27. Tel: 332 01 88.

France, Cirilo Amoras, 48. Tel: 352 41 25.

Germany, Avenida Primado Reig, 70. Tel: 361 43 54.

Iceland, Plaza Porta del Mar, 4. Tel: 351 72 75.

Netherlands, C/Gran Via Germanias, 18. Tel: 341 46 33.

Norway, Avenida del Puerto, 312. Tel: 323 08 87.

Sweden, C/Jorge Juan, 10. Tel: 394 03 75.

Switzerland, Camino Hondo del Grao, 78. Tel: 323 09 81.

USA, C/ Ribera, 3. Tel: 351 69 73.

(For other nationalities see under Alicante.)

EMERGENCIES

National Police, Tel: 091 and 351 08 62.

Municipal Police, Tel: 092 and 362 10 12, 362 12 06 and 362 13 08.

Ambulances, Tel: 350 01 00.

First Aid, Tel: 352 23 22.

Red Cross, Tel: 360 68 00.

Civil Guard, Tel: 333 11 00.

■ CAMPSITES BY PROVINCES ■

ALBACETE
(Telephone area code: 967)
Molinicos: Río Mundo, Ctra. Comarcal 415, Km 237. Tel: 43 32 30

Ossa de Montiel: Los Batanes, Lagunas de Ruidera. Tel: 37 71 29

Yeste: Río Segura, Ctra. Yeste-Segura de la Sierra, Km 20, La Donar.

ALICANTE
(Telephone area code: 96)
Alfaz del Pi: Tropical, Ctra. de Albir, s/n. Tel: 588 85 88

Albi: Partida Albir, Zona 6. Tel: 588 87 48

Alicante: Bahía, Playa Albufereta. Tel: 526 23 32

Altea: Cap Blanch, Playa del Albir. Tel: 584 22 11; Cap Negret, Partida Cap Negret, 13. Tel: 584 13 61; Miami: Partida Cap Blanch, 1. Tel: 584 03 86; San Antonio, Ctra. de Albir, 6. Tel: 584 09 17

Benidorm: Villasol, Camino Viejo de Valencia, s/n. Tel: 585 04 22; Arena Blanca, Rincón de Loex, s/n. Tel: 586 18 89; Armanello, Ctra. Alicante-Valencia,Km 123.Tel: 585 31 90; Benidorm, Ctra. Diputación Rincón de Loix.Tel: 586 00 11; Benisol, Ctra. Valencia Alicante, Km 124. Tel: 585 16 73; Don Quijote, Partida del Derramador, s/n. Tel 585 50 65; La Torreta, Ctra de la Diputación. Tel: 585 46 68

Benissa: Fanadix, Ctra. Moraira-Calpe, Km 6. Tel: 574 73 07.

Calpe: Ifach, Ctra. Calpe-Moraira, Km 5. Tel: 583 04 77; La Merced, Ctra. La Cometa, 1-E. Urb. La Merced. Tel: 583 00 97.

Campello: Costa Blanca, Partida del Convento. Tel: 563 06 70; Playa Muchavista, Ctra. A-190 Alicante-Playa de San Juan. Tel: 565 45 26

Denia: Los LLanos, Ctra. N-332, Km 203. Tel: 575 02 73; Los

Patos, Playa de las Devesas s/n; Diana, Ctra. Denia por la Costa, Km 6. Tel: 647 41 85; Las Marinas, Les Bovetes Nord-A I. Los Angeles. Tel: 578 14 46; Los Pinos, Partida Las Rotas. Tel: 578 26 98.

Elche: Internacional La Marina, Ctra. Alicante-Cartagena, Km 29. Partida La Marina. Tel: 541 90 51; El Palmeral, Ctra. Circunvalación Murcia-Alicante. Tel: 542 27 66; El Pinet, Partida La Marina, Playa del Pinet, s/n. Tel: 541 94 73; Sombra y Sol, Ctra. Arenales del Sol (El Altet). Tel: 568 72 02 Guardamar del Segura: Mare Nostrum, Ctra. Nacional, Km 38,5. Tel: 572 80 73; Palm Mar, Ctra. Alicante-Cartagena, Km 36,5. Tel: 572 88 56

Javea: Javea, Partida Pla, 7. Tel: 579 10 70; El Naranjal, Ctra. Cabo de la Nao, Partida Morer. Tel: 579 29 89

San Juan: El Caballo Loco, Ctra. Alicante-Valencia. Tel: 565 72 47; El Molino, Playa de San Juan. Tel: 565 24 80

Santa Pola: Rocas Blancas, Ctra. N-332, Km 88,2. Tel: 541 64 66

Torrevieja: La Campana, Ctra. Torrevieja-Cartagena, Km 4,5. Tel: 571 21 52; Torre del Moro,Ctra. de la Costa, Km 4. Tel: 571 02 64

Villajoyosa: La Cala, Ctra. N-332 Km 117,3. Tel: 585 14 61; El Paraiso, Ctra. N-332, Km 136. Tel: 685 18 38; Sertorium, Partida Torres, 83. Tel: 589 15 99

Castellon
(Telephone area code: 964)

Alcalá de Chivert: Playa Tropicana,Playa Tropicana Tel: 41 24 63; Alcocebre, Ctra. N-340, Km 4. Tel: 41 28 89

Benicassim: Bonterra, (300 m. north of Benicassim.) Tel: 30 00 007; Azahar, Partida Vilarroig. Tel: 30 31 96; Capricornio, Avda. Mohino, s/n. Tel: 30 16 99

Burriana: El Arenal, Playa Norte, Puerto de Burriana. Tel: 51 85 50

Eslida: Navarro, Ctra. Artana, s/n. Tel 61 12 52.

Oropesa: Blavamar, Partida Les Amplaries. Tel: 31 03 47; Los Almendros, Ctra. N-340, Km 87,2. Tel: 31 04 75; Oasis, Ctra. L'Atall, s/n. Tel: 31 06 77

Peñíscola: Bellavista, Partida Llandells. Tel: 48 01 35; Caravana, Ctra. N-340, Km 1,200. Tel: 48 08 24; El Edén, Ctra.

CS- 501, Km 6. Tel: 48 05 62

Torreblanca: Torrenostra, Playa Torrenostra. Tel: 42 05 37.

Cuenca
(Telephone area code: 966)
Cuenca: Pinar de Jabaga, Ctra. N-400, Km 174, Paraje Fuente de Albaladejito. Tel: 16 70 66

Teruel
(Telephone area code: 974)
Alcalá de la Selva: Los Iglos, Paraje Fuen la Reina. Tel: 80 31 47
Mora de Rubielos: El Morrón-Barrachinas, Masía El Colladico. Tel: 80 03 62

Valencia
(Telephone area code: 96)
Cullera: Santa Marta, Ctra. Faro de Cullera, Km 2. Tel: 172 14 40

Gandía: L'Alquería, Ctra. Gandía-Playa de Gandía, Km 2. Tel: 284 04 70; La Naranja, Playa Gandía, Partida La Marjal, Polígono 25. Tel: 284 16 16

Oliva: Ole, Ctra. N-332, Km 186, Partida L'Aigua Morta. Tel: 285 11 80; Azul, Partida Rapdells. Tel: 285 41 06

Pinedo: Coll Vert, Ctra. Nazaret-Oliva, Km 7,5. Playa de Pinedo. Tel: 367 13 40.

Pobla de Farnals: La Brasa, Playa Pobla de Farnals. Tel: 146 03 88
Puzol: Puzol, Camí dels Plans, Playa de Puzol. Tel: 142 15 27
Sagunto: Malvarrosa, Playa Almarda. Tel: 260 89 75
Sueca: Las Palmeras, Ctra. Nazaret-Oliva, Km 23. Tel: 177 08 61; San Pascual, Ctra. Nazaret-Oliva, Km 21, El Perelló. Tel: 177 02 73

Valencia: El Palmar, Ctra. Valencia-Cullera. Tel: 161 08 53; El Saler, Mata del Fang, s/n, El Saler. Tel: 183 00 23; Devesa Gardens, Ctra. Nazaret-Oliva, Km 15. Tel: 161 11 36 ❑

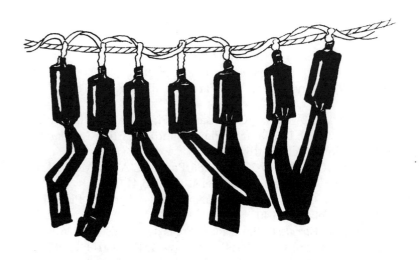

■ ON THE ROAD ■

Driving Tips

If you are coming from abroad with your own vehicle, bring the car documents, an international insurance certificate (green card), a bail bond in case of accident (also issued by your insurance company before leaving home) and an international driving licence.

You should have a spare set of car light bulbs in your car and a warning triangle (both obligatory). It's also a good idea to have a replacement fan belt in the boot and any other essential spare parts - especially if your car model is unlikely to be sold in Spain.

Driving in Spain is on the right. Spanish drivers have a reputation for careless, negligent or even dangerous driving evidenced by one of the worst accident rates in Europe. The best way not to join the statistics is to exercise extreme caution.

The Civil Guard's highway patrols can stop you at any time and they frequently stage road-blocks. Not only can they breathalyse you without giving a reason but they can impose heavy fines on the spot for many offences. You can even be fined for not producing the necessary documents mentioned above, together with your passport or identity card (which you should have with you all the time). Obviously, it is intelligent to remain polite, helpful and good humoured when dealing with them.

A massive building programme is transforming Spain's road system and you will find many changes to even the latest map. Eastern Spain's main artery is the two-lane A-7 Mediterranean coastal motorway (*autopista*) which will soon link France with Andalusia. You pay for the privilege of using it but it is the only sure way to avoid traffic congestion, and can considerably speed up longer journeys - although inevitably you miss the sights on the way. Where you can take the motorway to cover a route more rapidly without missing anything, we have indicated this in the text.

Many cities are now linked by stretches of *autovías*: dual-carriageways which are effectively toll-free motorways. Valencia by-pass and the A-7 south of Alicante fall into this category.

Other roads are divided into main roads (marked red on the map), provincial and local - which can often be in a bad state of repair. There are still many unsurfaced lanes in Spain and occasionally they are unavoidable if you want to see some point of interest. The terrain in this region, away from the coast, is especially mountainous and whatever the road surface a journey can take much longer than you expect, simply because of the number of curves.

The speed limit (for cars without caravans and motorbikes) in urban areas is 50 kph (30 mph). On main roads the limit is usually 100 kph (55 mph) - with an extra 20 kph allowed, where necessary and safe, to overtake an exceptionally slow-moving vehicle. On motorways you can do up to 120 kph (74 mph).

Spanish traffic regulations have recently tightened and now motorcyclists are obliged to wear crash helmets and motorists (and their passengers) to wear seat belts at all times.

Always give way to traffic coming from your right unless the signs indicate otherwise. On main roads and new roundabouts you almost always have priority.

With denationalisation, petrol stations are becoming more numerous but they can be few and far between in rural areas, and are usually closed at night. Petrol prices are still state-regulated with neglible local variations. You can now buy super (equivalent to three-star), and two grades of unleaded petrol which is now available at all stations. Car diesel is sold everywhere.

Finally, in the event of an emergency (if, say, you have to get someone injured to hospital), display a white hankerchief out of your car window and use your horn and headlights to warn other drivers to give way.

Public Transport

There are two railway systems in eastern Spain. Renfe operates the national network for intercity services. Some journeys can be painfully indirect and you will be wise to compare journey times with those offered by bus companies.

The other railway company is FGV which operates the narrow-gauge lines along the Costa Blanca and around Valencia.

Cycling

There are fewer recreational or commuting cyclists in Spain than in many other European countries and motorists are not generally respectful towards them (cycle racing, however, is a popular sport). Cycle lanes are almost non-existent; Valencia, which has a network of them, is the exception.

Country lanes, although usually quiet, are often badly pot-holed and many are totally unsign-posted - you have to ask for directions.

Walking

The pedestrian is not well-catered for in Spain. Although the law says otherwise, zebra crossings are generally invisible to motorists. Take care even when you think you have right of way at traffic lights or a pelican crossing: sometimes vehicles are permitted to cross your path even though you have a little green man flashing in front of you.

In the countryside there are hardly any marked footpaths and you will have to ask for directions from the locals - although this can sometimes be difficult as there are great tracts of land and some villages are underpopulated. If you do go hiking it's advisable to research your route well and tell someone where you are going; wear a hat; and carry plenty of water.

For comments on maps, see Introduction and under Valencia in the Town and City Guide.

Security

Never leave valuables or documents in an unattended car at any time. It's best not to leave anything at all on display when you park - what you cannot carry, lock in the boot. When staying overnight, take all baggage into the hotel.

If possible park your car in a garage or guarded car-park (shamefully, not many hotels in Spain offer either option). Thieves are especially interested in foreign cars.

Spain has three distinct police forces with different functions. The Municipal or Local Police (blue uniform, peaked cap) are employed by the local council for minor tasks such as controlling traffic. National Police (dark blue uniform) are concerned with the prevention and investigation of crime in cities. The Civil Guard (olive-green uniforms and, sometimes, distinctive patent leather tricorn hats) is responsible for crime and traffic duties in rural areas - and that includes most main roads ❏

■ FIESTAS ■

A baron is said to have once asked a convicted highway man on which day he wished to be executed, thinking he would choose the day of a saint of which he was a devotee. Cunningly, the highway man replied that he didn't want to die on any day on which his countrymen were enjoying themselves. He asked to be hung on a day when there was no fiesta taking place in any town or village in Spain. It proved impossible to hang him.

Even the smallest village manages to put on a fiesta in honour of its patron saint. It may last a day or a week but it will always be a special occasion in which the shops are shut and no work is done. If there is to be a procession or other event, streets are sealed off and parking restricted. Hotels and restaurants are usually booked up long in advance.

Even if based around a religious occasion, a fiesta is a chance to let off steam. Normal living is suspended and the noisy festivities - eating, drinking, pranks, risk-taking, dancing, licentiousness, parades - go on late into the night. Bull running, or some other eye-catching central event, also usually takes place. Unfortunately, in some fiestas animals are still treated with great cruelty – but opposition to such practices is growing steadily.

There is nothing like being in a town during a fiesta. If you happen to be staying there you won't be able to escape and you will be very unpopular if you raise any objection to the inconveniences caused. If you don't want to join in it's best to steer clear of fiesta-time altogether. Needless to say, it is not the moment to see the sights in peace.

Whether you want to know where and when to see them -

or where and when to avoid them - this calendar details the more interesting fiestas in eastern Spain.

January

New Year's Day, January 1. Public holiday throughout Spain.

Day of the Three Kings, January 6. Public holiday throughout Spain. The day on which Spanish children traditionally receive their Christmas presents. The day before, the Three Kings arrive near the port in Valencia.

Saint Antony, January 17. Pets and livestock are brought before a priest to be blessed on the day of their patron saint. The biggest such event is held in Valencia's Calle Sagunto.

February

Carnival is an excuse for fancy-dress parades everywhere. During *La Enfarinada,* in Belgida (near Albaida), boys throw flour at the girls. In Altea, children dress up and gather in the main square.

March

March 1, Public holiday in Ibiza and Formentera.

Fiestas de la Magdalena, Castellón, 3rd Sunday in Lent. The festivities, which commemorate the migration of Castellón's early settlers from the mountains to the plain, feature a spectacular procession of illuminated floats depicting scenes of local life.

The Fallas, Valencia, March 19. One of the incomparable (and noisiest) spectacles of Spain culminating with the burning of enormous papier-maché monuments at midnight on March 19, St Joseph's Day. Every day of the preceding week there is a *mascletá* - a deafening explosion of fireworks - in the Plaza del Ayuntamiento. The 360 *fallas* are put in place in the city-centre and suburbs on March 15. On March 18 the Plaza de la Virgen is filled with flowers. Fallas are also burnt in Benidorm, Denia, Gandia and Jativa. March 19 is a public holiday throughout Spain.

Palm Sunday, the procession in Elche, Spain's palm-tree capital, is famous for the quantity of palm branches which are carried.

Easter Week, one of the most famous of Spain's processions of hooded penitents and Biblical personalities is in Lorca (Murcia). Two brotherhoods vie to outdo each other in expense and finery. Costumes are elaborate and ostentatious; many of the participants are mounted on horses.

There are more restrained but nonetheless impressive processions in El Cabañal (near the port of Valencia) on Good Friday and Easter Sunday.

In Orihuela and Crevillente people carry sacred images by the 17th- and 18th-century artists Benlliure and Salzillo. On Easter Saturday in Orihuela you will also see a most unusual effigy - La Diablesa, a she-devil (kept on display in a museum the rest of the year - paraded around the streets.

Cuenca's Easter celebrations include the so-called "Drunkards Procession" which begins at dawn on Good Friday. Marchers are jeered and heckled by inebriated *turbas*, representing the Jews who scorned Christ. Unfortunately, the occasion has become an excuse for unruly non-participants to drink too much as well.

Las Tamboradas, Holy Thursday and Good Friday. Alcañiz, Calanda, Hijar and Andorra (in the north of the province of Teruel). Participants dressed in long black robes beat drums in mourning for Christ until their hands bleed.

April

Moors and Christians, Alcoy, April 22-24. The town divides into two armies to re-enact the Christians' victory over the Moors seven centuries ago. Some 15,000 people dress in elaborate and expensive costumes, which are best seen on April 22 as the armies march into the city in ranks ten or more abreast to the accompaniment of traditional Moors and Christians music. On the last day the armies fight symbolic "battles" by blasting blunderbusses into the air. Finally, St George appears on the battlements of the castle erected in the main square to proclaim the Christian victory. Similar Moors and Christians festivals are held all over the provinces of Valencia and Alicante throughout the summer.

The Pilgrims of Les Useres (Castellón). Last weekend in April.

Twelve men dressed in sombre tunics walk 80km of arduous mountain paths to the shrine of San Juan de Peñagolosa, singing pre- Gregorian chants on the way. April 23 is a public holiday in Teruel.

May

Labour Day, May 1. Public holiday throughout Spain.

The Race of the Wine Horses, Caravaca de la Cruz (Murcia). First week of May. The race commemorates a legend from the time when the Knights Templar were besieged in the castle by the Moors and running out of fresh drinking water. Several brave knights ran the gauntlet of their foes leading horses loaded with leather pouches to fetch wine. After fighting their way back to the castle they dipped the Cross of Caravaca (which is supposed to include a bit of the original cross) in the wine. The defenders drank the wine, recovered their fighting strength and defeated their enemies.

Cristo del Sahúco, Peñas de San Pedro (Albacete). The Monday following Whit-sunday. Men dressed in white carry a cross-shaped coffin at great speed to a shrine over 15km away.

Corpus Christi, Valencia. Stunning parades including giants and *cabezudos* - carnival figures with gigantic heads. May 31 is a public holiday in the provinces of Albacete, Cuenca and Ciudad Real.

June

June 9 is a public holiday in Murcia.

Las Hogueras, June 20-24. Alicante's spectacle of fire centres around the midsummer feast of San Juan on June 24, the *Nit del Foc*. At midnight the city is lit up by a thousand *fogueres*, papier-maché sculptures (erected on June 21). Fire, representing the triumph of light over darkness, features in celebrations for the shortest night of the year, June 23, all over the region.

July

Bulls in the Sea, early July. Denia. A semi-circular ring is set up on the quayside in which volunteers taunt bulls until one or the other - or both - ends up in the water.

August

Misterio de Elche, August 14-15. Unique liturgical drama performed in the Basílica de Santa María for the last six centuries. All 150 amateur performers are male - even the Virgin is a boy. The play, renowned for its ingenious special effects, is performed in two acts - *La Vespra* and *La Festa*. It tells the story of the Virgin Mary's death, ascension into heaven and her coronation.

Assumption, August 15. A public holiday throughout Spain.

Tomatina, August 26. Buñol (Valencia). A battle of tomatoes. Five lorry loads of ripe fruit (some 50,000 kilos) are provided for participants to hurl at each other until everyone and everything is dripping in sticky juice. The battle originated in 1944 when irreverent locals pelted civic dignitaries with tomatoes during the annual fair. Franco suppressed the *Tomatina* for several years on the grounds that "it wasn't very religious".

Sexenales de Morella, a fiesta held only once every six years, the last being in 1994. The various trade guilds (weavers, farmers, craftsmen and pilgrims) take turns to perform dances.

September

Human Towers, Algemesí (Valencia). September 8. Gaudily-dressed men form themselves into columns and a small boy, the *angel* scrambles to the top.

October

Valencia Day, October 9. A public holiday throughout the provinces of Valencia, Alicante and Castellón.

National Day of Spain, October 12. A public holiday which marks the discovery of America in 1492.

Consuegra Saffron Festival, last week in October. Saffron farmers gather in Consuegra (Toledo) to celebrate the saffron harvest. The fiesta includes a competition to select La Mancha's fastest saffron-plucker.

November

All Saints' Day, November 1 is celebrated all over Spain as a day in honour of the dead. Cemeteries become animated and colourful places for a few hours as people decorate the tombs of relatives with flowers.

Saint Raphael's Auction, La Nucia. Morning of November 15. The saint's chapel is only opened on this one day each year. A lively auction is held for the privilege of carrying the effigy of the saint in a solemn procession through the streets of the old town.

December

Immaculate Conception, December 8. Public holiday throughout Spain.

Christmas Day, December 25. Public holiday throughout Spain.

Day of the Holy Innocents, December 28. Spain's equivalent of April Fools' Day. In Ibi (Alicante) the outlandishly disguised *enfarinats*, their faces caked in flour, choose a mayor for the day and go around the town making fun of local life ❑

■ VOCABULARY ■

Basic Words and Phrases
yes: *sí*
no: *no*
please: *por favor*
thank you: *gracias*
good morning: *buenos días* (used until approximately 2pm)
good afternoon: *buenas tardes*
good night: *buenas noches*
goodbye: *adiós*
today: *hoy*
tomorrow: *mañana*
yesterday: *ayer*
How much is it? *¿Cuánto es?*
The bill please. *La cuenta por favor*
What time is it? *¿Qué hora es?*
It is one o'clock/two o'clock etc. *Es la una/Son las dos etc.*
What time does it start? *¿A qué hora empieza?*

Numbers
Zero, *cero*
1, *uno*
2, *dos*
3, *tres*
4, *cuatro*
5, *cinco*
6, *seis*
7, *siete*
8, *ocho*
9, *nueve*
10, *diez*

20, *veinte*
25, *veinticinco*
30, *treinta*
40, *cuarenta*
50, *cincuenta*
60, *sesenta*
70, *setenta*
80, *ochenta*
90, *noventa*
100, *cien*
500, *quinientos*
1000, *mil*

Finding Your Way Around

Which is the road to Valencia?: *¿Dónde está la carretera a Valencia?*
How do I get to the castle/the market?: *¿Cómo se va al castillo/al mercado?*
left: *izquierda*
right: *derecha*
straight on: *todo recto*
first right/second left: *la primera a la derecha/ la segunda a la izquierda.*
Can I park here?: *¿Se puede aparcar aquí?*
Where is the post office/railway station/police station?: *¿Dónde está correos/la estación/la comisaría?*
Is it far?: *¿Está lejos?*
Where is the toilet?: *¿Dónde están los servicios?*
Gentlemen's toilets: *caballeros*
Ladies toilets: *señoras*
Where can I buy a film/postcards/cigarettes/stamps medicine?:
¿Dónde venden carretes/postales /tabaco/sellos/medicinas?
Do you have a room free?: *¿Hay una habitación libre?*
I would like a (single) double room (with bath): *Quería una habitación (individual) doble (con baño)*
When does the bus to Denia leave?: *¿A qué hora sale el autobús para Denia?*

(local) bus: *autobús*
long distance bus (coach): *autocar*
What time does it arrive?: *¿A qué hora llega?*

For Motorists

car: *coche*
motorbike: *moto*
driving licence: *carnet de conducir*
insurance certificate: *póliza del seguro*
logbook: *tarjeta de inspección*
Is there a petrol station near here?: *¿Hay una gasolinera por aquí?*
Fill her up please: *Lleno, por favor.*
A thousand pesetas worth of...: *Mil pesetas de...*
premium/four-star: *super*
diesel: *gasóleo*
lead-free: *gasolina sin plomo*

Understanding Roadsigns

aparcamiento: parking
autopista: toll motorway, turnpike
autovía: dual carriageway/four-lane highway (effectively a toll- free motorway)
cambio de sentido: indicates a junction at which you can turn around.
carga o descarga: area for loading or unloading only; no parking.
carretera cortada: road blocked
ceda el paso: give way
centro urbano, centro ciudad: town centre, city centre
circunvalación: by-pass
cruce: crossroads
entrada: entrance
firme en mal estado: bad road surface
peaje: toll to pay
peatones: pedestrians
peligro: danger

prohibido aparcar, no aparcar: no parking
prohibido el paso: no entry
rotonda: roundabout
salida: exit
semáforo: traffic lights
tramo en obras: road works
vado permanente: keep clear; no parking
vado inundable: liable to flooding
vía única: one way street

Breakdowns

My car has broken down: *Mi coche está averiado.*
My car will not start: *Mi coche no arranca*
I have run out of petrol: *Me he quedado sin gasolina.*
I have a puncture: *Tengo una rueda pinchada.*
I have a flat battery: *La batería esta descargada.*
The lights don't work: *No funcionan las luces.*
Where is the nearest garage?: *¿Dónde está el taller de coches más cercano?*
Can you fix it?: *¿Puede arreglarlo?*
Do you do repairs?: *¿Hace reparaciones?*
oil: *aceite*
mechanic: *mecánico*
repair shop: *taller de reparaciones*
puncture: *pinchazo*
tow-truck: *grúa*
battery: *batería* brakes: *frenos*
bulb: *bombilla*
car keys: *llaves del coche*
clutch: *embrague*
distilled water: *agua destilada*
exhaust: *escape*
fan belt: *correa del ventilador*
fuse: *fusible*
gearbox: *caja de cambios*
headlights: *faros*
petrol tank: *depósito de gasolina*

points: *contactos*
radiator: *radiador*
spark plug: *bujía*
tyre: *neumático*
wheel: *rueda*
spare wheel: *rueda de recambio*
windscreen: *parabrisas*

For Cyclists
bicycle: *bicicleta*
Is there a cycle shop near here?: *¿Hay una tienda de recambios de bicicleta por aquí?*
Do you have a cycle pump?: *¿Tiene un bombín para bicicletas?*
wheel: *rueda*
spoke: *radio*
brake block: *zapata del freno*
cable: *cable*
chain: *cadena*
inner tube: *cámara*

In Case of Emergency
ambulance: *ambulancia*
surgery: *ambulatorio*
first aid post: *casa de socorro, puesto de socorro*
(National) police station: *comisaría de policia*
Civil Guard headquarters: *cuartel de la Guardia Civil*
Red Cross: *Cruz Roja*
chemist (pharmacy): *farmacia*
hospital: *hospital*
doctor: *médico*
casualty department (in a hospital): *urgencias*
I am lost: *Estoy perdido.*
There's been an accident: *Ha ocurrido un accidente.*
I have been robbed: *Me han robado.*
Call the police: *Llama a la policia.*
I have lost my luggage/passport/keys/husband: *He perdido mi equipaje, mi pasaporte, mis llaves, mi marido.*

I am ill: *Estoy enfermo* (if you are a man) *enferma* (if you are woman).

I need a doctor/dentist: *Necesito un médico/dentista.*

I am diabetic: *Soy diabetico/a*

I am pregnant: *Estoy embarazada.*

I have heart trouble: *Estoy enfermo del corazón.*

Sightseeing

In Valencia, Alicante and Castellón many people's first language is Valencian, a dialect of Catalan. Although they can speak the lingua franca, Castilian (what we call Spanish), they are often more comfortable in the local tongue. Signs are also often in Valencian. Here are some common words that you may see either in Spanish or Valencian.

Spanish	Valencian	English
abierto	overt	open
avenida	avinguda	avenue
ayuntamiento	ajuntament	town hall
balneario	balneari	spa
barranco	barranc	gully/ravine
barrio	barri	suburb/quarter
bodega	celler	wine cellar/wine producer
cama	llit	bed
camino	camí	road
campo	camp	the countryside; a field
calle	carrer	street
carretera	carretera	main road/highway
cascada	cascada	waterfall
castillo	castell	castle
cerrado	tancat	closed
ciudad	ciutat	city
colina	tossal	hill
corrida	corre-bou	bullfight
embalse	embassament	reservoir
fuente	font	spring

horario	horari	timetable/opening times
lago	llac	lake
mercado	mercat	market
montana	muntanya	mountain
paseo	passeig	promenade
plaza	plaça	square
playa	platja	beach
presa	presa	dam
pueblo	poble	village or town
puerto (de Montaña)	port	(mountain) pass
río	riu	river
salida	eixida	exit
senda	sender	footpath
urbanización	urbanizació	housing estate
valle	val	valley

Common Abbreviations

AC: BC

Avda. *(avenida)*: avenue

Bco. *(barranco)*: ravine or stream

C/ *(calle)*: street

Cast° *(castillo)*: castle

Ctra. *(carretera)*: main road

Etª. *(ermita)*: chapel or shrine

F: *(Fonda)*

H: *(Hotel)*

h: o'clock

P: *(Pension)*

Pl. or Plza. *(plaza)*: square

Pto. *(puerto)*: port or mountain pass

Rte.: restaurant

S. *(siglo)*: century

S. or Stª: saint

Sª *(sierra)*: mountain range

Eating and Drinking

Can I see the menu?: *¿Puedo ver el menú/la carta?*

Breakfast: *desayuno*
lunch: *almuerzo* or *comida*
dinner: *cena*
beer: *cerveza*
bread: *pan*
black coffee: *café solo*
white coffee: *café con leche*
salt: *sal*
sandwich: *bocadillo*
sugar: *azúcar*
tea: *té*
water: *agua*
red wine: *vino tinto*
white wine: *vino blanco*

Reading the Menu
ajo : garlic
atún : tuna fish
cerdo : pork
cordero : lamb
entremeses : starters
flan : créme caramel
fruta : fruit
helado : ice-cream
jamón serrano : cured ham
jamón york : cooked ham
mariscos : seafood
merluza : hake
perdiz : partridge
pescado : fish
pollo : chicken
queso : cheese
ración : bar snack (bigger than a tapa)
sopa : soup
tapa : snack
tortilla : omlette

■ FURTHER READING ON EASTERN SPAIN ■

With the exception of the Costa Blanca (and, perhaps, Cuenca and Ibiza), little has been written in English about eastern Spain. Even in Spanish there are few sources of reliable information for the layman. The following is a selection of the best available in both languages.

General Guides

Blue Guide Spain, Ian Robertson (A & C Black, London). A dense text especially good for information on art and archictecutre.

Charming Small Hotels Spain, edited by Chris Gill and Nick Inman (Duncan Petersen). Describes several hotels in the region selected for their décor, the warmth of their welcome and the quality of their service.

Guía Campsa (Campsa). Published annually in Spanish and available at Campsa petrol stations as well as bookshops. Describes (mainly expensive) restaurants in many of the places visited which are recommended for their excellence. Hotels are also listed with brief details.

Guía Oficial de Hoteles (Turespaña). Published annually by the Ministry of Commerce and Tourism, this fat - but inexpensive - book purports to list every hotel in Spain with its current facilities and prices. The symbols used are explained in a multilingual key but give little information.

Islamic Spain, Godfrey Goodwin (Penguin). Briefly covers the Moorish past of Valencia and Teruel.

Michelin guides. Michelin's multi-lingual "red guide" (revised annually) lists restaurants and hotels throughout the region. The "green guide" is a concise source of general information about many of the places visited.

Spain: Everything under the Sun (Harrap Columbus). A highly-detailed and reliable guide to the country, although sketchy and somewhat dated. A small companion volume covers Benidorm.

Spain: A Phaidon Cultural Guide, edited by Franz N. Mehling (Phaidon). Once you realise that there is an additional index to overcome the confusing layout (Guadalest, for instance, is under Alcoy) this is a useful guide to the major monuments to be seen in larger towns.

On Eastern Spain

Aventura Valenciana (ITVA, Valencia). A good introduction to the three provinces of the Valencian Community.

The A to Z of Settling on the Costa Blanca, Henry Lock (A to Z). For would-be residents.

Costa Blanca Walks, Roger Massingham (Parke Sutton). Detailed routes of twenty popular walks.

Walkers Guide - 100km Across the Mountains of La Marina, Alicante, compiled by Bob Stansfield. Self-published and available from the author, Costa Blanca Mountain Walkers, Casa Los Almendros, 10F, Pou Roig, Calpe. Tel: 96-583 25 27.

Els Ports de Morella y Benifassar - Ports de Beceite - Sus Tierras, Sus Gentes, Ricardo Muñoz Badía. In Spanish, for a deeper understanding of the Maestrazgo. Privately published but widely available in Morella and Valencia.

Geográfica Valenciana I: Valencian Polychrome (ITVA, Valencia). Published in several languages, including English. A general overview of the Valencian Community by a native journalist. Intelligent, perceptive and humourous.

Geográfica Valenciana II: The Living House (ITVA, Valencia). A tour de force on the archictecture of the region.

A Geological Field Guide to the Costa Blanca, Spain, by Frank Moseley (Geologists's Association Guide/Scottish Academic Press). For the specialist. Includes useful diagrams for understanding the landscape.

Not part of the package . . .

A Year in Ibiza, Paul Richardson (Macmillan)

Rock Art of the Spanish Levant, Antonio Beltrán (The Imprint of Man series, CUP). Further information on cave paintings.

Nature

Wild Spain, Frederic V. Grunfeld with Teresa Farino. (Ebury Press, London) includes chapters on the Serranía de Cuenca, the Montes Universales (around Albarracín), Lagunas de Ruidera and the Albufera.

The Birds of Britain and Europe, Hermann Heinzel, Richard Fitter and John Parslow (Collins) describes and illustrates almost every bird you are likely to see in eastern Spain.

A Handguide to the Wild Animals of Britain and Europe, Nicholas Arnold, Denys Ovenden Gordon Corbet (Collins/Treasure Press). The same for animals.

The Concise Flowers of Europe, Oleg Polunin (OUP). A brave attempt to cram the most commom wildflowers in Europe between two covers. Polunin wrote two other books, *Flowers of the Mediterranean* and *Flowers of South-west Europe*, which are more specific to this region but difficult to consult.

Guía de las Flores Silvestres de la Comunidad Valenciana, Ramón Figuerola, Juan B. Peris, Gerardo Stübing (Mestral). In Spanish. The only botanical work specifically covering this area.

Arboles de las Calles, Plazas, Parques y Jardines de Alicante, Francisco J Galan Baño (CAM, Alicante). In Spanish. A guide to almost every tree you are likely to find in the city of Alicante.

Guía de la Naturaleza de la Comunidad Valenciana. In Spanish. Originally produced in book form, later serialised by the daily papers, *Levante* and *Información*. Contains useful information on the nature reserves in the Valencian Community.

For Cyclists

Mediterráneo en Bici: De Tarifa a Jávea, J.L. Barrenetxea (Sua Edizioak, Bilboa). In Spanish.

España en Bici, Paco Tortosa and María del Mar Fornés (Integral, Barcelona) includes routes in the Maestrazgo, Cuenca, Lagunas de Ruidera, Sierra de Aitana and Albufera. In Spanish.

Free Booklets From Tourist Information Offices

Apart from the usual leaflets and maps, tourist offices often stock a series of highly informative glossy booklets in English and other languages produced by the Ministry of Commerce and Tourism's subsidiary Turespaña. Unfortunately, these booklets are not universally available (you generally find them far away from the areas they cover and then never in the language you want) but they are worth looking out for. Relevant ones include:

Mudejar Art and Architecture
Popular Architecture in Spain
Castles in Spain
Lorca

Fiction

Don Quixote, Miguel de Cervantes (Penguin).
The Cabin, Vincente Blasco Ibáñez

Periodicals

Lookout. Monthly colour magazine carrying in-depth reports and travel articles on eastern Spain.

Costa Blanca News. Published weekly. For news about the Costa Blanca's English speaking community ❏

■ GEOGRAPHICAL INDEX ■

■ MORE GREAT BOOKS ON SPAIN ■

Excursions in Southern Spain
by David Baird. 347 pages.
Forty easy-to-follow excursions by car take you to the most famous
sights and the least-known corners of Andalusia, Spain's most
fascinating region. Researched and written by David Baird, twice winner
of Spain's top travel award.

Birds of Iberia
by Clive Finlayson and David Tomlinson. 240 pages (Hardback, large format)
A journey through the different regions of this fascinating peninsula
which describes the main habits and birds found there, migration
patterns and ornithological sites. Beautifully illustrated throughout with
fine line drawings and more than 150 colour photographs, the book is an
appreciation of the extraordinarily rich and varied birdlife of Iberia

The Story of Spain
by Mark Williams. 272 pages
The bold and dramatic history of Spain, from the caves of Altamira to
our present day. This is a story of kings and poets, saints and
conquistadores, of Torquemada, Picasso, Cervantes, Franco, the
Alhambra, the Escorial... Mark Williams has drawn on years of rigorous
research to recreate the drama, excitement and pathos of crucial events in
the history of the western world. Illustrated in colour.

Gardening in Spain
by Marcelle Pitt. 216 pages
Your most valuable tool for successful gardening in Spain, from the author of
Lookout magazine's popular gardening column. How to plan your garden,
what to plant, when and how to plant it, how to make the most of flowers,
trees, shrubs, herbs. Illustrated with full-colour photographs.

Cooking in Spain
by Janet Mendel. 376 pages
The definitive guide to cooking in Spain, with more than 400 great
Spanish recipes. Plus complete information on Spain's regional
specialities and culinary history, how to buy the best in the market, a
complete English-Spanish glossary with more than 500 culinary terms,
handy conversation guide... all of it illustrated with colour photographs.

Spanish Property Owners' Handbook
by David Searl. 100 pages
Do you know your rights and obligations as a member of your community of property owners? Here, at last, are the answers! Including full text, in Spanish and English, of the Ley de la propiedad horizontal, with comments by legal writer David Searl.

The Best of Spanish Cooking
by Janet Mendel. 172 pages
The top food writer in Spain today invites you to a memorable feast featuring her all-time favourite Spanish recipes. More than 170 tantalizing dishes, so that you can recreate the flavour of Spain in your own home.

Expand Your Spanish
by Linda Hall de González. 272 pages
The unbelievable happens when you read this book. You can actually tackle the Spanish subjunctive and chuckle at the same time. Not a conventional grammar book, the author leads you with expertise and humour over the obstacles that put many people off learning the language.

A Selection of **Wildflowers of Southern Spain**
by Betty Molesworth Allen. 260 pages
Southern Spain is host to a rich variety of wildflowers in widely diverse habitats, some species growing nowhere else. This book describes more than 200 common plants of the region, each illustrated in full colour with simple text for easy identification and enjoyment.

You and the Law in Spain
by David Searl. 216 pages
Thousands of readers have relied on Lookout's best-selling You and the Law in Spain to guide them through the Spanish legal jungle. Now, author David Searl brings you a new, completely revised edition with even more information on taxes, work permits, cars, banking in Spain, buying property, Spain and the European Community, and lots more. It's a book no foreigner in Spain can afford to be without.

Inside Andalusia
by David Baird. 187 pages
A travel adventure through Spain's most fascinating region. David Baird invites you to explore an Andalusia you never dreamt of, to meet its people, and discover its exciting fiestas. Illustrated with brilliant colour photographs.

On sale at bookstores in Spain, or by post from: Ediciones Santana S.L., Apartado 422, 29640 Fuengirola, (Málaga) Spain.

TRAVEL NOTES

TRAVEL NOTES

TRAVEL NOTES